Helping Ourselves

Success Stories in Co-operative Business & Social Enterprise

EDITED BY

Robert Briscoe & Michael Ward

www.oaktreepress.com

OAK TREE PRESS
19 Rutland Street, Cork, Ireland
http://www.oaktreepress.com

A catalogue record of this book is
available from the British Library.

ISBN 1-86076-284-0

Printed in Ireland by ColourBooks.

CONTENTS

FIGURES

CASE STUDIES

EDITORS & CONTRIBUTORS

Robert Briscoe is the Programme Director of the Centre for Co-operative Studies, and a Senior Lecturer in the Department of Food Business & Development, University College Cork.

Michael Ward is the Deputy Director of the Centre for Co-operative Studies, and a Senior Lecturer in the Department of Food Business & Development, University College Cork.

Contributors

Colm Hughes is the former Manager of the Co-operative Development Unit of FÁS, the State training agency.

Olive McCarthy is a Researcher in the Centre for Co-operative Studies, and a Lecturer in the Department of Food Business & Development, University College Cork.

Mary O'Shaughnessy is a Researcher in the Centre for Co-operative Studies, and a Lecturer in the Department of Food Business & Development, University College Cork.

Bernard Thompson is General Secretary of NABCo, the National Association of Building Co-operatives.

INTRODUCTION

A BETTER WAY OF DOING BUSINESS

Robert Briscoe & Michael Ward

Extraordinary things are happening in the world of business. Here are just a few examples:

- In places as far apart as Colorado, Kobe in Japan and County Cork, farmers are working together with consumers and are finding it possible to provide high quality foods at attractive prices for the consumer while, at the same time, increasing farm incomes.

- In 2001, when the economy of Argentina collapsed and industrialists were abandoning their bankrupt factories, it was not slick consultants who turned them round. To everyone's amazement, it was ordinary workers, with no capital and no business experience, who transformed scores of the country's factories into thriving enterprises, many doing better now than before the collapse.

- Across Europe, motorists are finding it cheaper, more convenient and kinder to the environment to give up their own cars in favour of hiring vehicles as needed from their own car hire firms.

- Long before the Enron and Worldcom scandals caused stock prices to plummet, one far-sighted UK clearing bank was refusing to do business with firms that were unable or unwilling to abide by the bank's stringent ethical policy, although this meant that the bank turned away about 20% of new business. In spite of this, the profitability of the bank has been increasing faster than ever before.

- In Seattle, a network of health-care centres and hospitals, employing about 10,000 medical and administrative staff, is owned and controlled by its consumers, the people who use the network's health-care services.

- In 1994, when British Coal decided to shut down the Hirwaun coal mine in Wales, the miners bought the pit and now run it themselves, creating new jobs in a beleaguered community.
- In their efforts to ensure that third world producers are fairly treated, major retail chains in Europe are insisting on paying them higher than market prices for their produce. One of these retailers has banned the use of 20 specific pesticides in its own-label foodstuffs and, in its efforts to support organic producers, is breaking an EU regulation that sets a minimum size for peaches.

What these unusual businesses have in common is that they are all co-operatives, owned and controlled by the people who use their services. They represent a radically different way of running the businesses of the world, a strategy that is engaging the active commitment and creativity of more and more people world-wide. It is an approach to meeting our needs that gives ordinary people the chance to get involved in shaping the world they live in. It is a way of getting things done that is already transforming people's lives for the better. And it is not just a strategy for far-flung places: in Ireland and the UK, people are successfully adapting the co-operative idea to a whole new range of 21st century needs, such as environmental protection, health-care, and elder-care.

THE CO-OPERATIVE WAY

This book explores the co-operative way of doing business across a wide spectrum of activities and needs, ranging from basic needs for food, water, housing, finance, jobs, health-care and transportation, to needs for entertaining leisure activities, and the development of vibrant communities. In each of these areas, we show how ordinary people around the world are finding innovative ways of meeting their needs, with results that are proving more effective than the systems designed by big business and big government.

The co-operative agenda dates back to pre-history and has been widely used throughout the centuries in agriculture. However, its expansion into other fields has been slowed down by the mistaken assumption that co-operatives are relevant only in one or two sectors of life (such as agriculture and the provision of credit) or applicable only in marginal fringe businesses in disadvantaged communities. In reality, the co-operative approach is proving to be both enterprising and creative, and is applicable in areas that would have been undreamed of until recently.

Not only can the co-operative strategy deliver the goods more effectively, it is also a more environmentally friendly way of meeting needs and is more likely than conventional approaches to enhance the quality of life rather than degrade it. It is also a way of doing business that provides more effective ways of managing domestic and international trading relationships, ensuring that producers of basic commodities and the ultimate consumers are treated more fairly, thereby helping to resolve injustices that have been root causes of poverty and conflict.

QUESTIONS TO BE ANSWERED

Co-operative businesses are relevant, but how do they work in practice?
- How is it possible for idealistic businesses to succeed and survive the cut and thrust of a competitive market place?
- Is there a conflict between corporate success and responsiveness to users' needs?
- How do farmer-producers maintain control over food production and processing, while winning in highly competitive global markets?
- How do consumers make their voices heard in a world dominated by transnational multiples?
- How do ordinary people access affordable and ethical financial services that put their savings to work in their own communities?
- How do members of worker co-ops reconcile the conflicts of interest arising from employing and managing themselves at the same time?

These are just some of the practical questions that this book (and its companion volumes) will address across a wide range of activities and needs. In this book, we shall focus particularly on food & agribusiness, finance, public services, community development and the environment (including health, housing and leisure) and, finally, work (the creation of jobs).

Following two introductory chapters, there are three chapters on food and agribusiness issues and a chapter each on finance, service provision, community development and worker-owned co-operatives (including strategies for creating and saving jobs). Each of these chapters will illustrate what co-operatives are already achieving in the sector, with stories of individual co-ops showing how people have organised themselves to achieve success.

The book is divided into 10 chapters:

- **Chapter 1: From the Cradle to Retirement & Beyond!** – This introductory chapter will set the scene by exploring, with many examples, the wide range of services provided by co-ops of all kinds. It also discusses how and why co-ops get started in the first place and outlines some of the visions that inspired co-operative pioneers.

- **Chapter 2: What Co-operatives Have in Common** – What do the many different kinds of businesses outlined in **Chapter 1** have in common? This is one of the questions that this chapter attempts to answer. It also discusses the question of why some co-ops are more effective than others. It explains the principles that shape co-operative businesses and describes the co-operative process that makes them highly creative and successful. The important differences between co-operative and conventional businesses and some of the unique competitive advantages of the co-operative way of doing business are also discussed.

- **Chapter 3: Feeding Ourselves I : Consumer Co-ops & Food** – This chapter explores the different approaches to retailing and distribution used by consumer-owned food co-ops and gives examples of the competitive strategies that retail co-ops have used over the years. It examines strategies for achieving cost advantages as well as a variety of methods for differentiating the retailing product (for example, in terms of quality, safety, availability of product information, ethical marketing and fair trading).

- **Chapter 4: Feeding Ourselves II : Farmers' Co-ops & Food** – This chapter focuses mainly on the Irish experience and examines the variety of ways in which food producers have used co-operatives to increase their income and improve the quality of their lives. The chapter concludes with examples of ways in which farmers are working closely with consumers, to the benefit of both.

- **Chapter 5: Feeding Ourselves III : Workers' Co-ops & Food** – In this chapter, we explore the range of food businesses owned and controlled, not by farmers or consumers, but by the people working in them. This is the food industry sector, which successfully pioneered the sourcing and marketing of organic foods. We also look at co-operatives (including one of the largest food retailers in Europe) that are jointly owned by both workers *and* consumers.

- **Chapter 6: Financing Ourselves** – Financial co-ops are the fastest growing sector in the co-operative world. This chapter explores how user-owned financial institutions innovate to give their members greater control over their financial affairs and to promote enterprise and local development. Topics discussed include: Irish credit unions (how to turn your reputation into collateral); the Grameen Bank (how to build social collateral); the Desjardins Movement (credit unions and development in Quebec); VanCity (a multi-billion dollar credit union with a heart); Crédit Agricole Mutuel (an innovative French bank that involves 25,000 of its depositors in strategic planning); how to print your own money through LETS schemes & Time Banks; and the UK's Co-operative Bank (ethical banking as a competitive advantage).

- **Chapter 7: Serving Ourselves** – A growing trend in Europe is for co-operatives and other not-for-profit businesses to take-over and improve the quality of services previously provided directly by the state, by religious institutions or by investor-driven businesses. This chapter explains co-operative strategies for meeting neglected needs, such as some of the different ways of organising child-care businesses, and providing care for people with disabilities and the elderly, as well as rural transportation systems to improve access to remote areas. The co-operative approach involves the users of services in designing more appropriate and higher quality services. Topics discussed in this chapter include: Work Integration Social Enterprises in Ireland; New York's Home Care Co-op (owned and managed by the workers); residential services for the elderly; co-ops and leisure; co-operative health-care systems, and funeral co-ops.

- **Chapter 8: Developing Ourselves** – This chapter explores how we can work together to improve the environment and the quality of life in our local communities. It starts by visiting the West of Ireland to see how remote communities have used community co-operatives to build their economies, retain and attract public services and improve the quality of life. It then explores the co-operative contribution to a range of issues, which can provide pathways to more vibrant communities: affordable housing, tourism, a sustainable environment, and enjoyable and stimulating leisure activities.

- **Chapter 9: Working for Ourselves** – We now examine how successful worker-owned co-operatives are being set up in Ireland and internationally, to create jobs and harness the motivation, creativity and commitment of workers. The chapter starts with a brief visit to Argentina, where abandoned, bankrupt factories are being taken-over and resuscitated by their workers. It then explores the special management problems that can arise in this kind of co-op and explains how successful co-operative businesses address these problems. As well as reviewing famous success stories, such as the Mondragon network in the Basque region of Spain, it also examines some lesser-known strategies for developing new worker co-ops that have been pioneered in Ireland.

- **Chapter 10: The Way Forward** – This final chapter explores management dilemmas – those that confront conventional businesses and those that are peculiar to co-operatives. In particular, the discussion of co-operative dilemmas focuses on problems of raising investment capital and the issue of demutualisation, which has had a major impact on building societies and mutual insurance organisations. The chapter concludes with an overview of how effective co-ops have managed these dilemmas and offers suggestions on how co-ops might increase their effectiveness and build their competitive advantage.

ONE

FROM THE CRADLE TO RETIREMENT & BEYOND!

Robert Briscoe & Michael Ward

THE CO-OPERATIVE DIFFERENCE

To be successful, co-operatives must have a higher purpose than making money ... The centre of any co-operative's concern is human beings, not dollars, and the business is really a means to human ends.[1]

The quiet business

This is a book about co-operatives and their innovative ways of doing business. Co-ops prosper in every continent but are often poorly understood by the general public. It often happens that the very people who are being helped by a co-operative don't even realise that they are dealing with one. In Ireland, over two million people (more than half of the country's entire population) are members of credit unions. But it is likely that a good number of those members do not quite realise that their credit union is a co-operative and that they are part-owners of their own community banking system.

Typically, co-ops don't make a big song and dance about being co-operatives. They tend to work away quietly, providing services to their members. And, even though they *do* network nationally and internationally, they usually work together with like-minded

---

[1]   Max Kummerow, organiser of Wisconsin student housing co-ops.

organisations, which also go about their work efficiently but quietly. As a result, they don't do a good job of blowing their own trumpet!

Co-operatives are particularly plentiful in the production and distribution of food and have been playing a major role in the organic foods industry. Another major sector (and the fastest growing) is community banking services, providing accessible and affordable savings and loan services. These are the areas of co-operative activity that are best known. But most of us are unaware of the extraordinary range of other services provided by co-operatives, literally spanning the whole gamut of humanity's most urgent needs, from cradle to grave.

One of the aims of this book is to increase awareness of the range and significance of co-operatives and the key roles they play in the lives of so many people. We shall also see that co-operatives have remedies for many of the problems that threaten the well-being of our stressed-out planet. Another key objective is to underline the competitive advantages of the co-operative way of doing business, to emphasise that it is a better way of doing business, and to suggest ways in which co-operatives can build on their competitive edge. To date, the co-operative way of working has proven itself in a bewildering range of applications world-wide. An estimated 725 million people – a sizeable proportion of the world's 6 billion population – are members of the co-operatives affiliated to the International Co-operative Alliance.

In Ireland, the co-operative way of working has given Irish farmers greater control over food-processing and the purchase of inputs, freeing them from the clutches of the rural *gombeen men*[2] who emerged in the second half of the 19th Century. The Irish credit unions, inspired by Nora Herlihy in the late 1950s, grew in a mere 30 years into a flourishing nation-wide network embracing more than half the population. A new generation of Irish worker-owned co-operatives is demonstrating that the co-operative is a highly-efficient structure for building strong indigenous businesses firmly rooted in local communities. Ireland's community co-ops have brought mains electricity and piped water to remote islands and have helped create and protect many other services for neglected rural communities.

And co-operatives continue to grow – for example:

* In the United States, farmer co-ops currently market more than one third of the nation's farm commodities.

---

[2]   *Gombeen men* is an Irish term for unscrupulous business people, money-lenders and traders of all kinds, who took advantage of people in need.

- In Spain, the Mondragon network of worker-owned co-operatives employs over 68,000 people, almost 28% more than in 2000.

While some of the more established co-operatives fade in significance, new waves of co-ops are taking their place, addressing new needs in new kinds of ways. These include:

- Social economy co-operatives, which are mushrooming throughout Europe as a rapidly growing Third Sector of the economy, providing high quality, cost-effective public services (such as child-care and elder-care).
- Multi-stakeholder co-operatives (owned jointly by workers and consumers), which dominate food retailing in Spain.
- CSAs (Community Supported Agriculture), co-operative partnerships establishing direct links between farmers and consumers to the benefit of all, first developed in Switzerland and Japan, now growing rapidly in the USA and Canada, and beginning to take root in Ireland and the UK.
- The New Generation agricultural co-operatives, which are increasing the viability of farms and rural communities throughout the American Mid-West and reversing long-term trends in rural depopulation and loss of jobs.
- Tourism co-operatives, which offer a good deal to the consumer and support the move toward sustainable tourism.
- New small-scale dairy farmer co-operatives in Wisconsin, which, against all the odds, are rebuilding the viability of the family farm through new applications of the *meitheal*[3] approach.

There are a number of important reasons why co-operatives are receiving increased attention – for example, bio-diversity is a significant concept not just in the world of living organisms but also in the world of organisations. In a world increasingly dominated by footloose transnational corporations, co-operatives keep organisational alternatives alive, providing a local counterbalance to foreign-owned transnational businesses. They are invaluable organisational tools for enabling communities to design unique solutions to their own special

---

[3] Informal co-operation between neighbours, historically an important feature of Irish rural life. *Meitheal* was the word used for "the group drawn from the community for the co-operative effort" (Culloty, 1990, p.56).

problems, and making it possible for local businesses to participate creatively in the global economy.

When it comes to enhancing the quality of life, co-operatives have a number of key competitive advantages over other types of organisation:

- The different varieties of co-operatives empower groups of stakeholders often marginalised by conventional big business.
- They help build *social capital* and a vigorous community life, by developing opportunities for significant decision-making and effective action at the local level.
- They help reduce inequality by increasing the bargaining power and pooling the resources and skills of ordinary people.
- They provide opportunities for *mutual aid* and *cost-effective service provision* tailored precisely to people's needs.
- They encourage *local and individual self-reliance* and thereby offer significant alternatives to globalised, investor-driven businesses.
- They lead to the self-conscious *redesigning of goods and services around users' needs*.
- They have a *positive impact on the environment*, by placing less emphasis on environmentally-damaging strategies, such as short-term profit maximisation. They encourage *sustainable development* by helping communities build a better life from their own local resources.
- Co-operatives have often proved to be extremely efficient and cost-effective in circumstances where other forms of business find it hard to survive (see **Children of crisis and conflict** below).

THE VARIETY OF CO-OPERATIVES

A working definition

Let's start with a simple working definition of a co-operative:

> A co-operative is a self-help business, owned and democratically controlled by the people who use its services and share in its benefits.

This definition is over-simplified, but it does focus on the key features of the co-operative approach to getting things done.

Self-help
First of all, a co-op is a *self-help* organisation, owned and controlled by the people who use its services. It has been set up for the purpose of helping its members address their own needs and problems.

Designed to serve users
Unlike a conventional company, which is owned by a group of investors (who may never use the company's services and may even live on the other side of the world), a co-op's owners are intimately involved in the activities of the co-op. They use the co-op's services on a day-to-day basis. Thus:

- A **housing co-op** is owned by the people who live in the houses and flats, not by an absentee landlord.
- A **fishery co-op** is owned by the people who catch the fish, not by the wealthy owners of a fish-processing company.
- A **child-care co-op** is owned by the parents of the children and/or by the care workers providing the services.
- A **tourism co-op** is owned by the holiday-makers and/or by the small businesses that provide services to visitors (such as bed & breakfast guesthouses, tour-guides, etc.).
- A **dairy co-op** is owned by the farmers who produce the milk.
- A **credit union** is owned by its customers, the people who save money in the credit union and who borrow from it.
- An **electricity supply co-op** is owned by the people who use the electricity.

Democratically controlled
Another important feature of co-ops is that its members control the co-op *democratically*, one person, one vote. Things are done very differently in the typical business, where votes are allocated according to the number of shares you own, making it possible for one wealthy shareholder to out-vote all the rest.

Members share benefits according to their use of the co-op's services
When a co-operative business distributes profits to its members, it does so in proportion to their use of the business. The more they use the co-op, the greater the benefits they receive.

These features are summarised in **Figure 1.1**.

FIGURE 1.1: THE USER-FOCUSED CO-OPERATIVE MODEL

A co-operative is a user-owned and user-controlled business that distributes benefits on the basis of use. More specifically, it is distinguished from other businesses by three concepts or principles:

- **First, the user-owner principle**: Persons who own and finance the co-operative are those that use it.

- **Second, the user-control principle**: Control of the co-operative is by those who use the co-operative.

- **Third, the user-benefits principle**: Benefits are distributed to its users on the basis of their use. The user-benefits principle is often stated as "business-at-cost". [4, 5]

Clearly co-ops are unusual businesses and they tend to arouse strong feelings, both positive and negative. Also, the word *co-op* might summon up images for you of one particular kind of business, depending on where you were raised:

- If you had grown up in rural Ireland, your image of a co-op most likely would be a dairy, although if you were from an urban setting you might have thought first of credit unions, or housing co-ops. If you happened to run a bed & breakfast business, your co-op might be a tourism co-op, helping market your locality to foreign tourists. If you were an artist, you might think of a co-op as an agency through which you can sell your work and buy the materials you need.

- If you had gone to school in Britain, your idea of a co-op most likely would be a retail store selling groceries. Retail co-ops in the UK are also the biggest providers of funeral services in the country, so you might also associate them with undertaking!

- If you were raised on a prairie farm in Canada, you might think of a co-op as a business that runs grain elevators and markets your parents' grain.

- If you had studied at Harvard University, your idea of a co-operative would have been The Harvard Co-op, a student-owned department store, selling everything from books to boots and paying you a handsome year-end rebate on all the purchases you had made.

---

[4]   For example, farmer members of a dairy processing co-op share distributed profits in proportion to the quantity of milk they supply to the co-op; consumer members of a retail co-op share distributed profits in proportion to their purchases from the co-op.

[5]   D. Barton, 1988, Chairman of American Institute of Co-operation, quoted in Böök (1992).

- If you lived in the mountains of Nepal, you might think of the Mount Everest Co-op, which manages tourism sustainably for the benefit of the local people acting as guides or providing accommodation for visitors.
- If your home was in a rural village on the outskirts of Bombay, for you a co-op might be the firm that buys and sells the milk from the family's buffalo.
- At the other extreme, if you were born with a silver spoon in your mouth and inhabited one of the posher boulevards of East Manhattan, your co-op might be a luxurious apartment tower owned by the wealthy residents.
- If you grew up in the Basque region of Spain, for you a co-op probably would be a technologically-sophisticated factory, manufacturing and exporting appliances, or a co-operative university, owned and controlled by its students, staff and the industrial co-ops that fund it.
- If you were raised in a Fijian village, your co-op would be a small store where you could buy basic supplies and also earn a little cash by selling the copra you had cut.
- If your hometown was Seattle, on the West Coast of the USA, for you a co-op most likely would be a health-care network of hospitals and clinics, owned and controlled by their patients.

Not surprisingly, our image of a co-op is shaped and limited by our own experience. One of the reasons that co-ops have not yet reached their full potential is that most of us tend to have a very narrow view of the kinds of tasks co-ops can perform. Depending on where you live, you will see a co-op as just a *creamery* or just a *retail store*, and be totally unaware of all the other possibilities. It can be quite a shock to learn that co-operatives can do almost anything:

> It's a big culture change. Before, when we thought of the co-op, we'd think funerals and groceries. Now we think of our welfare and students services, and even owning a kicking nightclub.[6]

In fact, co-ops can be adapted to many different kinds of purpose. But they can succeed only if the people involved choose the *type* of co-operative business that is most suitable for meeting their needs. So let us

---

[6] Verity Coyle, president of the newly established Students' Union Co-op at the University of Lincoln, quoted in Woodin (2003).

begin our exploration of the co-operative by expanding our ideas about co-operative possibilities and examining the different types of co-operative available.

We have seen that a co-op is owned and democratically controlled by the people who *use* its services (see **Figure 1.1**). So, let's try classifying co-ops into categories according to how they are *used by their owners*.

TYPES OF CO-OPERATIVE BUSINESS

Consumer co-ops

One of the first successful co-ops was the Rochdale Equitable Pioneers Society, a consumer co-operative that opened its doors in 1844 in the English town of Rochdale. It started out as a small retail foodstore owned by its customers (the people who consume the products and services of the business). Initially, they used their co-op to provide themselves with pure, unadulterated food and honest weights and measures (hard to come by in those days!) but, as the business grew and prospered, it was able to provide them with a comprehensive range of goods and services. **Case Study 1.1** gives a brief history of the Rochdale Co-op.

CASE STUDY 1.1: THE ROCHDALE PIONEERS

The original Rochdale consumer co-op emerged in an era known as the "Hungry 'Forties". Incomes were low, prices high and jobs hard to come by. Textile workers in Rochdale had tried to improve their lot by organising a trade union and threatening to strike. But all to no avail, as there were plenty of unemployed ready to take the place of strikers. When all else failed, citizens of Rochdale began to think about an alternative way of increasing their spending power – something less obvious than trying to threaten the all-powerful employers with strike action. If they couldn't force their bosses to increase wages, maybe they could find ways to make their wages go further.

Twenty-eight pioneers decided to try setting up their own retail store. By pooling their purchasing power and buying in bulk, they would be able to get more food for their money. They also would be able to guarantee that the food they sold to themselves would be of good quality. This was an important issue in an age when it was common for retailers to increase their profits by adulterating food (adding clay to the flour and sand to the sugar) and by using weighing machines that gave short measure to the customer.

To finance the new business, they each agreed to buy a £1 share in the co-op. It took them a year to save this amount and, after they had paid for the equipment they needed and the rent for a shop, they had only a few pounds left to buy a small range of basic commodities such as flour, sugar, butter and oatmeal.

In 1844, they set up their co-op to be as inconspicuous as possible, selling its goods at market prices rather than trying to undercut directly the prices in company stores. The financial benefits to the members would come in the form of a refund, paid at the end of the year in proportion to each member's purchases. Membership was open to anyone who agreed to invest a £1 share and abide by the rules of the co-op.

Amazingly, the business grew rapidly, and the word spread to neighbouring towns. By the 1860s, there were Rochdale-style co-ops throughout the UK. It was not long before these small co-operatives got together to set up their own wholesaler and their own factories. Some even bought farmland to grow their own produce. It was not many years before similar co-ops sprang up across Europe and reached the USA via immigrants from Scandinavia.

Modern-day examples of co-ops are shown in **Case Studies 1.2** and **1.3**.

CASE STUDY 1.2: CONSUMER CO-OPS IN SWEDEN

In Sweden, in addition to an extensive network of consumer-owned hypermarkets and department stores, the consumer co-operative movement has acquired a number of high quality, conventional retail businesses and brought them into the co-operative fold. These new businesses include a major bookstore chain and a leading chain of toyshops. Co-operative members may now enjoy rebates on their purchases when shopping at these stores.

CASE STUDY 1.3: JAPANESE HAN CO-OPS

In Japan, Han co-ops consist of groups of neighbours who get together to pool their orders for food and other consumer goods, which are then delivered directly to their doorsteps from their own co-operative warehouse.

But consumer co-ops aren't just about running shops. The most successful example of this kind of co-op in Ireland is the **credit union**. The credit union serves the consumers of financial services and is owned and democratically controlled by its borrowers and savers. **Housing co-ops** (owned by their tenants) also fit into this category. A new field for consumer-owned co-ops is the rapidly growing field of **wind power**.

In North America, for example, you can find many kinds of co-ops that are governed by consumers. There are consumer **health-care co-ops** (health-care centres and hospitals owned by their patients – see **Case Study 1.4**), **electricity supply co-ops** and **telephone co-ops** (owned by the people who use the electricity and the phone services), and **water co-ops** (water supply systems owned by the people who drink the water). There are also **radio and viewer-owned TV stations** (owned by the listeners and viewers).

Case Studies 1.5 and **1.6** give more examples of the innovative consumer co-operatives that are emerging around the world.

CASE STUDY 1.4: THE GROUP HEALTH CO-OPERATIVE (GHC), SEATTLE[7]

GHC operates a care delivery system designed to ensure patients get the right services when they need them from the most appropriate place. This is done by co-ordinating between practitioners, emphasising prevention, and by using the best research available to help individualised treatment.

GHC is based in Seattle, but operates out of 20 centres in Washington State as well as two centres in Idaho. With about 10,000 people employed in health-care and administrative positions, GHC is the third-largest private sector employer in Washington State, with revenues in 2002 of $1.7billion. (For more on GHC, see **Chapter 7**.)

CASE STUDY 1.5: CONSUMER CO-OPS FOR THE 21ST CENTURY

Energy-purchasing Co-ops
With the growing movement toward deregulation of electricity supply, more and more countries will be experiencing the kind of energy market that already exists in the USA, where co-ops are playing an ever-increasing role. By working together, American co-ops are able to negotiate lower energy prices for their members and are developing ways of keeping energy costs down. They do this by working with their members to conserve energy and take greater advantage of off-peak rates.

---

[7]   See www.ghc.org.

In Australia, where co-ops are only just starting to work in this area, Co-operative Energy has helped a group of non-profit agencies for the elderly to cut their energy costs by an average 32%. (See **Chapter 8** for examples of electricity generating co-ops.)

Car-sharing Co-ops

This idea started in Switzerland in the late 1980s, but has spread already to Germany, Denmark, Holland, UK, Sweden, Austria and Italy, Norway and the UK.[8] Car-sharing is also available in hundreds of cities in North America.

The idea is simple: instead of the expense of owning a car that you might only use for an hour or so each day, you join a car-sharing co-op, which will enable you to book the right vehicle for your changing needs from a fleet of cars.

Swiss motorists save an average of 250 Swiss Francs per month by using the car-share co-op, and the movement is growing rapidly. In 1987, there were 28 co-op members sharing two cars. At the end of December 2003, there were 58,000 members in Switzerland alone, sharing 1,700 vehicles at 980 locations in 400 communities across the country.

Producer co-ops

This is a type of business that is owned and democratically controlled by independent producers, such as farmers, fishermen, artisans, handicraft producers and artists, as well as other small business operators as varied as taxi drivers, pharmacists, general medical practitioners, hauliers and plumbers (see **Case Study 1.6** for a co-op owned by garage operators).

The purpose of this kind of co-op is to help producers improve the effectiveness and profitability of their own individual businesses. For example, a *dairy co-op* can help its farmer-members get a better price for their milk by processing and marketing it for them. *Agricultural* producer co-ops can also provide a range of other services, including the supply of farm inputs (such as fertilisers and seeds), and access to equipment and machinery. *Handicraft co-ops* help members get a better price for their products by providing training to improve members' skills, as well as marketing services and the supply of raw materials. In many parts of the world, independent taxi drivers combine to form *taxi co-operatives* to help market their taxi businesses. Typically, such a co-op provides taxi owners with a base and a dispatching service.

---

[8] "Vu ses avantages, l'autopartage est en train de décoller en Europe", *Le Courier de Geneve* – 20.7.1999. Also see http://www.mobility.ch/e/index.htm for more details. For up-to-date information in French, try http://www.mobility.ch/index.cfm?dom=2. For information on North American car-sharing, see www.carsharing.net.

CASE STUDY 1.6: A GARAGE CO-OP

Capricorn Garage Co-op provides the majority of parts and services to mechanical workshops, service stations and smash repairers throughout Australia. It is a registered co-op, owned by over 8,000 industry members across Australia, as well as in New Zealand and South Africa. Membership is open to registered automobile repairers, panel beaters, auto electricians, service stations and general repairers.

One of the benefits of belonging to the co-op is that members have instant credit lines with all of Capricorn's preferred suppliers, as well as negotiated price discounts on all purchases. Goods ordered from suppliers are invoiced through Capricorn's office, which then mails a single consolidated monthly statement to each member, listing all the purchases made. Preferred suppliers can also communicate with members via the Capricorn website to inform them of special offers and to manage bonus point schemes.

For more information, see www.capricorn.com.au.

Worker co-ops[9]

This type of co-op is less common in Ireland than the producer co-operative but is attracting increasing interest and is proving to be a useful means of job-creation and small business development. A worker co-op is a business owned and democratically controlled by its workers (for example, a fishing boat, owned and controlled by its crew). A very successful worker co-op in Ireland is Heron Quality Foods in West Cork, a specialist bakery that is Ireland's largest supplier of gluten-free breads.

Worker co-ops have been particularly successful in Southern Europe, notably Spain, where the Mondragon network of capital-intensive worker co-ops competes successfully in demanding export markets, and Italy, where co-operatives even undertake major civil engineering tasks such as road and bridge building.

Community co-ops[10]

These are businesses that are owned and democratically controlled by the people living in a particular community. The purpose of such a co-op is to improve the viability of a community, by creating jobs, marketing the community's assets and providing needed services. For example, a community co-op might create jobs by promoting the tourism potential

---

[9]   For more on this type of co-op, see **Chapter 9**.
[10] For more on this type of co-op, see **Chapter 8**.

of the community or by helping to create new worker co-operatives and other kinds of small business. It might provide needed services by, for example, setting up a village shop or running a community bus to link the village with neighbouring urban centres.

Although community co-ops have been particularly valuable in so-called peripheral regions, notably in Western Ireland, the highlands and islands of Scotland and remote parts of Atlantic Canada, they have also sprung up in many other parts of the world – and not always in rural areas. You will also find them in disadvantaged urban areas in many of the major cities of the UK and North America. As in rural areas, their role in the inner city is to improve the viability of a local community, by creating jobs, marketing the community's assets, keeping resources within the community and protecting and/or providing needed services.

Multi-stakeholder co-ops

Also referred to as a *multi-user co-op*, this type of co-operative is owned and controlled by two or more of the groups of users described above. It might be a business owned and controlled jointly by its customers and workers (for example, the Eroski supermarket chain in the Basque region of Spain – see **Case Study 1.7** – or an American health-care co-op, some of which are owned jointly by medical staff and patients). Another possibility is a producer/consumer co-op owned jointly by farmers and shoppers (like the Community Supported Agriculture partnerships that are spreading rapidly through North America and establishing a firm foothold in Europe).

CASE STUDY 1.7: EROSKI

This is a highly successful retail co-operative, owned by workers and shoppers. Its Board of Directors consists of equal numbers of consumer and worker representatives, but the President is always a consumer and has the casting vote. Eroski was born in the Basque region of Spain but now dominates food retailing throughout the country.

For more on Eroski, and how it got so big so fast, see **Chapter 6**.

Social economy co-ops are an important, growing co-operative sector, often using the multi-user structure. For example a child-care co-operative is often jointly owned and controlled democratically by both the parents of the children being looked after and the workers looking after the kids (see **Case Study 1.8**).

CASE STUDY 1.8: CO-OPERATIVE CHILD-CARE

The Oxford, Swindon and Gloucester consumer co-op (OSG) is one of the UK's most successful consumer co-ops, which operates a wide range of retail stores owned and controlled democratically by their customers. In recent years, OSG has been finding new ways of meeting the community's needs by helping to develop new kinds of co-operatives capable of addressing a wider range of needs.

Recognising that there is a lack of quality child-care services, OSG has developed a multi-stakeholder model for child-care co-ops. OSG aims to sponsor the development of a network of nurseries and child-care services, each of which will involve a local group representing the key stakeholders (parents, carers, employees, community groups and even, when appropriate, local employers). The first of these co-ops was launched in 2003; two more followed in 2004.[11]

HOW CO-OPERATIVES GET STARTED

Children of distress?

Co-ops have often been referred to as *children of distress* and, indeed, they frequently do emerge when people are experiencing severe problems. For example, see **Case Study 1.1** if you are not familiar with the oft-told story of the Rochdale Pioneers and the first successful consumer co-op, which they set up in 1844, in the industrial town of Rochdale in the north of England.

We can also draw some tentative hypotheses about the motivations for starting co-operatives by looking at the kinds of business situation in which they emerge. Many types of co-operatives are involved in the food industry, so let us look at the food business chain (**Figure 1.2**) and see where co-ops have been most likely to emerge.

---

[11] Jenkins (2003).

FIGURE 1.2: THE FOOD BUSINESS CHAIN:
FROM FARM TO FORK

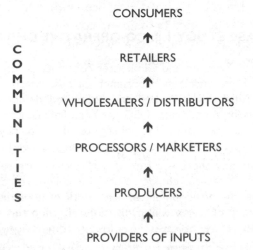

CONSUMERS

↑

C   RETAILERS
O
M   ↑
M
U   WHOLESALERS / DISTRIBUTORS
N
I   ↑
T
I   PROCESSORS / MARKETERS
E
S   ↑

PRODUCERS

↑

PROVIDERS OF INPUTS

Co-ops have tended to emerge at those points of the chain where people are poorly served by conventional businesses and where reliance on the marketplace fails to meet people's needs – for example:

- **Small producers** (farmers and fishermen) set up co-ops in situations where they had little bargaining power in their dealings with a comparatively small number of distributors, processors or suppliers of inputs. By combining in a co-operative, they were able to get a better profit from their produce – for example, by pooling their purchases of inputs (equipment and fertilisers), by collectively processing and marketing their outputs, and by providing collective services to members, (training, insurance, finance, etc.).
- **Consumers** (particularly in Northern Europe and UK) set up retail co-ops when they felt themselves at a disadvantage in their relationship with retailers and other distributors. By combining their purchasing power in co-operatives, they were able to provide themselves with food of reliable quality at lower cost.
- **Workers** (particularly in Southern Europe) set up co-ops to provide themselves with more secure, better-paid and more meaningful jobs than were available from conventional employers.
- **Communities:** A community is also an important stakeholder of the businesses located within its boundaries. After all, the community depends on its businesses to provide jobs and services. The negative

products of its businesses, such as toxic waste, also affect it! Remote, endangered communities (particularly in places like Western Ireland, and the islands and highlands of Scotland), where markets are small and costs of operation high, set up community-owned co-ops to provide goods and services, which made insufficient profits to be of interest to conventional businesses and were too costly for local authorities. In addition, important objectives for many of them were to protect the local environment and safeguard a cultural heritage under threat.

Children of crisis and conflict

Co-ops have often proved invaluable in extreme situations of crisis and conflict. A recent publication by the International Labour Organisation (the UN's oldest agency) provides numerous examples of the effectiveness of co-operatives and other self-help organisations in facilitating socio-economic recovery from extreme crises, including:[12]

- There are more than 2,400 labour-contracting co-ops in India's Gujurat state, many of which have played a significant role in rebuilding devastated communities after the earthquakes of 2002.
- Co-operative micro-finance systems have assisted the recovery of villages in Papua New Guinea, which had suffered severe depopulation after 10 years of civil war.
- In Guatemala, credit and agricultural co-operatives played an important role in improving the social and economic conditions of impoverished communities, thereby addressing the problem of gross inequality, a root cause of conflict.
- Following widespread livestock infection in Somalia, co-operatives provided their members with veterinary services, enabling them to secure the disease-free certification they needed to resume the trading of their cattle.
- Before the establishment of cattle marketing co-operatives in Botswana, farmers were obliged to sell to local traders who paid rock-bottom prices. Often, farmers would be indebted to the same traders for consumer goods and were trapped in a cycle of perpetual poverty. The co-ops enabled farmers to ship their cattle to abattoirs that paid fair prices, and to beat drought by moving all their cattle to holding grounds with a bore-hole.

---

[12]   Parnell (2003).

- After the Kobe earthquake in Japan, the local consumer co-operative played a major role in getting food supplies to people throughout the affected region.
- Kurdish refugees fleeing from Iraq to Turkey relied on agricultural, credit, housing and employment co-ops to ease their problems.

Children of vision

Yet it would be a mistake to assume that co-operatives are solely products of crisis, desperation and misery. They have also been motivated by powerful visions of a better world. Even in the gloomy world of Rochdale in the 1840s, distress was not the sole – or even the main – motivation of the co-operative pioneers.

> They were not half-starved operatives, driven by the desperation of hunger to start a co-operative store. Most of them were comparatively well-paid skilled artisans, some in business on their own account. Idealism, the vision of a better social order, not hunger, inspired these men.[13]

Their idealism and vision showed up in the catalogue of ambitious objectives drawn up for this modest co-operative, which was to be launched with set-up capital of a mere £28. Here is what they planned to achieve:
- The establishment of a store for the sale of provisions, clothing, etc.
- The building, purchasing or erecting of a number of houses, in which those members desiring to assist each other in improving their domestic and social conditions may reside.
- To commence the manufacture of such articles as the Society may determine upon, for the employment of such members as may be without employment, or may be suffering in consequence of repeated reductions in their wages.
- As a further benefit and security to the members of this Society, the Society shall purchase or rent an estate or estates of land, which shall be cultivated by the members who may be out of employment or whose labour may be badly remunerated.
- That, for the promotion of sobriety, a Temperance Hotel be opened in one of the Society's houses as soon as convenient.
- That, as soon as practical, this Society shall proceed to arrange the powers of production, distribution, education and government; or, in

---

13   Bonner (1961).

other words, to establish a self-supporting home colony of united interests, or assist other societies in establishing such colonies.[14]

So, the first step was to open a store, and the pioneers set out a list of businesslike rules to ensure that the store would be operated efficiently and in the best interests of all its members (these became known as the *Rochdale Principles*). The store would enable them to build the capital and skills needed to create houses for the homeless and a factory for the unemployed. The ultimate goal would be to set up a self-managing, self-supporting co-operative community, which would run its own schools, factories and farms.

> This was their Utopia, for which their storekeeping and the rest of their projects were regarded only as an imperfect and partial preparation.[15]

An ambitious vision for a group of 28 people who had taken a whole year to save between them the modest sum of £28!

Co-operative visions from Ireland

The Rochdale co-operators had developed a successful co-operative model, which stimulated the birth of large-scale co-operative movements in country after country. But long before Rochdale, the Irish economist, William Thompson of Cork, had also developed a vision of a co-operative system. His ideas influenced the Welsh social reformer, Robert Owen, who in turn influenced the Rochdale Pioneers.[16] Thompson developed not only a powerful critique of the existing economic system, but also a positive vision of a better future.

> Thompson encouraged the working classes to take the initiative in bringing about a new co-operative system through working class organisations such as trade unions. He appealed to the trade unions to use workers' savings to set up local co-operative villages with their own industries.[17]

Early Irish co-operators had a broad view of the usefulness of co-operatives, which were not just seen as a means of obtaining a fair price for milk, but as the hub for community development. The poet George

---

[14]   Webb (1910).
[15]   Cole (1944), p.76.
[16]   Tucker (1983).
[17]   Briscoe *et al.* (1982), p.19.

Russell (better known as AE) painted a powerful vision of the future of co-operatives in rural Ireland:

> A ... co-operative community ought to have, to a large extent, the character of a nation. It should manufacture for its members all things which it profitably can manufacture for them, employing its own workmen, carpenters, bootmakers, makers and menders of farm equipment, saddlery, harness, etc. It should aim at feeding its members and their families cheaply and well, as far as possible out of the meat and grain produced in the district. It should have a mill to grind their grain, a creamery to manufacture their butter; or where certain enterprises like a bacon factory are too great for it, it should unite with other co-operative creameries to furnish out such an enterprise. It should sell for the members their produce, and buy for them their requirements, and hold for them labour-saving machinery. It should put aside a certain portion of its profits every year for the creation of halls, libraries, places of recreation and games, and it should pursue this plan steadily with the purpose of giving its members every social and educational advantage which the civilisation of their time affords. It should have its councils or village parliaments where improvements and new ventures could be discussed.[18]

POSITIVE *vs* NEGATIVE VISIONS

Peter Senge, a leading systems theorist, argues that the kind of positive vision shared by Thompson and the Rochdale Pioneers is a much more powerful and reliable motivator than the desperate desire to avoid distress. Senge argues that negative visions are less effective than positive visions for three main reasons:

- First, energy that could build something new is diverted to "preventing" something we don't want to happen.
- Second, negative visions carry a subtle yet unmistakable message of powerlessness: our people really don't care; they can only pull together when there is sufficient threat.
- Last, negative visions are inevitably short-term: the organisation is motivated so long as the threat persists; once it passes, so does the organisation's vision and energy.[19]

---

[18] Quoted in Keating (1983), pp.54-55.
[19] Senge (1990), p.225.

According to Senge, the first quality or capability of a learning organisation (one that learns from its experience and responds appropriately to changing needs) is aspiration. People learn through aspiration (driven by hope and ambition) *and* through desperation (driven by fear), but there is a great difference in the quality of that learning. If a co-op is a child of desperation alone, it learns only as long as it has to, stopping when the external pressures are removed. This is exactly what happens in incompetent and lacklustre co-operatives, which have lost their original sense of purpose and are finding it difficult to develop a new reason for their existence.

Senge emphasises the importance of a compelling, positive vision:

> The purpose of thinking about and articulating the vision is to generate energy for change – to create a focus, enthusiasm, a sense of what might be possible. Now who knows what will actually develop? Who knows the ways in which it will develop? It may be as we imagine it, or it might also be in a way that is completely unimaginable today. The important thing is that it produces change in the right direction.[20]

"Change in the right direction" was the immediate outcome of the vision formulated by the Rochdale Pioneers in their 1844 list of objectives. Their inspiring vision of the self-supporting, co-operative community was never achieved, but it did move things in the right direction toward the almost unimaginable world-wide co-operative movement of today, involving more than 725 million people working together in 750,000 co-operatives.

Similarly, in Ireland, the co-operative visions of the poet George Russell (AE) helped move the Irish co-operative movement in the right direction and, further afield, influenced the thinking of people like Rabindranath Tagore and Mahatma Gandhi. AE developed a vision of a new rural civilisation and urged individual co-ops to look beyond their immediate problems and work together to create a new social organism.

> It is not enough to organise farmers in a district for one purpose only – into a credit society, a dairy society, a fruit society, a bacon factory, or in a co-operative store. All these may be and must be beginnings, but if they are to develop and absorb all rural business into their organisation, they will have little effect on character. No true social organism will have been created. ... If co-operative societies are specialised for this purpose or that ... the limitation of

---

[20] Peter Senge, quoted in Di Carlo (1996), p.229.

objective prevents a true social organism from being formed. The latter has a tremendous effect on human character. The specialised society only develops economic efficiency. The evolution of society beyond its present level depends absolutely on its power to unite and create true social organism.[21]

SUMMARY

In this chapter, we have taken a quick tour through the world of co-operatives, looking at some of the ways in which different stakeholders (consumers, producers, workers and communities) are able to use the co-operative concept to meet their varied needs, and how different groups of stakeholders have developed new ways of working together for their mutual benefit. We have seen that co-ops help people meet a bewildering variety of needs, from power generation to job creation, from child-care to funerals. We have seen that co-ops help *producers*, small business people of all kinds, by reducing their outgoings and improving income. *Consumers* use them to improve the quality of the goods and services they use; *workers* use them to create meaningful jobs; and *communities* to enhance livelihoods, protect the environment, and improve the quality of life. We also considered how co-ops get started. Often they are *children of distress* forced into action to address an intolerable situation for which there is no immediate remedy. But also they are often *children of vision*, inspired by a powerful vision of a better way of running the world.

What do all of these disparate businesses have in common? **Chapter 2** attempts to answer this question, and also to analyse some of the factors underlying co-operative success and failure.

---

[21] Russell (1982, reprinted).

TWO

WHAT CO-OPS HAVE IN COMMON

Robert Briscoe & Michael Ward

So far, we have explored the extraordinary variety of businesses operating as co-operatives. We have seen that they serve many different types of user and offer a multitude of goods and services, ranging from comprehensive, state-of the-art health services in North America to processing and marketing the milk of a villager's buffalo in India. In spite of such huge differences of scale and technology, all of these businesses share common characteristics. In this chapter, we explore these common characteristics and define more precisely the concept of a co-operative.

We start by discussing the widely accepted *co-operative principles*, which have been used to define the legal structure of co-ops. We then look at how co-ops go about achieving their goals. In the most effective co-ops, things get done by means of a very distinctive *co-operative process*. It is this co-operative process that is the source of a co-operative's competitive advantage. The use of the co-operative process clearly differentiates fully-functioning co-operatives from conventional businesses. It also distinguishes an effective co-operative from a lacklustre one.

THE PRINCIPLES OF CO-OPERATION

So far we have used a rough working definition of a co-op as *a self-help business, owned and democratically controlled by the people who use its services*. This definition gives us a useful, general picture but is incomplete. We also looked at the user-focused definition of a co-op (**Figure 1.1**), which takes us a step further.

The Rochdale Pioneers had the problem of deciding how to operate this new kind of user-owned business. How should a user-owned business be designed to ensure that it remains true to its purpose of putting the user of the business first? They came up with a number of operating principles to ensure that their business would consistently operate in the interests of their customer/members:

- **Open membership:** To ensure that their co-op would be owned by its customers, they decided that ownership of the co-operative should be open to anyone who could make use of its services and was also prepared to invest in a share as a contribution to the co-op's capital.

- **Democratic control:** To ensure that their co-op would be controlled by its users, and *only* by its users, it was agreed that only members of the co-op would be allowed to elect and serve on the co-op's board of directors (management committee) and that the board should be answerable to the membership at periodic general meetings (held at least once a year). And to ensure that the co-op couldn't be taken over by a small clique of wealthy individuals, the rule was one member one vote, regardless of the number of shares they held, very different from the practice in conventional companies where the rule is one share one vote.

- **Economic participation:** Shareholders should be paid no more than a modest rate of interest to reward them for the use of their capital. After all, the co-op aims to reward people according to their use of the business, not according to how much money they have invested in it. This is very different from a conventional company, which distributes benefits in proportion to the number of shares owned by the shareholder.

The pioneers also came up with a number of other operational principles, but the basic principles above summarise most of the distinctive characteristics of the co-operative organisation structure. Co-operatives in most parts of the world are required by co-operative legislation to abide by these basic principles of co-operation (often still referred to as the *Rochdale Principles*). For a more detailed and comprehensive discussion of *co-operative principles*, see the **Appendix**.

Among the other important principles developed by the Rochdale pioneers, but not usually required by legislation, are:

- **Investment in education:** The co-operative is required to spend a fixed proportion of its profits on education. In Rochdale, they agreed to spend 2.5% of their net profits in this way. Because their co-op had been set up to assist the development of disadvantaged people, it was only reasonable that they should spend some of their profits on developing their members (to improve their ability to run their own affairs). They should also try to inform the general public (to show them how the techniques of co-operation could be applied to the solution of societal problems). Many co-operators would go so far as to insist that education is the real purpose of all kinds of co-operatives (see **Figure 2.1**).

- **Pure and unadulterated food:** It might pay the unscrupulous shopkeeper to add sand to the sugar and use inaccurate weighing scales, but such abuses should never be countenanced in a consumer co-operative. Their co-op was designed to benefit the customer, not the shopkeeper. Therefore, it was only reasonable to redesign retailing in the interests of the customer. In an era before BSE, the pioneers were as interested as we are in traceability of foodstuffs. The new co-ops integrated backwards as fast as they could, joining together to set up their own wholesaler as well as flour mills and bakeries, dairies and meat-processing plants. They went so far as to buy agricultural land and even a coal mine,[22] to ensure that their customer would get the best deals.

---

[22]   Today, the Co-op Group, which is the largest co-operative in the UK, is also the country's biggest farmer. The coal mines were nationalised in 1947, when the government took over the industry. However, when the industry was virtually closed down by the Thatcher government, the last remaining coal mine in Wales was bought by its miners who now run it as a very successful worker-owned co-operative (Tower Colliery).

FIGURE 2.1: WHY EDUCATION?[23]

To the question 'Why do co-operative societies assume educational tasks?', we are justified in replying that educational tasks have in fact assumed co-operative societies. The purpose for which we exist is not grocery or laundry but education, in the sense of cultivating men and women of co-operative quality.

Co-operation between co-operatives

Co-ops should co-operate with other co-ops. They usually start out as tiny businesses run by relatively poor people with very limited resources. They are much more likely to prosper if they can work closely with other co-ops. This is why you find credit unions working together to set up a central body to provide affordable services to them all, and small retail co-ops co-operating to run a wholesaling organisation so they can enjoy the cost advantages of bulk buying.

THE COMPETITIVE ADVANTAGE OF CO-OPS

The guru of strategic management, Michael Porter, has argued that there are only the following sources of competitive advantage[24]:

- Low costs, which are hard for your competitors to match.
- Focusing on the needs of a highly specialised niche market, which is less attractive to large-scale competitors.
- Differentiation of your products or services from competitors'.

How do co-ops create competitive advantages?

Low Costs?

Sometimes, as a co-op, it is possible to achieve low operating costs unavailable to your competitors – perhaps by using no-frills premises or by using volunteers to do some of the work. Also, as a co-op, you might be able to motivate your employees so that they do not need the costly supervision other firms must use to ensure their workers do the work they are supposed to do (this is particularly likely to be an advantage of

---

[23]   Marshall (undated).
[24]   Porter (1985).

a worker-owned co-op). And, as mentioned above, co-operation with other co-ops is also a viable strategy for keeping costs down.

Focusing on a niche market?

Many co-ops have done this successfully, specialising in a business area that has few competitors. This was done with particular success in the 1960s to 1980s in the USA and the UK, when many co-ops were set up to sell organic foods or run vegetarian restaurants – alternative bookshops and bicycle repair shops were also popular options. Many of these co-ops still exist, even though major supermarkets, in response to growing consumer demand) have moved into the marketing of organic foods.

Differentiation?

The most likely competitive advantage for a co-op stems from its ability to differentiate itself from conventional businesses. Because a co-operative exists to serve users rather than to maximise profits for investors, it does not have to spend most of its profits to satisfy investors. This gives a co-op greater freedom to redesign its business, in order to make it more useful and usable for its members. The concept of *design for use* is a co-op's main tool for differentiating itself from its competitors. Design for use is a key element in what we call the US strategy for getting things done, and is discussed in the next section.

THEM & US: Two Ways to Run the World

There are two fundamental ways of getting things done. Let's try to avoid sociological jargon, and use instead very simple terms to describe these two approaches:[25] the THEM way of getting things done, and the US way.

Let's start by looking at the THEM approach, which is based on the idea that:

> … the best way of solving problems and meeting needs is to leave
> it all to THEM – to small elites of unusually resourceful, powerful
> or wealthy people.

If you think about it, this is the usual way things get done in industrialised countries. We have a problem or a need to be met, so we

---

[25]   The following discussion is based on Briscoe *et al.* (1982), pp.27-36.

complain a bit and wait around for THEM to do something about it. In other words, we wait until somebody important – a businessperson, a politician, an expert of some sort – decides that it is in their own interests to do something about *our* problem.

Because we leave it to THEM, the supposed answer to our problem usually comes in the form of a product or service, which is offered to us at a price that will give THEM a good profit. It may, however, take a long time before anyone gets around to doing anything about our problem, years, decades, even centuries! But, if and when it eventually *does* happen, we simply buy the new product or service to see if it does indeed solve our problem for us. Of course, if there are no easy profits to be made from addressing our problems, we may never get a solution.

The important people, who take action on our behalf, show *initiative*. They take the responsibility and risks involved in starting something new. The rest of us have little part to play in the process, apart from complaining – and waiting. Our role is that of shoppers – and patient shoppers at that. We spend much of our lives waiting and, the poorer we are, the more of our time is spent waiting. We are the passive audience of great events performed by important actors.

Now, the THEM approach is such a widely accepted notion of how things get done that it is often very hard to see any alternative to it. The vast majority of the world's organisations are THEM organisations. Most businesses, most government agencies, most intergovernment organisations (like the United Nations), most churches, hospitals, schools and universities and a high proportion of voluntary organisations are in the THEM camp. The phenomenon even transcends political systems. Both capitalist and communist societies are, and have been, organised on THEM principles.

If THEM enterprises have such a widespread dominion, what else is possible? Do other alternatives exist? This is where the US approach comes in. US organisations emerge in situations where conventional structures are unable to meet important human needs.

The US approach turns the conventional way of doing things upside down. According to this approach:

> ... things get done most effectively when the people experiencing the problems get together with others like themselves and combine their energies, skills and resources to set up their own organisations. With these organisations, they provide themselves with products, services or experiences especially designed to meet their common needs.

In other words, the US way of getting things done is for the ordinary people with the needs and the problems – you and me – to combine together and do things for ourselves. US organisations are designed around the needs of their users, and the users themselves are active in tailoring the organisations to their own special needs. Usually, profits are less important than the quality and nature of the services and the relationships provided by the organisation.

Now, this is very different from the way most organisations operate. The people in charge of the typical organisation have not the slightest interest in using its services themselves. The people in charge of THEM organisations have other goals to achieve. Their goals are not totally restricted to profits, but may also include self-fulfilment, security, power and influence, freedom of action, self-esteem – or any combination of the above.

The US approach is also very different from the way most public service organisations are run. Many public agencies were originally designed around their clients' needs, but usually they do not invite their users' participation in major decisions. And because users are not involved in any significant way, the original aims of the organisations tend to be displaced by the needs of those in charge. So well-intentioned health-care systems can end up being run for the benefit of the consultants, and universities for the benefit of professors and administrators. See **Case Study 1.4** and **Chapter 7** for examples of health-care systems that have been designed for use.

THEM: THE CONVENTIONAL THEORY OF ACTION

Let's try to understand all of this better by taking a closer look at some of the distinguishing features of these two ways of getting things done.

The key characteristics of the THEM approach to organising include:

- Treating users as passive objects.
- Treating users as isolated and competing individuals.
- Concentrating the power to design and manage the organisation in the hands of a small elite.

Let's look at each of these characteristics in turn.

Users as passive objects

Clients and users are generally seen as rather ill-informed, incompetent people who must rely on experts to provide the answers to their problems. Because the users are thought to have little to contribute to the management of the organisation, it makes sense to concentrate decision-making in the hands of the *experts* and treat the rest of us as passive objects to be serviced, and even manipulated, for our own good.

Strangely enough, this is much the same argument used by democratic theorists such as Dahl and Sartori[26] who argue, in effect, that parliamentary democracy can only work because most people don't take democratic values seriously. According to this view, wholesale apathy is vital. Without it, the system would grind to a halt!

Users as isolated and competing individuals

The THEM approach is likely to work best if people relate to the organisation as isolated individuals, competing against one another for a good bargain. The competitive quest for one's own self-interest is seen as the most efficient way to meet needs and allocate resources. Pressure groups of users, like consumers associations or trade unions, are discouraged because they create inflexibility in the system, thereby reducing efficiency and profitability.

Power concentrated in a small elite

As a result of this concentration of power, most THEM organisations end up being designed for the well-being of a narrow elite, and the needs of the people who use its products and services are not the prime purpose of the organisation. Its prime beneficiaries are the dominant elites, whose main interests are not in the specific products of the organisation but in things like profits, return on investment, security, self-fulfilment and freedom of action. Indeed, many of the investors who own shares in a company may know very little about what the company does.

Clearly, the THEM approach is a convenient theory of action for the elites of the world. It is also accepted by most of us as inevitable. Most assume that it is the only possible way of getting things done in a reasonably orderly and efficient manner.

Ways of implementing this mode of organising have changed dramatically over the years. In its nastier versions, an elite ruled simply because it had the power to club you over the head if you didn't go

---

[26]   Their arguments are discussed in Pateman (1970), pp.8-12.

along with it. Under the more liberal forms of capitalism, elites could remain as elites only if their goods and services competed successfully in terms of quality and price, which made life pleasanter for the ultimate consumer. Perhaps the most comforting version of this approach to organising is parliamentary democracy, which makes it possible, from time to time, to swap one elite for another, though it is often hard to find any significant difference between the elites on offer.

This approach to organising has proved remarkably efficient at getting things done, but only in a limited range of situations and often at enormous social and environmental costs. It is useful for mass-producing tangible, consumer goods and for providing simple services, and is outstandingly efficient at building the wealth and security of tenure of the small elites who call the tune. It is far less successful in important areas of human need, such as meeting the basic needs of impoverished humanity, health, education, the appropriate development of underdeveloped regions, the husbanding of scarce resources, environmental protection, peace and security. In these less tangible but supremely important areas, the conventional approach to organising often undermines the quality of life for the majority of people. To address such issues effectively, we need to turn to a radically different way of getting things done.

US: THE CO-OPERATIVE THEORY OF ACTION

The theory of action implicit in the operations of effective co-operatives is very different from the THEM approach. Look at the US approach again:

> We address human needs and problems most effectively when the people experiencing those needs and problems combine with others in a similar situation and get actively involved in the design of organisational strategies that will enable them to solve their own problems and meet their own needs.

This revolutionary theory of action, in which organisations are likely to be most effective, may be summarised in these key characteristics:

- Activating and involving users of goods and services.
- Encouraging users to engage in mutual aid.
- Involving users in design for use.

Activation of users

The people experiencing problems and needs are actively involved in the process of designing services, activities and structures to address those problems; they are treated as origins of action, not passive objects to be serviced and manipulated. In other words, people are encouraged to do things for themselves, and to acquire the skills needed to run their own affairs. The assumption behind this principle is that things get done more effectively when the people using the organisation are knowledgeable, conscious of the nature of their needs and problems, and actively involved in seeking effective solutions.

Who are these users who are to be *activated* in the solutions of their own problems? Consider our earlier discussion of the various categories of beneficiaries of co-ops. The users who are to be activated might be *consumers* seeking more effective products or services, *workers* trying to create worthwhile jobs, farmers or other *producers* looking for more effective ways of marketing their produce, or even whole *communities* seeking to increase employment and prosperity in their region.

Most conventionally-trained managers might consider this activation principle a recipe for disaster! Used appropriately, however, it can greatly enhance effectiveness. People are more likely to understand and be committed to courses of action they choose for themselves; and the strategies they choose are more likely to fit their needs than are the grand schemes handed down from on high by would-be exploiters or do-gooders.

Mutual aid

Those experiencing the problems and needs pool their efforts and resources to help one another to develop collective solutions to their mutual problems. In other words, things are likely to work more efficiently, if we work together to develop collective solutions. The underlying assumption is that co-operation and mutual support produce better solutions than the attempts of isolated people.

For example, a poor person can meet her need for credit individually by borrowing from a money-lender – at exorbitant rates of interest. When she combines with others, she can help set up and run a credit union, which can free her from unmanageable debt.

We can solve our housing problems individually by buying or renting our own house. Collectively, we could set up a housing co-operative, combine our skills and resources to do the work more cheaply and even design our own neighbourhood to meet our needs.

Design for use

The organisation itself, its products, services and activities are consciously designed for use – to be helpful to the people who use its products and services (instead of being designed around the goals of a limited elite). The people with the needs and the problems are actively involved in this design process.

If the prime purpose of our co-operative organisation is to promote the well-being of its users, it would seem logical for every aspect of the organisation to be tailored consciously to users' needs. Everything about it, its structure and management styles, its products and services, its facilities and location, its member education programmes should *all* be designed to address the key problems experienced by the organisation's users.

FIGURE 2.2: UNDERSTANDING DESIGN FOR USE[27]

What happens when we don't design for use?

Conventional organisations typically do not design products or services for use. Their services derive from the profit-making process; they are not ends in themselves, but particular strategies for making money or for ensuring the strength and growth of the organisation.

Perhaps that is why we end up with transportation systems that rely predominantly on the use of the private car and thereby maximise the depletion of natural resources and the dangers of gridlock; tower flats that no-one wants to live in; school systems that sometimes seem to be designed to fail students; food companies that sell highly-processed snacks rather than nutritious food; and whole economies that seem to be ingeniously designed to starve the poor and overfeed the rich.

What does design for use look like?

An effective co-operative with activated members working together to solve mutual problems is more likely to design its services self-consciously for use because it is clearly focused on the interests of members. For example, an effective *dairy co-operative* will be concerned with providing services to ensure its members' continuing prosperity as dairy farmers, whereas the conventional processing firm will probably care less about the well-being of the farmer in a particular geographic region than about securing the most economical supplies from whatever source. "The aim of the co-op is to make money *for* the farmer; the aim of the conventional firm is to make money *from* the farmer."[28] (See **Chapter 4**.)

---

[27] Briscoe *et al.* (1982), pp.35-36.
[28] Thirkell (1998).

In the consumer field, effective co-ops have redesigned the process of retailing in the interests of the consumer, through innovative policies and practices in the fields of marketing, merchandising, consumer information, store design, division of labour between customers and staff and/or product design. (See **Chapter 3**.)

Similarly, many *worker co-ops* put great emphasis on the quality of working life and producing high quality goods and services rather than producing for profit alone. (See **Chapters 6** and **9**.)

FIGURE 2.3: COMPARISON OF THEM & US APPROACHES

THEM	US
Users are kept passive and dependent.	Users are encouraged to be active shapers of the organisation.
Users are dealt with as isolated individuals, and are encouraged to compete against one another.	Users are encouraged to help one another to develop solutions to their common problems.
The organisation is designed primarily to serve the needs of a small elite of, for example, investors and leaders.	The organisation is tailored to the needs of its users.

LOSING WEIGHT – ACCORDING TO THEM & US

Let's take a look at a dramatic example to underline the difference between the two approaches. Increasing numbers of people in developed countries have the problem of being overweight. Maybe we should say they *think* they have a problem, because it's not just those whose health is endangered by their weight who are worried about their size. Plenty of quite skinny people are obsessed about their weight, because they have been led to believe that all of those emaciated models and movie stars are ideals worth emulating. It is a common ploy of the THEM approach to try to convince us that we are suffering from a spurious problem that only they can solve.

You might think that losing weight would be the sort of problem best solved by cutting down on your calories, taking more exercise and buying less from THEM rather than buying more. But just think of the ingenious range of products and services that conventional businesses have invented to help you lose weight and relieve you of your money!

THEM solutions include:

- Crash diet programmes based on the apparently magical qualities of particular foodstuffs (last year, it was pineapples you had to eat; the year before, grapefruit; this year, lots of protein and fat).
- The books and consultations sold by the inventors of these courses.
- Tiny frozen meals costing more than normal-sized portions.
- Bulk foods and drugs to kill your appetite.
- Artificial sweeteners and diet drinks. Unfortunately, the body can't be fooled – non-sugar sweeteners do not satisfy the sugar addict.
- So called "fat farms", luxurious quasi-prison camps where you pay huge sums of money to exercise under supervision and be subjected to starvation diets.
- Subscriptions to gyms and swimming pools for exercise regimes of varying degrees of severity.
- The attention you may need from sports medicine specialists to repair the damage you have done to yourself from unaccustomed exercise in the gym.
- Expensive surgical treatments like liposuction, the grim medical procedure for sucking away excess fat cells from various parts of your anatomy with a sort of surgical vacuum cleaner. Unfortunately, when you start to put weight on again, you may well be left with unsightly pits and hollows where the old fat cells used to be.
- You can even get your stomach stapled so that it's physically impossible for you to over-eat!

What might an US approach to weight-reduction look like? A suitable strategy might look something like this:

- Groups of people with the same problem would get together to set reasonable and safe goals for weight loss. They would give each other mutual support and share in gentle exercise programmes unlikely to shock their poor bodies into a heart attack.

This would be a viable strategy, all at a fraction of the cost of buying ineffective and often dangerous treatments from THEM. It is also a strategy that groups of people can practise themselves without great expense. However, some clever THEM organisations have recognised the power of this US strategy and are charging us to participate!

You will find lots of examples of design for use in producer, consumer and worker co-operatives in the chapters that follow.

A STIMULUS TO IMAGINATION?

Just in case this is sounding like a one-sided attack on the THEM approach, it is important to emphasise that both THEM and US approaches have their uses. The problem is that THEM is often used inappropriately, in situations where it cannot possibly work effectively. This happens because most of us think that it is the only approach available to us. It is the inappropriate use of THEM strategies that lie at the root of some of our most serious problems.

Classifying our ways of getting things done into THEM and US approaches can be enormously useful. Above all, it is a stimulus to the imagination and helps us to think creatively about the problems we are confronting. If you try it yourself, you will find yourself looking at problems and tasks with new eyes. Whenever a cooperative is confronted by a management dilemma, or members are concerned that their co-op is losing its competitive edge, the best strategy is likely to involve using the US approach to redesign the situation.

A useful exercise to open up your thinking is to try to imagine what an US approach might look like in a range of different fields. Here are some fields that would benefit from US thinking:

- What might an US approach to education look like; how might you redesign learning situations; how might you redesign systems of governance for schools, colleges and universities?
- How might you redesign the field of health-care – everything from preventative programmes, professional services, to hospital care and services for people with special needs?
- How might you improve the effectiveness of a policing system using the US approach?
- How might you redesign our approaches to foreign aid and third world development?

This way of thinking is particularly valuable to established, co-operatives of all kinds. *The effectiveness of a co-op depends on the extent to which it uses the US approach for meeting its member needs.* A management consultant in Australia makes a living from challenging the thinking of successful credit unions. When a credit union has reached the stage where it seems almost indistinguishable from a bank, he is brought in to goad them into thinking from an US perspective. The process is a powerful method for revitalising a complacent organisation and making it more responsive to the changing needs of its members.

Managing co-operatives is not an easy task. As we have seen, not only do you have to run a successful business, you also have to ensure that it continues to adapt to members' changing needs. A pioneer American co-operator, Murray Lincoln, writing about his experiences working with electricity co-ops serving farmers, argued that, to remain successful as a co-operative, it was necessary to appoint a top executive charged with the responsibility to foment perpetual revolution![29]

Complacency is the big enemy of successful co-operatives and credit unions. But you don't have to hire an Australian consultant or appoint a VP in charge of revolution. You can do it yourself by practising "upside-down thinking" with the help of US.

THE CO-OPERATIVE DIFFERENCE

Corporation, n. An ingenious device for obtaining individual profit without individual responsibility.[30]

Capitalism can be a useful social tool or a weapon of unabashed human exploitation. Which it will be depends entirely on the way it is regulated. Capitalism itself contains no ethical values. Those who use it decide by their actions whether it is a force for good or evil.[31]

The US strategy and design for use are at the heart of what distinguishes a co-operative from a conventional business. It is a difference that is frequently evident, not only in the way a co-operative treats its own members, but also in the way it relates to other co-operatives or to needy people wherever they may be found.

The following examples illustrate the difference between the conventional approach and the US approach to addressing the needs and problems of developing countries.

---

[29]   Lincoln (1960).
[30]   Bierce (1971), p.79.
[31]   Saul (1995), p.54-55.

The conventional approach

In November 2002, when Ethiopia was facing its worst drought in decades, Nestlé, one of the world's largest food companies was pressing its claim against the Ethiopian government for US$6 million, as compensation for assets seized by the Stalinist regime that had ruled Ethiopia in the 1970s. Oxfam got hold of the story, which was made public in the *Guardian* newspaper. Within a week, 40,000 angry people, appalled by this example of corporate insensitivity, wrote to Nestlé which, faced with a consumer boycott, back-pedalled fast. It agreed to accept the US$1.5 million compensation already offered by the Ethiopian government and then donated the compensation to Ethiopia's famine fund. The story is all the more shocking against the background of falling coffee prices, which have further impoverished Ethiopian producers while boosting Nestlé's handsome profits.[32]

Contrast this with the way Britain's largest co-operative, the Co-op Group, set about sourcing cocoa beans from third world farmers.

The co-operative approach

The Co-op Group is a major retailer in the UK and deliberately seeks out ways of paying third world growers decent, sustainable prices for their produce. Because of the Co-op's concerns about appalling labour conditions in the chocolate chain, it deliberately sought a supplier that treats growers fairly and produces the highest quality products. The supplier it identified was Ghana's biggest cocoa co-operative – Kuapa Kokoo (see **Case Study 2.1**) – an organisation owned and democratically controlled by the cocoa growers themselves. The Co-op Group can now offer a fair and stable price to cocoa growers by dealing directly with the farmer's co-op. This shortens the supply chain, by cutting out exploitative middlemen, and encourages small-scale growers to work together to increase their bargaining power and reduce their costs.

It is important to emphasise here that we are not trying to argue that all co-operatives always act ethically and all conventional firms are unethical. What we are arguing is that co-operatives, because of their special structure, process, objectives and accountability to users, are more likely to act in ways that most of us would consider ethical.

---

[32]   This story was featured by Charlotte Denny in *The Guardian*, 24.01.2003.

CASE STUDY 2.1: KUAPA KOKOO[33]

Kuapa Kokoo was set up with the help of the UK NGO Twin Trading. Its mission is to empower its members, increase their income level and raise their standard of living. Kuapa Kokoo is a union of 40,000 growers, each with their own passports to record their membership and the amount of cocoa they deliver.

There are four sections to Kuapa Kokoo:

1. **Kuapa Kokoo Limited**, the cocoa buying company.
2. **Kuapa Kokoo Farmers' Trust**, which manages Fair Trade funds and projects for the village societies.
3. **Kuapa Kokoo Credit Union**, which offers growers credit facilities.
4. **The Day Chocolate Company**, the UK arm, of which Kuapa owns a third and which produces *Divine* and *Dubble* chocolate, as well as the Co-op range of Fair Trade chocolate.

The benefits of Fair Trade to Kuapa Kokoo and its members are significant: from the secure and guaranteed fair price they receive for their cocoa beans to the knowledge they have gained of the international chocolate market. The extra money earned from Fair Trade sales is invested back into the community, into projects such as water supplies, latrines, crop improvement, gender relations and education.

For Kuapa Kokoo, owning a third of The Day Chocolate Company is a source of great pride, as well as status on the international market. The Day Chocolate Company has enabled the co-op to gain a better understanding of how the market works and their role within it. Ironically, most of the growers had never seen, much less tasted, chocolate.

The stories of Nestlé and the Co-op Group are not isolated examples. Co-operatives have a long history of running businesses that put people before profits. In an earlier study of the international activities of co-operatives, John Craig (1976) contrasted the behaviour of CF Industries (CFI), an agricultural supplies co-op, which is a major producer of fertilisers in the US, with the strategy of Chevron of California and International Mineral Corporation (IMC). Both CFI and the Chevron/ IMC partnership became involved in helping to establish fertiliser factories in India, but they went about the task in very different ways.[34]

---

33   This story is reprinted in an abridged form (with kind permission) from Co-op Group (2002).

34   Craig (1976), pp.11 *et seq.* and pp.43 *et seq.*

CFI helped Indian co-operatives establish their own fertiliser factory. They did this by raising seed capital of US$1 million from American co ops and by lending technical and managerial staff to train Indian management in the operation of the plant and the distribution system. CFI owned no shares in the plant and received none of the profits.

Chevron and IMC developed a company with an Indian partner to manufacture and distribute fertiliser in India. The American partners own 49% of the company, provide the senior management and get 49% of all profits.

Case Study 2.2 contains other examples of the co-operative approach, while **Case Study 2.3** summarises the results of a Canadian survey that shows some of the ways in which co-ops differ from conventional organisations.

CASE STUDY 2.2: CO-OPERATORS VOLUNTEER

Canada's Co-operative Insurance Services (CIS, now known as *The Co-operators*) was approached by a delegation of credit union officers from Colombia to provide insurance services for the credit unions in Colombia. The CIS manager declined, but offered to help the Colombian co-operators set up their own insurance co-operative. This help was provided at no cost to the Colombians, resulting in a highly effective co-operative owned 100% by the Colombian credit unions.[35]

ACDI/VOCA (Agricultural Cooperative Development International /Volunteers in Overseas Cooperative Assistance) currently works in 35 developing and transitional countries helping them set up and improve the effectiveness of their own co-operative movements. (www.acdivoca.org)

In a similar vein, the Irish League of Credit Unions (ILCU) operates an International Division, which has been lending trained staff to help credit unions establish themselves in The Gambia.

The Credit Union Foundation of Australia (CUFA) provides experienced staff to assist South East Asian countries and the island countries of the South Pacific to establish and strengthen their own credit unions. When did you last hear of a conventional bank that donated staff to help develop other banks in a developing country?

---

[35]   Craig (1976), pp.11-12.

CASE STUDY 2.3: THE CO-OPERATIVE DIFFERENCE: A CANADIAN SURVEY[36]

In a 2002 survey on community involvement by co-operatives, 61.1% of respondents said co-ops provide distinctive contributions to the community compared with other businesses. They target disadvantaged groups and individuals, offer security and education, and provide personalised, democratic, and alternative services.

As one respondent put it, 'The goal of the co-operative is to provide a valuable service to the people it serves. The goal of a business is also to be valuable, but only to itself.'

SUMMARY

In this chapter, we have tried to answer the question, "What do co-operative businesses have in common?" First we discussed the *Principles of Co-operation* (promulgated and updated by the International Co-operative Alliance (ICA), and based on operating principles formulated originally by the pioneers of the first Rochdale Co-op). We saw that those principles, which relate to *open membership, democratic control, limited returns on capital* and *distribution of profits*, are typically incorporated in co-operative legislation as the defining characteristics of a co-op. We also discussed the importance of the *education principle*. (See also the **Appendix** for a fuller discussion of the ICA's co-operative principles).

But the effectiveness of a co-operative is not defined by its legal structure alone. What a co-op does within that legal structure is arguably more important than the structure itself. We therefore identified a *co-operative process* (the US approach), which is used by fully-functioning co-operatives, a process that underpins the ability of effective co-ops to succeed both as ethical co-operatives and as competitive businesses. The co-operative process is at the heart of the co-operative difference, and we concluded this chapter with some contrasting examples of the international activities of co-operatives and those of conventional multinationals.

In the next chapter, we focus on food co-ops that are owned by their customers. **Chapter 3** outlines many ways in which these consumer-owned co-ops have built their competitive advantage by designing their services for use.

---

[36] Source: www.buildingcommunityassets.coop/en/model.html.

THREE

FEEDING OURSELVES I :
CONSUMER CO-OPS & FOOD

Robert Briscoe

The impetus to cut costs, and produce and sell more underpins the way the world rears its animals, grows its crops and manufactures and markets its food, sometimes with alarming effects. Indeed, these perceived food-related felonies are usually committed with the full force of the law and the scientific community working against consumers' views. The trouble is they just don't recognise that science and the law frequently lag behind consumer opinion, which often condemns as abhorrent the practices the Co-op has identified as the "seven food crimes".[37]

The quotation above comes from a report based on a Gallup study of consumer attitudes to the food industry (the results of the study are summarised in **Figure 3.1**). The study was commissioned by the largest consumer co-operative in the UK, the Co-op Group[38]. The report bears the dramatic title, *Food Crimes*, and identifies seven "crimes" committed in the conventional approach to the production and marketing of the food we eat.

In this and the next three chapters, we shall learn how many co-operatives are trying to tackle these food crimes and we shall see examples of how co-ops do things differently. We'll explore innovative business strategies in the food and agribusiness industry, enabling both producers and consumers to improve their bargaining power in the food

---

[37] Co-op Group (2000), p.4.
[38] Formerly the Co-operative Wholesale Society Ltd. (CWS).

business chain, and encouraging them to work together in integrated food co-ops. The main actors in this drama will be:

- Co-operatives owned by consumers (like the Co-op Group).
- Co-operatives owned by farmers.
- Worker-owned co-operatives, which have played a major role in the promotion of healthy eating.

Along the way, we'll also look at the growing cohort of co-operative ventures that are owned by more than one group of stakeholders. For example, co-ops that are jointly owned by farmers and consumers, and retail co-ops owned by the customers and the staff.

In this chapter, we begin at the top of the food business chain and look at how consumer co-operatives have attempted to re-design food distribution for the benefit of customers. We examine how consumers designed their own co-operative food supply systems, and give examples of the business strategies they have used. Starting with retail stores, many consumer co-ops have then *integrated backwards* down the food business chain, setting up their own wholesale distribution systems, processing and manufacturing businesses, and purchasing agencies. Some have even bought farms and are growing their own raw materials! Let's start by exploring the co-operative approach to retailing and comparing the conventional THEM approach with the co-operative US way of doing things.

THE THEM APPROACH TO FOOD RETAILING

Food Crimes[39] identifies seven "crimes" committed in the conventional approach to the production and marketing of the food we eat:

- **Blackmail**: Putting massive marketing efforts (often aimed at children) behind products that are incompatible with healthy eating.
- **Contamination:** Using unnecessary chemicals on farmland and livestock.
- **GBH** (Grievous Bodily Harm): Disregarding animal rights.
- **Vandalism:** Damaging ecosystems with intensive food production systems.

---

[39]   Co-op Group (2000).

- **Cannibalism:** Feeding animals with remains of their own species, and herbivores with animal by-products.
- **Pillage:** Multi-national corporations carelessly exploiting countries, cultures and creeds.
- **Fraud:** Adulterating food with artificial additives.

These so-called food crimes stem directly from a THEM approach to food production and distribution. The THEM approach to retailing involves selling as much as you can to customers, with little apparent concern for the nutritional value of foodstuffs, their impact on people's health, their repercussions for the environment, their implications for animal rights, or their effect on the livelihood of third world producers.

Conventional approaches to retailing demonstrate a preference for well-advertised, high mark-up lines that will build company profits. As a result, the following kinds of promotional gimmicks are widely used on the shop-floor:

- Prime shelf allocations for high-margin goods.
- Display dumps of highly-advertised, high-margin snacks.
- Child-eye-level displays at the checkout.

Consumers dislike such tactics and are becoming aware of the food crimes committed by segments of the food industry (see **Figure 3.1**).

FIGURE 3.1: CONSUMER ATTITUDES TO FOOD CRIMES

A Gallup consumer survey commissioned by the UK's Co-op Group revealed that consumers were increasingly concerned about *food crimes*: [40]

- 33% of respondents reported that they had boycotted a shop or product in the past; 57% said they were now ready to do so; 62% said they were prepared to pay more for products that met their standards.
- 66% of respondents thought it important that the food industry should treat animals humanely.
- 70% were concerned about the environmental impact of the industry.
- 62% wanted information on labels to be clearer and more informative, so as to enable them to eat more healthily.

---

[40] Abridged from Co-op Group (1995).

THE US APPROACH TO FOOD RETAILING

In **Chapter 1**, we saw that a key aim of the original Rochdale Co-op was to provide customers with unadulterated foods and full measure. In 2003, the Co-op Group is still fighting an uphill battle against the food crimes of today. Its concerns now go far beyond the use of questionable food additives, to include such issues as the impact of our food industry on the environment, the well-being of producers in under-developed countries, and the treatment of farm animals.

We have seen that the first successful retail food co-operative in Rochdale helped its members in many ways. Among the store's distinctive advantages were the provision of quality, unadulterated foods and a patronage refund (known as the "divi"), which effectively reduced the cost of food. The divi earned by members was substantial. And the Co-op operated a "penny bank", where members could keep their savings and earn interest on their nest-eggs.

Rochdale also networked with other co-ops to set up wholesaling and manufacturing businesses and buy land for growing fresh foods. Some of these ventures were second level co-ops (co-ops owned by the primary co-ops). The profits from these second level co-ops were then distributed to the primaries in proportion to their purchases. This increased the profitability of the primary co-op and, in turn, boosted the refunds payable to members.

But, these unusual businesspeople were not interested solely in selling groceries. Their range of goods expanded dramatically, until the co-ops were selling a department store assortment. They also provided a whole gamut of useful services for members. They enabled people who had spent their lives imprisoned by debt to accumulate savings. The oppressed and isolated could enjoy the support and comradeship of the co-op's community life and could even derive a modicum of social security in a chronically insecure world. With the help of their co-op, the uneducated could piece together an education and the disenfranchised secured citizenship.

Holyoake, who was a frequent visitor to Rochdale, collected a series of anecdotes from the members and listed some of the very real financial and social benefits they had derived from their store (see **Case Study 3.1**). In the following vivid picture, he summarises some of the material benefits of co-operation for the Co-op member and his[41] household:

---

[41] In spite of Holyoake's politically incorrect assumption that the member was always a male, it soon became evident that more and more women were taking out memberships in the

He appeared better fed, which was not likely to escape notice among hungry weavers. He was better dressed than formerly; which gave him distinction among his shabby comrades in the mill. The wife no longer had to "sell her petticoat" but had a new gown. Some old hen coops were furbished up, and new pullets were observed in them; the very cocks seemed to crow of Co-operation. ... After a while, a pianoforte was reported to have been seen in a Co-operative cottage, on which it was said the daughters played Co-operative airs, the like of which had never been heard in that quarter. [42]

CASE STUDY 3.1: ROCHDALE ANECDOTES[43]

The effects of the Rochdale Store in improving the finances of its members was seen in the instance of one known as Dick, who had lived in a cellar for 30 years, and was never out of debt. One morning, he astonished his milkman by asking him to change a £5 note. The sly dog had never had one before ... Dick has now twenty pounds of "brass" in the Store. And most of those who have the largest balances standing to their credit are persons who have never paid many shillings in. The whole is the accumulation of their profits.

Member No.12 joined the Society in 1844. He had never been out of a shopkeeper's books for 40 years. He spent at the shop from 20 to 30 shillings per week, and has been indebted as much as £30 at a time. Since he has joined the Pioneers' Society, he has paid in contributions of £2 18s; he has drawn from the Society as profits £17 10s. 7d., and he has still left in the Society funds of £5. Thus he has had better food and gained £20. Had such a Society been open to him in the early part of his life, he would now be worth a considerable sum.

Mrs. Mills, a widow, came to the Store for a steak but, as the Store had none, and she wanted it for a sick person, she went into the public market and bought a pound and a half. On reaching home, she weighed her purchase and found that the pound weighed but 14 ounces and the half pound weighed only seven. She now says that, when there is no steak at the Store, "they lump it".

Many married women become members because their husbands will not take the trouble, and others join it in self-defence, to prevent the

---

Co-op. Thanks to the patronage refunds (known locally as the "divi"), the Co-op helped many women to gain a degree of financial independence since the divi was money they didn't have to account for to their husbands. This is all the more significant when one considers that, at that time, married women had no legal property rights.

[42]   Holyoake (1907).

[43]   Holyoake (1907), extracted from pp.44–46.

husbands from spending the money in drink. The husband cannot withdraw the savings at the Store standing in the wife's name unless she signs the order.

REDESIGNING RETAILING FOR THE CONSUMER

How have businesses owned by consumers managed to develop competitive strategies in the cut-throat business of retailing? How have they achieved *cost advantages* or gained competitive advantage by *differentiating* their businesses from conventional firms?[44] Let's explore some of the strategies co-ops have used. The most effective consumer co-ops have been able to offer distinctive advantages to members, not by copying the competition, but by radically redesigning the process of retailing in the interests of the customer. The active involvement of members, in this process of *design for use*, helps keep costs down and earns commitment by getting them to participate in group decision-making about issues such as the balance between costs and levels of service.

THE MONEY-SAVING STRATEGY

Many consumer co-ops have attempted to redesign retailing to save the customer money. Rochdale did this by returning the profits to shoppers in proportion to their purchases. This is still the most popular co-operative strategy for saving the customer money. A more dramatic, but complicated, approach to saving customers money was the model developed by Canada's direct charge co-operatives.

Direct charge co-ops

In the 1960s, consumer groups in Canada developed an approach to food distribution, which radically redesigned the process of retailing in the interests of the customer. A *direct charge co-op* is a form of retail store, which is open to members only and which sells its merchandise at wholesale prices. It keeps costs down by removing unnecessary frills and services and by involving members more actively in the running of the store. (See **Case Study 3.2** for more details on the workings of direct charge co-ops.)

---

[44]   See **Chapter 2** for a summary of Porter's ideas on the sources of competitive advantage.

CASE STUDY 3.2: CANADA'S DIRECT CHARGE CO-OPS

For the privilege of buying goods at wholesale prices, members of a *direct charge co-op* undertake to finance the business by investing in redeemable shares and paying a fixed weekly fee to cover the operating costs. This fee is calculated by dividing the weekly operating expenses by the number of members.

The weekly fee is kept low by tight management of costs. This may involve housing the store in a simple metal building on an inexpensive site, stacking foods in cut cases on warehouse shelving, and encouraging members to perform all or some of the labour involved in running the store. In some cases, members do the bulk of the shelf-stocking and cleaning on a volunteer rota; in others, most of the work is done by paid staff but members may be required to pack their own goods, return shopping carts to the store, etc.

Direct charge stores claim to save the consumer money, not just by keeping prices down but also by removing some of the pressures on people to buy. Because the members' weekly fee covers the costs of running the store, the co-op has no vested interest in inducing people to buy more than they need. In effect, it is *purchasing for* members rather than *selling to* them. It can therefore dispense with promotional gimmicks, such as display dumps of high-margin junk foods, child-eye-level displays at the checkout or prime locations for high-margin goods.

The direct charge strategy worked well for many Canadian co-operatives for at least two decades. Particularly impressive was the performance of Hub Co-op in the town of Nanaimo on Vancouver Island, which in a short space of time became the leading food retailer in a community previously dominated by a mighty multi-national supermarket chain. The strategy was also popular in Canada's Atlantic provinces. However, many of the co-ops using this approach have returned to more conventional styles of retailing. The low cost, no-frills approach worked for a while in particular economic circumstances, but probably lost its popularity as increasingly affluent members looked for a more up-market approach to retailing. It is interesting, however, to see the growing popularity of no-frills retailers like Aldi and WalMart (which recently acquired the Asda chain in the UK). It is probable that new versions of the direct charge approach could still, however, be a powerful retailing strategy. Low cost operations, combined with close relationships with local food producers, can ensure favourable prices for farmers and consumers alike (by cutting out the profits of middlemen), with produce of the highest quality.

Japan's Han co-ops

The Japanese have developed an even more radical way of redesigning retailing to save the consumer money. In Japan, there are about 600 co-ops, with a combined membership of more than 21 million (out of a total population of 127 million). Many of the Japanese consumer co-ops have been designed according to the Han system, which eliminates much of the cost of expensive retail stores and instead uses a central warehouse despatch centre from which orders are delivered to a network of neighbourhood consumer groups – the Han groups (see **Case Studies 1.3** and **3.3**).

CASE STUDY 3.3: THE SEIKATSU CLUB CONSUMER CO-OPERATIVE UNION (SCCU)

The SCCU is an association of 22 Japanese consumer co-operatives with a total of 250,000 members, most of them women. It also operates eight wholly-owned companies, including a milk processing plant and serves 140,000 Han consumer groups. On behalf of its member co-ops, SCCU develops, purchases, distributes and controls the quality of a wide range of food and other consumer goods.

Because the Han groups pre-order their supplies, SCCU can plan its purchases and control inventory costs. Another way in which costs are radically cut is by reducing the range of goods stocked from the 30,000 commonly found in conventional supermarkets to only 2,000. Size choices are typically limited to two per item. As well as saving the consumer money, SCCU ensures higher than usual quality, sourcing fresh foods whenever possible from local sources. It also operates a *Producer Cost Guarantee Scheme*, which ensures that prices paid to local farmers are sufficient to provide a sustainable livelihood for their families.

THE INFORMATION & INNOVATIVE
SERVICES STRATEGY

Co-ops can save people money without having to go to the direct charge extreme. In addition to returning profits to members in the form of patronage refunds (the Rochdale divi), many co-ops have also tried to make shopping less expensive by improving the information available to the consumer. Some have also added services such as free supervised child-care to make shopping a more comfortable experience.

Calgary Co-op

Calgary Co-op is one of the largest consumer retail co-operatives in North America, operating 19 retail shopping centres in the city of Calgary and neighbouring communities in the Canadian province of Alberta. It started out in 1956 with a small supermarket in downtown Calgary, but soon distinguished itself from its competitors by pioneering a system of unit pricing, which enabled its customers to compare the price of goods across brands and sizes and select the best buy. It also provided a supervised crèche, where members could leave their children while shopping. In itself, this saved shoppers money by freeing them from pressures from their kids to buy the pricey junk foods promoted on children's TV.

The strategy has proved a powerful one for Calgary. It has won the trust of consumers in a wide range of businesses, including petrol stations, travel agencies, liquor stores and pharmacies (all of which provide patronage refunds to members). See **Case Study 3.4** for more information on this successful co-operative business.

CASE STUDY 3.4: CALGARY CO-OP

Calgary Co-op was founded in 1956 when one small supermarket was opened to provide competition for an American multi-national, which dominated the city's retail trade at that time.

In December 2003, the Co-op was one of the largest consumer retail co-operatives in North America, operating 20 retail shopping centres in Calgary, Airdrie and Strathmore, in the Canadian province of Alberta, with assets of CAN$272 million and sales of CAN$750 million. It achieved its highest net profit ever in 2003 and has a workforce of more than 3,600 employees.

The patronage refund, paid in cash and shares, represents substantial savings for members, averaging 3.46% over all purchases (slightly higher on petroleum purchases and slightly lower on the rest).

Quality awards
Quality of service is also emphasised, as well as savings. In 2002, Calgary Co-op was chosen best food store and best travel service in the *Calgary Herald*'s Readers' Choice Awards. It also won awards in the bakery, catering and liquor departments. The Co-op also works hard at keeping the children happy, with over 33,000 members in its Kids' Club. The Co-op was awarded the 2002 *Child Friendly* designation from *Calgary Child* magazine. In 2002, the Co-op was also won the *A's of Excellence* award for business, commercial industry and institutions from the Alberta Recycling Council, for its efforts in protecting the environment through recycling. In 2003, it won the "Environmental Achievement Corporate Award" from the City of Calgary and, in 2004, it won four first place awards in the "Calgary Child Parents Choice Awards" and was named "Best Grocery Store" for the seventh year running.

Community efforts
Calgary Co-op has committed itself to demonstrating its concern for the local community by investing heavily in a variety of fund-raising and community development projects. A small but innovative example of these is the *From Bags to Riches* initiative. Shoppers can take part in this programme simply by re-using their plastic bags – for every bag recycled, the customer gets a three-cent credit on their grocery purchases or can donate the credit to charity. In 2002, CAN$8,000 was raised for charity in this way.

Sources: Personal visit, 1985; www.calgary-coop.com (2004).

RESPONSIBLE RETAILING

The Co-op Group has developed an approach to retailing that builds competitive advantage by emphasising the co-operative difference and demonstrating the Co-op's commitment to ethical business. It did this by responding in a multitude of ways to the consumer concerns about the seven *food crimes* outlined at the beginning of this chapter.

> As a consumer-owned business, answerable to more than 100 regional democratic consumer groups around the UK, the Co-op is in a unique position among retailers to gauge the consumer mood at grass-roots level. Even more importantly, because the Co-op

isn't a publicly quoted company, it can take action on behalf of consumers without fear of its share price plummeting.[45]

Its actions included:

- From 1985, it banned animal testing on its own brand toiletries and household products.
- Radically improved the usefulness of the information on its own label products – for example:
  - It was the first retailer to label eggs as "intensively produced".
  - It moved salt information to the front of the pack.
  - It was the first retailer to give information on the ingredients and processing aids used in wines and spirits.
  - It was the first retailer to give its customers the power (through a consumer jury) to change its labels if they found them misleading.
  - It was the first retailer to introduce the new "cruelty-free" label.
- As a major element in its responsible business strategy, the Co-op Group became the country's leading retailer in the number of new fairly-traded products that it sourced and promoted in its shops.
- In 2000, it banned the use in its own-brand food products of 40 widely-used pesticides. It also banned advertising of unhealthy foods and drink to children.
- In 2002, it launched Britain's first fully biodegradable plastic carrier bag.

Many of these innovations were introduced before the 1995 survey, when decision-makers were not at all confident that co-operative values would actually improve the Co-op's sales (some sceptics even feared that overt expression of such values would damage business performance). There was great delight, therefore, to find that the new Co-op labelling and the introduction of a wide range of Fair Trade products were very popular with Co-op customers. Also popular was the discount enjoyed by members of 3% on all Co-op brand goods and 1% on everything else, including holidays purchased at Travelcare, the group's travel agency. There are now 4,000 Co-op own-brand products, which have become so popular that they account for half of all the Co-op's retail sales.

---

[45]   Co-op Group (2000), p.5.

Industry awards

The responsible retailing strategy seems to be working for the Co-op Group and the UK's co-ops in general (many of them have adopted the Co-op Group's strategies). In 2002, co-op food stores outperformed their grocery rivals, with a 6.9% turnover increase when all food retailers recorded growth of only 4%. In addition, the Co-op Group won a number of prestigious industry awards:

* The Co-op Group's achievements in developing its own brand Fair Trade products was recognised in 2001, when it won the award for in-store Promotion of the Year at the national *Retail Week Awards*.

* In 2002, the Group was declared the multiple retailer of the year at the Retail Industry Awards, beating Tesco and Asda.

SMALL IS POSSIBLE

With sales of over £8 billion at the end of 2003 and consolidated operating profits of £327 million (a rise of 4%), the UK's Co-op Group is big business, employing 70,000 people, and operating more than 3,000 retail outlets (some examples of other gigantic co-ops are outlined in **Case Study 3.5**). The Co-op group is also engaged in food production on a massive scale, and is the UK's largest farmer. But co-ops do not always have to be huge to succeed. You'll also find highly successful medium sized co-ops, comparable in size to Canada's Calgary Co-op (see **Case Study 3.6** for some UK examples).

CASE STUDY 3.5: CO-OPERATIVE GIANTS

United Co-op[46]

United is the direct descendant of the Rochdale Society of Equitable Pioneers. More than 150 co-ops, including the original Rochdale, are part of the vast trading area of United. It is now one of the largest co-ops in Europe with over a million members and 15,000 employees. By 2003 annual sales were more than £1.5 billion, with a trading profit of £34.5 million. In the first six months of 2004, sales increased by 8% and profits by 19%.

---

[46]   www.coop.co.uk (click on "About Us", then "Reports", then "Annual Report 2004").

An interesting feature of United is its innovative attempt to get members actively involved in the co-op's democratic process. To become an active member and be eligible for substantial refunds on your purchases (last year's active member refund was 10% of grocery purchases), members must attend a number of co-op meetings, have a minimum shareholding of £10 and purchase sufficient goods or services from the co-op to accumulate 500 points each year. In the co-op's food stores and pharmacies, one point is earned for each pound spent. In travel branches though, you'd need to spend £10 per point.

Switzerland's Consumer Co-ops[47]

In 2001, 14 regional co-op societies and Coop Suisse (a second-level wholesale and manufacturing co-op) merged to form a single consumer co-operative society called simply "COOP". In 2002, this massive national co-operative had its best ever results. While retail trade in the country as a whole fell by 0.3%, COOP's sales were up by 7.2% to SFR14.54 billion and overall profit grew by 13.9% to SFR593 million; in 2003, sales increased by 6.5% and profits by 3%. COOP's market share was 21.9% of food sales, 10% of non-foods and 15.6% of retail sales. Surprisingly, COOP's main competitor is another national co-operative (the Migros Organisation[48]), which achieved similar results.

Midlands Co-op[49]

Midlands is one of the UK's largest regional co-operative societies, with an active membership of about 120,000. With sales of over £750 million and about 7,500 employees, it trades across all six Midlands counties and encompasses the cities of Birmingham, Leicester and Derby. Midlands Co-op has 124 retail stores, including 9 superstores. It is one of the UK's leading regional dairy operators, processing over a million pints of milk daily and delivering milk and other goods to over 400,000 homes, hospitals and schools in 14 local authorities. Midlands is the largest independent travel agent in the region with over 100 branches; and the leading funeral director, handling over 12,000 funerals from 80 funeral homes.

The co-op has a two-tier representative structure to facilitate democratic control. Members elect representatives to local area boards. These area boards then nominate representatives to the Central Board, which appoints the chief executive and oversees the management of the co-op for the members.

---

[47]   COOP (2003) at www.coop.ch.

[48]   www.migros.ch/migros_FR.

[49]   www.midsco-op.co.uk/, 25.9.2003.

CASE STUDY 3.6: MEDIUM-SIZED CONSUMER CO-OPS

Oxford, Swindon and Gloucester Co-op (OSG)[50]

OSG is one of the most successful co-ops in the UK, serving an area that includes Oxfordshire, Wiltshire and the Cotswolds. In 2003, sales reached more than £309 million, with a profit before distributions of £6.7 million. It has 86 food stores, 28 funeral homes, 8 motor showrooms, 12 Co-op Travelcare agencies and more than 77,000 members. OSG fosters community development by assisting the development of new community-based co-operatives and social enterprises.

Lincoln Co-op[51]

This is another successful medium-sized co-op, offering a range of services similar to OSG's. It serves the whole of Lincolnshire, England's second largest county and has about 140,000 members and an annual turnover of £220 million. It fosters member participation in the democratic control of the co-op by encouraging members to join local community-based groups made up of members, local managers and directors to work on local issues such as the allocation of co-operative funds to community groups.

In many parts of the world, you'll also find plenty of tiny co-ops, which manage to compete with the giants (see **Case Study 3.7**). Small co-ops have proved capable of competing against giant retailing combines mainly by *differentiating* themselves. They do this in a number of ways, for example:

- Offering an unusual range of products (such as vegetarian, organic, and Fair Trade foods and environmentally-friendly products).
- Offering unusual services (often including educational programmes on *how to eat better for less*, and opportunities for protesting against food crimes with like-minded associates!).
- Stocking good value and high quality produce (by creating links with local growers who produce excellent food but cannot produce enough to satisfy superstores).

Many of them manage to survive comfortably by locating themselves in small communities, where the profit potential is too small to attract major competitors. Strangely enough, the enormous UK Co-op Group

---

50   www.osg.coop, 25.9.2003.
51   www.lincoln.coop, 25.9.2003.

has itself come up with a strategy, which suggests a possible model for small-scale local co-ops.

CASE STUDY 3.7: SMALLER CO-OPS

The Dublin Food Co-op (DFC)[52]

DFC is a small consumer co-op, which opens its doors every Saturday from 9.30am to 3pm at the St. Andrews Centre, Pearse Street, in the centre of Dublin. It was founded in 1983 with the aim of providing its members with wholesome food and environmentally-kind products and services. Almost all of its food is organically grown, much of it grown in Ireland by a selected group of producers. The co-op supports Fair Trade sources and prices its goods as near as possible to the wholesale cost, with a only small mark-up to cover their modest operating costs and make a contribution to reserves.

Non-members must pay a €2 admission fee to shop at St. Andrews Centre. Memberships can be bought for periods ranging from 3 months (€5 for an individual) to one year (€20). Reduced concession fees are also available, and volunteering to work will qualify you for discounted membership.

Moose Jaw Co-op[53]

This co-op in the northern Canadian town of Moose Jaw is one of many smaller co-ops that serve communities in the Province of Saskatchewan. It offers a comprehensive range of foods and services, including a shopping centre, a fitness centre, a petrol station and a farm supply business. In the past decade alone, the Co-op has returned over CAN$5 million in patronage refund to its members.

The Durham Co-op Grocery[54]: A social meeting place or a grocery store?

In the opposite corner of North America, this co-op began life in 1971 as *The Intergalactic Food Conspiracy* in Durham, North Carolina. It started out as a buying club of 50 students from Duke University and was housed in the basement of a chapel. Now it has 400 members and its own retail store, selling organic and vegetarian foods and working closely with local organic farmers.

---

52   www.dublinfoodcoop.com/, 29.09.2003.
53   www.moosejawcoop.com.
54   Gregory (2002).

Serving smaller markets: the Market Town strategy[55]

Concerned about the impact of massive out-of-town shopping centres on the viability of retailing in small towns, the Co-op Group developed the concept of an eco-friendly *Market Town Store*. The essence of this idea was to design a smaller size of supermarket, which offers the facilities, range of goods and services of a much larger store.

Key elements in this concept are:

- A big enough **range** to meet the food shopping needs of most consumers, so shoppers can get the bulk of their supplies locally without having to drive to out-of-town shopping centres.

- A **modern look**, with lower fixtures and fittings to improve customer access, clear signs, colourful graphics featuring local organisations and issues.

- A **local identity** with signage including the name of the town, and a frontage that complements the location.

- **Facilities** usually available only in larger stores.

For example, the Market Town supermarket opened in the Yorkshire town of Maltby:

> ... employs 60 staff, and includes a Post Office, cash machine, parent and child facilities, customer toilet, provision for disabled shoppers, parking, delicatessen, Cuisine de France, wide choice of fresh foods, full range of grocery products, and non-food ranges such as CDs, videos and mobile phones.

The Market Town concept is also seen as a more environmentally friendly approach to retailing than the out-of-town shopping centre. By providing high quality retailing in the midst of the community, the Market Town concept not only helps sustain and build a vibrant community, it also reduces the need to drive long distances to shop and provides a range of shopping centre services for those without cars.

---

[55]   This section is taken from a Co-op Group press release issued in 2000.

SUMMARY

In this chapter, we have been looking at shops owned and controlled by shoppers. These unusual retail stores, designed to meet the needs of consumers, range in scale from the Dublin Food Co-op (open for just a few hours each week, like Rochdale in its early days) to the integrated co-operative systems that dominate food retailing in Switzerland. We have explored briefly some of the strategies they use to compete against the multiples. Some (like the Seikatsu Club) save the consumer money by radically redesigning the process of retailing, others differentiate themselves by emphasising their ethical stance and fighting food crimes. The smaller ones focus on niche markets like organic and vegetarian foods, and many of them are located in small communities. Some of these also develop direct relations with local suppliers, so that they can provide fresh foods at reasonable prices while paying a fair price to the farmer.

In the next chapter, we move to the other end of the food business chain and explore the wide range of food systems designed by producers, to give them greater control over their own livelihood and improve the viability of their farms.

FOUR

FEEDING OURSELVES II : FARMERS' CO-OPS & FOOD

Michael Ward

In **Chapter 3**, we started our exploration of food co-ops by looking at how consumer co-ops have attempted to redesign food distribution and production for the benefit of consumers. In this chapter, focusing on the Irish experience in particular, we examine the variety of ways in which co-operatives have been used by food producers to increase their income and improve the quality of their lives.

In particular, we shall explore the strategies used by processing and marketing co-ops to improve farm incomes. We shall also see how farmer co-ops have integrated backwards, to purchase and manufacture inputs for farmers and how they have integrated forwards to open their own retail outlets. The chapter concludes with examples of ways in which producers are working closely with consumers to the benefit of both.

AN ETHIOPIAN MILK CO-OP

In the late 1990s, 34 small-scale dairy farmers in the Oromia region of Ethiopia decided to set up a co-operative to collect and transport their milk. It was hoped that this would increase their bargaining power in their dealings with milk processors and help them to find new outlets for their milk.

In a little over four years, the membership had increased more than 10-fold and the quantity of milk collected more than five times the amount they had handled in their first year. Profit had increased from a loss to a surplus of nearly 500,000 Birr. This happened even though the co-op had very little equipment (apart from a cooler and a truck) and no processing facilities of its own and was therefore obliged to sell its members' milk unpasteurised. But, in spite of these problems, the co-op had already made a significant difference for the milk producers. The bargaining power they gained from pooling their milk supply, and the ability to transport it further afield, was already helping increase members' earnings and encouraging more producers to join the co-op. At the end of the 1890s, dairy co-ops in Ireland would not have looked very different from that co-op in Ethiopia.

IRISH AGRICULTURAL CO-OPERATIVES

An historical overview

One of the earliest Irish agricultural co-operatives was set up at Ralahine, County Clare, in 1831, on the estate of John Scott Vandeleur, who was influenced by the thinking of Robert Owen and his co-operative experiments at New Lanark. Vandeleur rented the land to a co-operative formed by the tenants. The 82 members were each entitled to one vote – this included women, almost 100 years before female suffrage was established in Britain. The experiment was highly successful. Its demise was not due to internal problems, but to the fact that Vandeleur gambled away his wealth and the estate was taken over to pay his debts[56]:

> The fundamental problem of landownership had not been dealt
> with and the experience of Ralahine vindicated Thompson's
> criticism of schemes which relied on the whims of the wealthy.

The 19th century was a time of extreme hardship for Irish farmers, a time of grinding poverty and exploitation by landlords and *gombeen men*. Ireland was primarily rural, a land of tiny farms, and rural poverty was rampant. Farmers urgently needed help to improve their standards of production and marketing, to get access to good quality farm supplies at reasonable prices, and access to credit to keep them going during the off-season. For too long, they had depended on landlords and traders to market and sell their produce with little or no return to the farmer. A strategy was needed to enable farmers to take control of their industry and redesign it in the interests of producers. In fact, it has been argued

---

[56]   For a detailed discussion on the Ralahine experiment and the thinking of William
       Thompson of Cork, see Tucker (1983), pp.14-23.

that it was not economic benefits alone that prompted the establishment of co-operatives, but a desire to have a business structure in which the farmer had direct control.[57] The degree to which the co-operative structure has facilitated this need for farmer control in Ireland is an issue under intense discussion in the 21st century.

The first Irish dairy co-operative was established at Dromcollogher, County Limerick, in 1889, by Sir Horace Plunkett,[58] who saw co-operation as the way to improve the overall quality of life in rural Ireland. His motto was "Better farming, Better business, Better living". He and his associates had seen how co-operative creameries had raised farming standards in Denmark since 1882 and believed that the co-operative idea could also be an effective remedy for the problems faced by Irish farmers.

By 1891, 16 co-operative creameries had been set up in Ireland. In 1894, the Irish Agricultural Organisation Society (IAOS, now known as ICOS) was formed to promote the methods of agricultural co-operation, not only to the members of the 50 or so co-operative creameries of the time, but also to the wider agricultural community. By 1905, the number of co-operative creameries had grown to 275.

Credit co-operatives also gained a foothold in Ireland at this time. They were undermined, however, by the agricultural co-operatives themselves, which also extended credit to their members. The credit co-ops died out in the 1920s, but re-emerged in the 1950s in the form of credit unions, although these were more in response to urban, than to rural, poverty.

The years 1900 – 1920

The first two decades of the 20th century were a time of great vitality and prosperity for Irish agricultural co-operatives:

> … by the beginning of the 20th century, the population of most rural communities had been reduced and transformed from a teeming mass of impoverished labourers and very small tenant farmers, into a stable, conservative, land owning peasantry, established on family farms which, for the most part and by modern standards, are quite small. [59]

---

[57]   ICOS (1989), celebrating the 100th anniversary of Drumcollogher.
[58]   For more on the life and ideas of this practical idealist, see Keating (1983).
[59]   Breen *et al.* (1990), pp.185.

Co-operative creameries were established in nearly every district of southern and north-eastern Ireland, as a result of a major organising campaign at local level. These creameries were built by the farmers themselves with their own money. World-wide interest in the Irish co-operative movement was keen and many came to Ireland to study the structures and methods of Irish co-operation. In 1900, there were 374 co-operative societies of all types in Ireland and, by 1913, this had grown to almost 1,000, half of which were creameries. Already, most of these co-operative creameries had developed into multi-purpose agricultural societies.

Economic depression

But the period of prosperity was not to last. The end of the First World War saw the disappearance of the large demand for food and clothing for troops. Increased supplies from other countries, coupled with reduced purchasing power at home, strangled the Irish economy. In the 1920s, co-operatives faced severe financial difficulties, aggravated by the fact that many had extended unlimited credit to farmers during the prosperous years between 1900 and 1920. In addition, co-operative consciousness declined, as farmers tried to maximise individual income in a depressed economy. Although approximately 55% of the male labour force in Ireland was employed in farming, the sense of co-operative organisation began to die away. The War of Independence from Britain had also had a devastating impact on the co-operative creameries. Perceived by the British as centres of rebellion against the Crown, many were burned to the ground.

After independence, it was increasingly recognised that the economic wealth of Ireland lay in its dairy industry, and milk wars were waged between co-operative and private creameries, as they fought for market share. The Irish government recognised, however, that dairying could be developed more efficiently through co-operation than through internecine wars, and intervened in 1928 to form the Dairy Disposal Board Company, the aim of which was to take-over private creameries and bring about some rationalisation of their activities.

However, there was little improvement in the situation as the economic depression throughout the world brought the co-operative movement to a low ebb. To compound matters, the original co-operative founders had died and the co-operative philosophy they expounded began to be forgotten. It was not until the 1950s, with the end of the Second World War, that Ireland began to emerge from its economic gloom. Farming had been kept alive and it had provided much local employment. Agricultural output and incomes had remained reasonably stable throughout the period, although growth was severely inhibited. Ireland had 160 dairy co-operatives at this time, ranging in size from 500,000 to five million gallons. Twenty per cent of all milk production was handled by the Dairy Disposal Board Company, while most liquid milk processing remained in private ownership. Butter was the main product being manufactured from manufacturing milk.

Renewed co-operative interest

From the mid-1950s to the mid-1960s, agricultural co-operatives in Ireland expanded again, but the new growth focused on livestock and the establishment of co-operative livestock marts as a more effective replacement for the old village fairs. Co-operative endeavour was also focused on the establishment of grain co-ops and stores, particularly as a result of the discovery of a new high-yielding barley. Existing dairy co-operatives diversified their interests into grain handling and storage facilities. This, in turn, led to milling and animal feed compounding by several co-operatives. Pig breeding and fattening co-operatives also began to emerge at this time. O'Leary (1983, p.119) points out that:

> … most of the co-operative growth developed around the existing co-op creameries, if not directly then at least by encouragement and often by financial help and management advice from the existing co-ops.

Moves toward merger

The Knapp Report[60] is considered by many to be a watershed in Irish agricultural co-operation. After consultation with the IAOS, the Irish Minister for Agriculture advocated this report be carried out by Joseph Knapp as:

> … a general appraisement of the agricultural co-operative movement in Ireland and to make such recommendations as he might deem desirable with a view to further strengthening the movement and increasing its influence. [61]

Knapp criticised the lack of co-operative education and proper communication structures in Irish co-operatives. He felt that Irish co-

---

[60]   Knapp (1964).
[61]   Knapp (1964), from the *Foreword*.

operative managers were running their co-ops as if they were private companies. His main recommendation was that the dairy processing industry should be rationalised through amalgamation into bigger and better co-operatives.

Ireland was also at this time anticipating its entry into the European Community and there had been a new awakening to the commercial and economic aspects of farming. In the early 1960s, many of Ireland's 160 dairy co-operatives were very small and sold their milk on to bigger co-operatives for processing. In February 1966, on the strength of the Knapp Report, the IAOS released its first major proposals for the rationalisation of co-operative creameries. These proposals were updated in 1972 to encourage further amalgamations. Many neighbouring co-operatives took the plunge and amalgamated to form bigger organisations, although many of these amalgamations did not necessarily make geographical sense or result in rationalisation.

By the late 1970s, the Irish dairy co-operative structure had been radically altered through amalgamation. Four categories of co-operative had emerged:

- The "Big Six", handling approximately 80-100 million gallons of milk each per annum and together accounting for 60% of Ireland's total milk supply.
- Six medium sized co-operatives, each with a milk supply of approximately 30 million gallons of milk per annum and constituting about 20% of total milk supplies.
- A group of 10 co-operatives, each with a milk supply ranging from 10-20 million gallons per annum, representing about 13% of total milk supply.
- Twenty very small non-manufacturing co-operative creameries.

The period from 1970 to 1990 was one of amalgamation, merger, take-over, and joint venture. Some Irish co-operatives formed strategic alliances with multi-national food processors, bolstering the bargaining power of Irish co-operatives. The 12 largest societies invested heavily in plant equipment in order to process an increasing milk supply throughout the country, particularly as EU price supports were available to Irish milk producers. However, these increases began to be reversed as a result of policy changes within the EU that restricted milk output and reduced price supports. This led to planned rationalisation in processing facilities and investment instead in new product and market development on a co-operative-wide basis.

In the 1980s, it had begun to be recognised that Irish agricultural co-operatives were not being adequately controlled by their members and that the members' level of understanding of the co-operative ethos was very low. Ward *et al.* (1982) in their study of co-operatives in the North-Eastern part of Ireland concluded that poor access to information, autocratic management, and member apathy were the root causes of these problems.

Members *vs* investors: the spectre of demutualisation

Other significant issues affecting Irish agricultural co-operatives in the 1980s and 1990s related to capitalisation. Major questions confronting the larger, merged co-operatives included:

- How to raise sufficient capital to achieve the size and scale of operations necessary to trade internationally?
- How to ensure that the value of members' share holdings could grow to reflect the increased scale of their co-operative businesses?

The first problem, that of *raising sufficient capital*, is linked to the second problem of *keeping members happy with the return on their investment*. Clearly, co-ops are going to find it hard to raise capital from their members, if the members feel that their share capital is dead money, which does not grow even when the business is prospering. And this indeed seems to have been the case in the typical Irish co-operative. Members saw their co-op getting bigger and bigger, investing more and more in modern plant, making bigger profits, and paying higher and higher salaries to managers, yet at the same time there was virtually no growth in the value of their share capital and no flow of dividends to reward them as owners of the business. In such circumstances, members would have no incentive to invest more than the minimum required to be a shareholder.

But the situation was even worse than this. In most co-ops, it was possible for a farmer to use the services of the co-op without having to become a shareholder at all! This meant that there was virtually no economic incentive for the farmer to invest anything in the co-op with which he did business. The inevitable result was that a substantial proportion of milk suppliers refused to become shareholders and contributed nothing to the co-operative's capital. This situation had come about because the typical dairy co-operative retained virtually all of its profits as unallocated capital, and was not distributing profits to its members according to their use of the co-operative's services.

By contrast, the practice in the typical North American co-operative was to allocate the bulk of the profits to members' share accounts in proportion to the use they made of the co-operative's services. This had the triple benefits of:

- Rewarding farmers when they used the co-op.
- Building members' share capital.
- Retaining distributed profits within the co-operative.

Under such conditions, farmers would have every incentive to:

- Become shareholders.
- Make maximum use of the co-op's services
- Invest adequate capital to ensure the continued growth and competitiveness of the business.

In Ireland, however, because of the failure of Irish co-ops to reward members for using the business, the actual value of co-operative *shares* typically bore no resemblance to the actual value of the co-operative's *assets*. This, in turn, eliminated all economic incentives for farmers to invest in their co-operative. To raise additional capital, several of the larger co-operatives abandoned co-operative principles and set up their own public limited company (PLC), to which they sold the co-operative's assets. Some of the shares in the new PLC were distributed to members, and substantial proportions of the PLC's shares were sold to the general public via the stock exchange. This is almost an exclusively Irish co-op approach to raising capital and rewarding management. There have been very few attempts to copy this approach in other countries.

The birth of Kerry Foods plc[62]

The first example of a co-operative taking the PLC route in Ireland occurred in June 1986, when Kerry Co-operative Creameries Ltd. exchanged its assets for a majority shareholding in a public limited company (Kerry Foods) as a means of raising finance to assist in acquisitions. Kerry Co-operative received 90 million B ordinary shares.

---

[62]   The story of the growth of Kerry Foods is told in Kennelly (2001).

Kerry Foods proceeded to engage in a series of placings of A ordinary shares, which are tradable on the stock exchange, to raise the much needed finance. At this time, Kerry Co-operative had about 6,000 shareholders, about 1,000 of whom were not active.

Bailieboro Co-operative, in County Cavan, with a membership of 4,000 shareholders (only half of whom were active), went a step further in 1988 when it terminated its co-operative operation completely and sold its business to a publicly quoted company. This was as a direct result of:

- The failure of the co-operative to allocate its profits to individual members in proportion to their use of the business.
- The fact that a majority of members had been allowed to continue as shareholders, even though they had ceased to be milk suppliers and were now only interested in making the most of their financial investment!

This development was described in the ICOS *Annual Report* for 1998[63]:

> That decision in isolation may not have been important until it is realised that there was another offer from a neighbouring co-op which was equally as good as the one finally accepted. Yet the members (only one-third of them were milk suppliers) decided to opt out of the co-operative system and transfer their business to a company in which they would have no say. This raises serious questions about the relationship between co-operatives and their membership.

Avonmore, Golden Vale, and Waterford Co-operatives (all of which had between 3,000 and 4,000 active shareholders) and IAWS Co-op (see **Case Study 4.1**) were soon to follow the PLC route in the footsteps of Kerry. While all of these co-operatives originally intended to retain a majority shareholding in the PLC, it has been worrying to note that the co-operatively-owned shareholding has decreased in recent years. For example, Kerry Co-operative now holds less than 35% control of the PLC.

---

63   ICOS (1989).

CASE STUDY 4.1: IAWS CO-OP

The Irish Agricultural Wholesale Co-operative was founded in 1897 by Irish agricultural co-operatives as their wholesale supplier of quality farm inputs, and later diversified into fish processing and fertilizer manufacturing.

IAWS was structured as a secondary co-op – a co-operative owned by the primary co-ops that used its services – but, in 1988, it followed Kerry's example and established a subsidiary publicly quoted company on the stock exchange: IAWS PLC. The IAWS Co-op received shares in the PLC in return for most of the Co-op's assets and businesses. The influx of public investment facilitated further significant diversification in value-added foods such as bakeries – for example, Cuisine de France (Europe) and La Breq (US).

IAWS Co-op now has only a minority holding in IAWS PLC (40%, valued in 2002 at €450 million), and there is a danger for the future of the Co-op and its farmer members losing control of IAWS.[64] In the meantime, the success of the IAWS acquisition has provided member co-ops with capital to fund their own expansion. For example, Lakeland Co-op used the proceeds of some of its IAWS shares to acquire Bailieboro and bring it back into the co-operative fold.

Non-user members and non-member users

As we saw in the Bailieboro case, another issue that has contributed to the rise of the co-operative PLC is the tendency in the Irish co-operative movement for a separation to develop between users and members. Members who ceased to supply the co-operative with milk over the years have all too often been allowed to remain as shareholders. This has led to the situation where many co-operative shareholders are inactive members of the co-operative. Conversely, some suppliers of the co-operative have been allowed to supply the co-operative, although they are not members of the co-operative, and although the rules require them to be so. For example, in a 1989 survey of 15 dairy co-operatives in Ireland, with a total of 71,597 shareholders, only 35,558 were active milk suppliers[65]. The remaining shareholders were inactive, dead, or untraceable.

---

[64] At the time of going to print, IAWS was in the process of considering further reduction of its holdings in IAWS plc. This will be discussed and updated in our forthcoming book, *Feeding Ourselves*.

[65] See Jacobson & O'Leary (1990).

Despite efforts during the 1990s at individual co-op level, and with the leadership and support of ICOS, the problem of inactive shareholders and non-shareholder users continues to be serious. So much so that ICOS felt obliged to issue a best practice share policy document in March 1999, 10 years after the publication of the first policy position on membership and shareholding. [66] This document concludes:

> For many co-operatives, the current shareholding structure is imbalanced because there is a high proportion of inactive shareholders. Inactive shareholders are shareholders who do not trade with the co-operative.

Had the co-operatives been allocating bonus shares in proportion to usage, the user/member problem would not have arisen. Allocation of bonus shares to users of the co-op would automatically enable them to accumulate sufficient investment to become members. It is instructive to look again at the Bailieboro case, summarised above. Bailieboro Co-op was sold off to a private company, largely by members who did not supply milk to the co-operative. This would have been less likely if Bailieboro had insisted that only users of the co-op could become, and remain, shareholders, as required by co-operative principles.

The failure of many Irish co-operatives to follow best international co-operative practice in terms of member shareholding and distribution of benefit in proportion to use has considerably reduced their ability to attract funding from their member shareholders. Jacobson & O'Leary (1990, p.125) argue that a co-operative could do anything a PLC could do:

> Co-operatives can be as successful as PLCs in attracting investment when they treat member ownership with respect … co-operatives can move swiftly in correcting this situation by adopting appropriate profit allocation procedures and equity redemption policies.

Torgerson (1999, p.34) supports this point of view, when he argues that well-managed co-operatives are well able to amass adequate capital. As evidence, he points to the fact that farmer-owned co-operatives in the USA have been more successful than conventional businesses at increasing their equity capital. Between 1980 and 1996, the top 100 co-operatives have increased their equity capital, as a percentage of total assets, from 29.4% to 35.2%. Over the same period, the Fortune 100

---

[66]   ICOS (1999).

corporations have seen their equity capital decrease, as a percentage of total assets, from 44.9% to 26.2%. As additional evidence, he discusses the remarkable success of new generation co-operatives in building new, market-orientated, added-value processing businesses.

> It is estimated that between 75 and 100 new co-operatives have been organized in the 1990s, with a combined investment of over US$3 billion ... The new wave co-operative idea has even extended to the livestock industry often regarded as the last bastion of independent behaviour by farmers.[67]

Already in Ireland, a co-operative of organic livestock farmers is exploring the possibility of setting up a capital-intensive new generation co-operative on the American model.

Co-op renewal

Two of the larger Irish co-operatives, Ballyclough and Mitchelstown, especially the former, had traditionally given more attention to bonus sharing, distribution of benefit in proportion to use and activating milk suppliers. As a result, they were less threatened than many other co-ops by share valuation problems and inactive shareholders, which influenced their decision to keep well clear of the PLC route. In 1990, they decided to amalgamate and form Dairygold Society and made a commitment to maintaining it as a full co-operative. This stemmed the PLC tide and gave renewed public confidence in the co-operative way. The largest dairy business in the country, catering for 3,000 members and with a turnover of approximately €1 billion, was remaining true to its co-operative roots.

A few months later, Lough Egish and Killeshandra Co-operatives in the North East shook off a take-over bid by Larry Goodman's Food Industries and amalgamated to form Lakeland Dairies, which again committed itself to co-operative ownership (see **Case Study 4.2**).

---

[67]   Torgerson (1999), p.35.

CASE STUDY 4.2: LAKELAND DAIRIES CO-OPERATIVE & ITS STRATEGY OF REMUTUALISATION

In 1990, Killeshandra Co-op in County Cavan (founded in 1896) and Lough Egish Co-op in County Monaghan (founded in 1901) amalgamated as Lakeland Dairies Co-operative.

Lakeland acquired Baileboro (a former co-operative with a 40 million gallon milk pool), which had previously been taken-over in turn by Food Industries, Golden Vale PLC and Kerry Foods PLC. Lakeland went on to acquire the Nestlé Omagh whole milk powder plant, which had a 40 million gallon milk pool. Its next acquisition was L.E. Pritchett, Newtownards, County Down, with a 16 million gallon milk pool.

To demonstrate its commitment to the concept of co-operative ownership, Lakeland has integrated all of the suppliers of these acquired companies into Lakeland's co-operative structure.

With a milk pool of 160 million gallons, and milk suppliers north and south of the border, Lakeland is now the fourth largest milk processor in Ireland and is concentrating on building a food service milk business.

As an approach to build farmers' trust in, and commitment to their co-operative, Lakeland has installed a system of independent milk testing for every test that affects milk payment to farmers.

The present structure of Irish agricultural co-operatives can be found in the ICOS Annual Report for 2003.[68] The Irish agricultural and dairy co-operatives, along with other rural societies, such as marts and fishing co-operatives, are members of the Irish Co-operative Organisation Society (ICOS), which is itself a co-operative, representing the interests of its member co-operatives, nationally and internationally.

At the end of 2003, there were 30 dairy co-operatives in Ireland, including co-operatives with holdings in PLCs. These co-ops had a total of 88,646 members and net total sales of almost €10 billion. Membership and milk supplier numbers vary from co-operative to co-operative, depending not only on the size of the co-operative but also on farm size structure in its own geographical area. The number of co-operatives has steadily declined from the 1960s, as a result of amalgamations.

---

[68]   ICOS (2003), p.27, and www.icos.ie.

A renewed focus on amalgamations

In the late 1990s, Avonmore and Waterford co-operatives, which had both followed Kerry's PLC strategy, were performing sluggishly. They agreed to merge and formed Glanbia Co-op, which held a majority holding in Glanbia Foods PLC. Interestingly, the co-op maintained its majority holding in the PLC and promised to do so in the future. However, the economies expected from the merger of the two organisations were slow to emerge and it is only now benefiting from a refocusing and rationalisation drive.

In 2000, an ICOS publication argued the case for more mergers and rationalisation:[69]

> Irish milk processing scale is falling behind that of its main competitors and that of its customers in the retail and food services sector (and that) there is scope for increased efficiency and value added strategies to be implemented in the dairy sector.

In order to enjoy the benefits of increased scale, investment and product diversification, and to offset changes in the policy environment, ICOS recommended that co-operatives seriously consider:

> Combining at regional level to process the main dairy products either through mergers or joint venture investments[70] ... or ... [Establishing] a single large scale processing business for the country's main dairy products.[71]

Farmers and co-operative response to date would not appear to favour the single business option, at least in the short to medium term. Instead, the option of merging at regional level seems most favoured. But even here, progress has been slow, with movement initially confined to the merging of smaller, neighbouring societies. North Connacht Farmers and Kiltoghert amalgamated in 2000 to form Connacht Gold, while Mid West and Nenagh have amalgamated into the new Arrabawn Co-op.

The Co-op *vs* PLC debate

The dawn of a new millennium saw some milk supplier dissatisfaction with PLC involvement, particularly in the business of primary milk processing. This was fueled by the desire of some PLCs, such as Golden

---

[69]   ICOS (2000), p.5.
[70]   *Ibid.,* p.7.
[71]   *Ibid.,* p.8.

Vale, to apply to primary milk processing the same return on investment targets as in secondary added-value food sectors. This was not welcomed by the farmer milk suppliers. Golden Vale gave serious consideration to remutualisating this portion of its business, but eventually decided to sell its entire business to neighbouring Kerry Foods PLC, in which Kerry Co-op has a minority holding. The Kerry and Golden Vale South milk pools were merged while Golden Vale North (formally Bailieboro Co-op, which had been acquired by Golden Vale PLC from Food Industries) was sold on to Lakeland Dairies (see **Case Study 4.2**) and thus returned to co-operative control.

In 2003, discontent with the PLC structure erupted in Glanbia. Its fresh milk producers group, accounting for approximately 30% of the Glanbia milk pool, proposed a remutualisation of Glanbia PLC with a buy-back by Glanbia Co-op. This proposal did not enjoy the support of Glanbia Foods PLC management. Perhaps the real significance lies in the fact that remutualisation was being discussed at all. It raises questions about the suitability of the PLC structure, at least in the business of primary milk processing.

Within the last year, the chief executives of both Dairygold and Lakeland Dairies independently have committed their societies to maintaining 100% co-operative control as, in their opinion, it is the most advantageous structure for the dairying business. It would seem that the centenary of the birth of Irish agricultural and dairy co-operatives is being celebrated with renewed appreciation of co-operative values.

IRISH CO-OPS IN AN INTERNATIONAL CONTEXT

Notwithstanding the recent consolidation brought about by key players such as Kerry and Lakeland, the *Prospectus Report* (Prospectus, 2003) on behalf of government and industry has called for much greater consolidation (see **Figure 4.1**).

FIGURE 4.1: THE PROSPECTUS REPORT 2003[72]

The main points in the report are as follows:

* The Irish dairy industry is falling behind its international competitors and faces significant challenges. Much larger processing units are required.

* "A consolidated player needs to emerge in the medium term with a scale where it is processing around 70% of the processed milk ... it needs to begin with a consolidation between some of the five largest processors and also consolidation and joint ventures amongst some of the smaller processors." (p.12)

* Larger individual farm units are required. More emphasis is needed on value-added products, together with greater investments in R&D.

In terms of scale, the Irish dairy industry lags behind internationally. In New Zealand, Fonterra Co-op (**Case Study 4.3**) handles approximately 97% of New Zealand milk. In the Netherlands, Friesland Coberco Co-op and Campina Co-ops account for approximately 80% of Dutch milk between them. Arla Foods, with 16,700 dairy farmers and a turnover of €3.9 billion is the dominant co-op in Sweden and Denmark. By comparison, Ireland's four largest processors – Glanbia, Dairygold, Kerry and Lakeland – would need to combine to achieve similar scale. Irish dairy co-ops, however, are well-served internationally by a second-level marketing co-op called the Irish Dairy Board (IDB) (see **Case Study 4.4**), although even here, there is potential to reduce duplication in international marketing effort by some of the bigger PLC/Co-ops.

CASE STUDY 4.3: FONTERRA CO-OP, NEW ZEALAND

With a turnover of approximately NZ$8 billion, Fonterra is New Zealand's largest company and is the fourth largest dairy company in the world, handling 97% of New Zealand's milk – an estimated 35% of the world's dairy trade. It serves 13,000 dairy farmers, has 18,000 staff in 120 countries and operates 27 manufacturing locations.

---

[72]   Prospectus (2003).

In an attempt to avoid the dangers of monopoly, the milk price is set independently of the Board by an outside regulator appointed by the shareholders' council and government. Fonterra is governed by a young, well-educated Board of Directors with university degrees, mostly in their 40s and includes women.

It has linkages and joint venture agreements with Nestlé, Dairy Farmers of America, Arla and Australian Dairies.

CASE STUDY 4.4: THE IRISH DAIRY BOARD (IDB)

IDB was founded in 1961 as Bord Bainne, with the key objective of marketing Ireland's dairy product internationally. It is a co-operative, owned by member co-operatives and it has proved particularly useful for the smaller to medium sized co-ops, enabling them to reach export markets. Inevitably, it duplicates to some extent the marketing activities of larger co-ops / PLCs.

Its key competitive advantage is the extremely effective "Kerrygold" brand, which is a trusted brand for butter in approximately 60 countries. In recent years, IDB has been highly profitable, with an annual turnover of approximately €2 billion.

There is a greater potential to use the Kerrygold brand image to promote other consumer products in Europe.

SMALL IS BEAUTIFUL & COMPETITIVE!

Internationally, merger and amalgamation continue apace in dairy co-ops. Irish co-op farmer shareholders are relatively slow, however, to agree to amalgamation. The merger of Waterford and Avonmore Co-ops and PLCs in 1997 was only accepted when a merger commitment was made to pay a set bonus per gallon of milk above the national milk price audit average for the next three years. Another inducement to support merger was the selling of another tranche of the Co-op's PLC shares to provide an additional financial incentive for farmers.

Many farmer shareholders have a strong sense of loyalty and pride in their co-operative, which goes well beyond commercial considerations alone. They worry about the impact of amalgamation on local employment and the sustainability of rural communities, concerns that are reflected in the multi-purpose nature of Irish dairy co-operatives. Above all, farmers believe that healthy competition between co-operatives, in terms of services and the milk price paid to farmers, leads to efficiencies and is an important method of ensuring farmer influence. However, farmers may not have total confidence in the effectiveness of the existing democratic decision-making processes, especially when a co-op is in a near monopoly situation. This again draws attention to the importance of considerations such as active membership, surplus allocation, equity redemption and representative structures as discussed above.

The presence of co-operatives side by side with PLCs is an added complication in any Irish amalgamation activity, both in terms of financial structure, organisation strategy and member attitudes. The PLCs tend to regard acquisitions, particularly overseas acquisitions, and in-house diversification as even more important routes (than amalgamation with local co-ops) to the kind of growth they require. The PLCs are less concerned with low margin primary milk processing and do not see their major profits coming from this source. Many Irish farmers and co-operatives are far from convinced by the efficiency and economy argument for large-scale milk processing. They point to medium-sized societies such as Town of Monaghan Co-op in Ulster (**Case Study 4.5**), or very small co-operatives such as Newmarket in Munster, which regularly outperform the largest co-ops and PLCs on milk price and service to farmers.

> The performance of Newmarket is remarkable. With only 8 million gallons of own quota, it is a pace-setter. Newmarket is virtually an all cheese manufacturer, which was a very difficult product to sell last year.[73]

CASE STUDY 4.5: TOWN OF MONAGHAN CO-OP (TOMC)

TOMC was established in 1901 and now serves 1,100 milk suppliers north and south of the border. It has a 95 million gallon annual milk pool and supplies branded products direct to local consumers.

In 2002, TOMC acquired the Leckpatrick milk powder plant at Artigarvan, County Tyrone, and now processes milk in Northern Ireland for the first time.

> Monaghan tops the league ... it has performed very well over the last three months paying impressive spring bonuses.[74]

---

[73] Joe Rea, commenting on the April 2003 milk price league in *Irish Farmers Journal*, 21.6.2003, p.20.

[74] Joe Rea, commenting on March 2003 milk price league compiled by the *Irish Farmers Journal*, 20.3.2003, p.24.

The efficiency of small, well-managed co-operatives, operating in niche markets also has international parallels. In New Zealand, Tatua Co-op and Westland Milk Products, with less than 5% of milk supply, often outperform the giant Fonterra on milk price.

There is much admiration in Ireland for the West Cork federal co-operative model, delivering as it does a top milk price and quality service, combined with profitability. Here, four co-ops – Bandon, Barryroe, Drinagh and Lisavaird – operate a joint venture milk processing facility, while remaining independent in other respects (**Case Study 4.6**). These four co-operatives, together with Dairygold Co-op, also own a highly innovative rural services co-op, which aims to develop its catchment area by retaining locally as many jobs and services as possible (see **Case Study 4.7**).

CASE STUDY 4.6: WEST CORK CO-OPS:
CARBERY CREAMERIES LTD.

Four West Cork Co-ops hold the following percentages of shares in the jointly-owned Carbery Creameries:

Bandon	Barryroe	Drinagh	Lisavaird
22.6	18.4	39.0	20.0

Carbery is a leading cheese manufacturer ("Dubliner" cheese is its best-known brand) and does all the processing of the milk, which is collected by the individual co-ops, which decide independently on the milk price they will pay to their members.

> For the second year in a row Bandon has emerged to pay the highest price in the country ... the second and third highest milk prices in the country last year were also paid in West Cork by Barryroe and Lisavaird respectively ... Wexford creameries disrupted the West Cork four in a row by emerging just ahead of Drinagh Co-op.[75]

The individual co-ops also operate their own networks of farm input stores.

Active milk suppliers are building up small direct ownership in Carbery via issue of B shares 2002 –2007 in proportion to milk supply. By 2007, milk suppliers will own approximately 9% of the shares in Carbery with entitlement to a separate vote on special resolutions such as merger. The remainder of the shares will be owned by the four co-ops according to the percentages listed above.

---

[75] Eric Donald, *Irish Farmers Journal*, commenting on KPMG annual milk price audit 2002.

CASE STUDY 4.7: SOUTH WESTERN SERVICES CO-OP[76]

This is a second level co-op owned by Bandon, Lisavaird, Drinagh, Barryroe and Dairygold Co-operatives. It has an annual turnover of about €15 million, a net profit of about €2.7million, 230 employees and contract staff and provides farmers with a range of agricultural services including: milk recording, farm relief, artificial insemination, business and accounting services and auctioneering.

In addition, it provides IT services: including data processing for government departments, etc. It is also engaged in forestry and wind energy and is at present developing a joint venture biomass plant to produce electricity.

Co-operatives in America are also beginning to rediscover the benefits of small-scale co-operatives. More and more farmers are finding it necessary to work together with neighbouring farms to meet the needs that are not met by large-scale co-ops. See **Case Study 4.8** for examples from the state of Wisconsin.

CASE STUDY 4.8: BACK TO THE DRAWING BOARD: A NEW GENERATION OF DAIRY CO-OPS?

After decades of mergers and consolidations of dairy co-ops, it seems that dairy farmers in Wisconsin are finding it necessary to start from scratch and create new smaller co-ops that meet their needs more effectively than the giant conglomerates. These new neighbourhood co-ops are able to provide smaller farms with many of the advantages of farming on a larger scale. They can do this by reducing input costs by pooling purchases, sharing best practice ideas to increase productivity and quality, sharing equipment and facilities to reduce overheads and providing themselves with a sufficient pool of milk to serve local speciality markets. For example:

- Scenic Valley Protein Cooperative in Darlington, WI has 10 member farms producing premium milk from Jersey cows.

- Wisconsin Dairy Grazers Co-operative has five member farms, making the best use of their joint holdings.

- Green Ribbon Creamery, with five member farms, is planning to create a new marketing co-operative to be located in an old creamery.

---

[76] At the time of going to print, SWSC is considering merging at least some of its activities with IAWS plc. This may result in some degree of demutualization, which will be discussed and updated in our forthcoming book, *Feeding Ourselves*.

BUILDING ON EXISTING CO-OPERATION

It is important to acknowledge that there is already considerable co-operation between Irish co-operatives and PLCs in relation to the use of processing facilities at both off-peak and high season. For example, Newmarket Co-op in North Cork works closely with neighbouring co-ops and PLCs. The further development of this type of co-operation into the formation of joint ventures or federations to spearhead new businesses would appear to be the preferred option for Irish co-operatives, judging by their response to the recent Prospectus Report (2003):

> [Glanbia's emphasis would be on] co-operation, shared assets and joint ventures in processing rather than on mergers or amalgamation.[77]

> Co-operation among dairy processors at regional level must precede the national consolidation goals arising from the Prospectus Report.[78]

SERVING THE CONSUMER – FEEDING OURSELVES

The 20th century has witnessed phenomenal growth in agricultural production, marketing and distribution. Food criss-crosses the world in millions of food-miles before reaching our tables. It is highly processed and packaged after leaving the farms, where it is produced with the aid of artificial fertilizers, chemicals and foodstuffs. The food chain, from farm to factory, is highly modernized and automated, resulting in fewer and fewer workers, particularly at farm level. In the last decade alone, the number of Irish dairy farmers has halved approximately and the Department of Agriculture predicts a further 50% reduction to around 14,000 in 2010 (Department of Agriculture and Food, 2003).

Giant international food retailers have taken over from the corner shop and use their concentrated power to squeeze margins at farm and processor level. For example, in the Republic of Ireland own-label liquid milk sold at discount prices continues to win market share from milk sold under processors' brands. This milk is being sourced in Northern Ireland, which is outside the remit of Ireland's national milk agency.

---

[77] Group Managing Director of Glanbia Co-op at the Agricultural Science Association annual conference, Kilkenny as reported in the *Irish Examiner*, 20.9.2003, p.10.

[78] Chief Executive, Lakeland Dairies, at the Agricultural Science Association annual conference, Kilkenny as reported in the *Irish Examiner*, 20.9.2003, p.10.

Ultimately, farmers both north and south of the border will lose out if they are unable to work together to countervail this retailer power.

During the 20th century, Irish agricultural co-ops have worked tirelessly to maintain farmer power and influence. In common with agricultural co-operatives internationally, they have done so within the prevailing conventional scientific model of farming. Farmers and consumers remain separate and distinct, allowing the development of middle-men in the form of giant retailers to exploit both. Even when consumers have organised to form consumer co-ops, as in the UK, they have remained aloof from the producer co-ops.

Many in agribusiness respond to changes in EU Common Agricultural Policy and increased concentration of the industry by advocating accelerated concentration at both farm and factory levels and a continuation of the conventional model as discussed above (see Prospectus, 2003).

AN ALTERNATIVE CO-OPERATIVE APPROACH

An alternative co-operative approach to organising the food industry and feeding ourselves is gaining momentum both internationally and in Ireland. This approach combines less intensive, mainly organic production with joint collaboration between producers and consumers in the form of farmers' markets and Community Supported Agriculture initiatives. It promotes respect for the environment and the countryside by putting the emphasis on quality, taste, value for money, traceability and connectiveness with the land rather than packaging and convenience. It is grounded in the local community and is more craft- and designer-based. It is given international expression in movements such as the "Slow Food Movement", founded in Italy in 1989 by Carlo Petrini and by the publication of more and more cookbooks urging us to cook with fresh, seasonal, organic local produce.

This alternative approach to food is not just an intellectual movement or pastime for the wealthy. Thousands of people are voting with their feet by regularly attending farmers' markets and similar events (see **Case Study 4.9**). Others are voting on the Internet by ordering online (see **Case Study 4.10**) on Cambrian Organics.

CASE STUDY 4.9: AN ALTERNATIVE APPROACH TO FEEDING OURSELVES

Irish Farmers' Markets say that "on an average day … the market at Leopardstown race course in County Dublin will attract between 1,500 and 2,000 customers, while a couple of weeks ago Castlebellingham, County Louth clocked a record 2,500 to 3,000".[79]

There are now regular farmers' markets in places such as Macroom, Galway, Midleton, Milltown (Kerry), Bantry, Cashel, Kenmare, Kilrush, Dublin's IFSC, Glendalough, Dun Laoghaire etc, etc. There are at least 400 farmers' markets in the UK, with a combined turnover in excess of £100 million, and an estimated 3,000 farmers' markets in the USA.

CASE STUDY 4.10: CAMBRIAN ORGANICS[80]

This co-op was set up in 2001 by a group of Welsh farmers who decided to find a way to sell their organic meat direct to their customers. Cutting out the middlemen enables the co-op to provide the customer with an excellent product at reasonable prices, while paying a fair price to the farmer. The co-op sells organic beef, pork, lamb and chicken direct to their customers' homes via an Internet ordering system. This is how the co-op is described on its web site:

> Cambrian Organics is a group of organic farmers who are passionate about the way we produce food. All of our meat comes from animals born, reared and processed with care in Wales, using skilled local butchers and traditional methods of production to ensure the best possible flavour.

It markets itself to those customers who want their meat to be traceable back to a specific farmer who cares about quality and food safety. To ensure the meat arrives in excellent condition, it is dispatched in boxes, with each cut individually vacuum-packed and labelled.

It even does its bit for the local tourist industry, inviting customers to relax in this unspoiled corner of Wales and suggest that, whilst staying in the area, they visit the farm that produces their favourite cut of meat!

---

[79]   *Sunday Tribune Magazine*, 26.10.2003, p.10.
[80]   www.cambrianorganics.com.

SHARING THE HARVEST: THE CSA APPROACH

A more radical approach to linking farmers with consumers is the concept of Community Supported Agriculture (CSA). CSAs are co-operative partnerships between groups of consumers and nearby farmers. They aim to cut out the middlemen between the farmer and the consumer and to use the profits saved to increase the prices paid to the producer and to reduce prices for the consumers.

The name Community Supported Agriculture[81] is a bit of a misnomer, as it suggests that the farmers are getting a better deal than the community of consumers, which is not the case. There are considerable mutual benefits. Farmers get better prices for their produce and a guaranteed market; consumers can enjoy quality fresh food (often organic), locally grown and recently harvested, at less than the prices charged by supermarkets for foods that have been on the road for a long, long time and often taste like it!

The idea of the CSA developed first in the Han consumer co-ops of Japan (see **Case Studies 1.3** and **3.3**). Han members began to question why foods that could be grown locally were being shipped from the other side of the world, damaging the environment, putting local farmers out of business, and delivering tired and tasteless produce to the kitchen table. They decided to make direct links with local farmers, entering into agreements on the range of foods that farmers could produce and the prices consumers would need to pay to ensure that local farms were viable.

In effect, the idea was that each family of consumers would agree to purchase each year a share of the local harvest. The price of this share would be agreed mutually by farmers and consumers to ensure that each side got a good deal. The share might be paid in advance or by instalments throughout the season, with perhaps 20% paid up front to help the farmer finance the enterprise. Typically, distribution would be handled by the consumer groups, with the help of volunteers and community pick-up points; farmers could concentrate on farming, without having to worry about how to market the crop. To ensure that less well-off consumers could take part in the programme, many CSAs gave a discount to members who were willing to donate their labour.

---

[81] The Soil Association, which has been promoting CSA development in the UK, has been trying to devise a more accurate name for this type of partnership. *Mutual farming* is one suggestion. See www.cuco.org.uk.

The idea spread to Germany and Switzerland and from there to the States, where CSAs took off. Today, there are an estimated 1,000 CSAs in the USA. In Wisconsin alone, 65 CSAs grow food for about 3,000 households.[82] Search for CSA on the Internet and you will discover an explosion of information: the web sites of individual CSAs, of support organisations, networks of CSAs and discussion groups. See **Case Study 4.11** for more information.

CASE STUDY 4.11: COMMUNITY SUPPORTED AGRICULTURE

US Department of Agriculture's definition of a CSA[83]:

> In basic terms, a CSA consists of a community of individuals who pledge support to a farm operation so that the farmland becomes, either legally or spiritually, the community's farm, with the growers and consumers providing mutual support and sharing the risks and benefits of food production. Members or shareholders of the farm or garden pledge in advance to cover the anticipated costs of the farm operation and farmer's salary. In return, they receive shares in the farm's bounty throughout the growing season, as well as satisfaction gained from reconnecting to the land. Members also share in risks, including poor harvest due to unfavourable weather or pests.

Angelic Organics
Angelic Organics[84] is a CSA in Northern Illinois, offering consumers three different types of harvest shares: i) a 20-week share (mid June – late October); ii) 4 winter deliveries (November –December); iii) a 12-week share (late summer & fall).

Here's how Angelic Organics describe its CSA services:

> With a preseason payment, you can purchase a "share" of our summer's harvest. You then receive a weekly box of our freshest, seasonal produce during the course of our 20-week harvest season, from mid-June to late-October. Further, you may choose to extend the season with a Winter Share - 4 additional boxes of storage vegetables to be delivered every other week in November & December.

---

82   See www.macsac.org.
83   http://attra.ncat.org/attra-pub/csa.html.
84   See www.angelicorganics.com/farm.html.

The importance of CSAs

The University of Massachusetts[85] emphasises the following advantages of the CSA model:

- A fair return to farmers and growers.
- The food dollar is kept in the community and builds regional food production.
- It encourages co-operation between farmers to meet the diverse needs of consumers.
- A guaranteed market allows farmers to concentrate on farming.
- Biodiversity is promoted by preserving small farms with a wide variety of crops.
- Farmers and consumers get to know and respect each other.
- CSA creates a sense of social responsibility and stewardship of local land.

THE FUTURE

Consumer interest in alternatives to mass-produced foods and desire for traceability and local farmer contact and knowledge are likely to influence the structure of the Irish and international agricultural co-operative movement in the years ahead. Smaller, locally-based co-operatives, or those with a decentralised structure, may be better able to link in to this type of consumer movement. Perhaps the best of both worlds can be achieved by amalgamating and centralising the processing of commodity products, while organic production and marketing can be handled more locally.

Interestingly, in the years ahead, Irish and European farmers will be much freer to produce for organic and local markets with the decoupling of EU product support payments from actual production. Perhaps the activities of Amul Co-operative in India (see **Case Studies 4.12**) may have much more relevance to Ireland and Europe than might appear at first glance.

---

[85] www.umass.edu/umext/csa/.

CASE STUDY 4.12: AMUL DAIRY CO-OP

A recent issue of *Business Week*[86] tells the remarkable story of India's largest dairy business. Anand Milk Union Ltd., better known as Amul, is a highly successful milk processing and marketing co-operative, with sales of US$612 million, growing by 25% per year. Because of its low-cost sources of raw milk, Amul's cheeses, ice-creams and chocolates compete successfully in local markets with the products of global giants, such as Nestlé and Unilever. Amul also has a growing presence in international markets, with exports to the USA, Africa and the Middle East.

Amul is a second level co-op owned by 175 local primary co-ops, involving two million people, who share Amul's profits. In 2001, Amul distributed half of its US$12 million profits to its member farmers. The existence of such an efficient processing and marketing co-op has transformed the lives of small farmers, even those with only one cow! Take, for example, Navali village in Gujarat State, where 932 of the 6,000 villagers are members of the Navali co-op. As well as earning enough to meet basic needs and pay for the education of their children, the proceeds from milk production have been sufficient to help build a new road and housing for schoolteachers. Last year, the farmers of Navali even donated money to earthquake victims in other parts of Gujarat.

SUMMARY

In this chapter, we've taken a quick stroll through the history of agricultural co-operatives in Ireland. We started in the 19th century, when Ireland's dairy co-ops would have looked much like newly launched dairy co-ops in 21st century Ethiopia. We saw the rapid growth of Irish co-ops in the early decades of the 20th century and how they weathered the economic depression that followed. In the early 1960s, the Knapp Report criticised Irish co-ops for not being *co-operative* enough, but further weakened their identification with their local communities by advocating wholesale rationalisation through mergers. The amalgamation process accelerated with Ireland's entry into the European Community and global ambitions. The failure of many co-ops to follow best international co-operative practice led to the partial demutualisation of some of Ireland's biggest co-operative businesses.

The loss of farmer control in major segments of the dairy industry and the high milk prices paid by some of Ireland's smaller co-ops have

---

[86] Kripalani & Engardio (2002).

led to a questioning of the once fashionable stampedes toward merger and demutualisation. Such doubts have been reinforced by the ability of the tiny Tatua Co-op and Westland Milk Products in New Zealand to give farmers a significantly better deal than the giant Fonterra Co-op, which through merger now accounts for about 95% of New Zealand's milk industry.

The uneasiness of farmers seems to be paralleled by the concerns of consumers. The rapid growth of farmer/consumer partnerships, such as CSAs, suggests the possibility that a very different approach to food production and distribution might be in store for us.

Will Irish agricultural co-operatives of the 21st century look more like those of our great grandparents in the 19th century, as they continue to protect the interests of the ordinary farmer and rural dweller? But this time round, will they perhaps do things somewhat differently? Will they co-operate with the urban consumer to free themselves from the tyranny of the multinational PLC food retailers?

FIVE

FEEDING OURSELVES III : WORKER-OWNED CO-OPS & FOOD

Robert Briscoe

Imagine a food store so adored by its customers that they rally round and lend it £300,000 to expand its business in their community. Imagine another food store, which, in a mere decade, has become the social hub of a town and is helping to set up a similar store in a neighbouring town. It works with local producers to ensure the best of fresh foods. And, in addition to traditional food shop services, it features a wide range of organic and whole foods, an open air café with pastries freshly baked in its own bakery, an in-store kitchen cooking a wide range of quality take-out hot meals, and a nutrition centre. It's even solving the community's housing problems by helping to develop housing co-ops, and it boosts the local economy by accepting a local currency[87] in part payment for its goods and services.

The first of these unusual businesses is the Unicorn Grocery Co-operative, located in a suburb of Manchester in the North of England. Unicorn is loved by its customers, but owned by its workers! The second of these co-ops is the Weaver Street Market (WSM) in the small town of Carrboro, North Carolina. WSM is owned jointly by its workers *and* its customers.

So far, in our investigation of food co-ops, we've been looking at the co-operatives that emerge at both ends of the food business chain, those

---

[87] Find out more about local currencies in **Chapter 6**.

run by consumers and those run by food producers. In this chapter, we explore the range of food businesses that are owned and controlled, not by farmers or consumers, but by the people working in them, and we'll also look at a few (like the Weaver Street Co-op) that are jointly owned by both workers and consumers.

Worker co-ops engage in a wide variety of food businesses in many countries. They are involved in retailing and in food services, such as restaurants and catering firms. They can also be found in the middle of the food chain, manufacturing food products. They pioneered the retailing and wholesaling of organic and vegetarian foods, long before the mainstream distributors recognised that there was money to be made from such foods. In the 1970s and 80s, worker co-ops and consumer co-ops (particularly in the USA, Canada and the UK) grew rapidly in this market niche. In recent years, however, the major supermarket chains have moved into the growing market for organics, creating problems for the multitude of tiny co-ops in this field. Nevertheless, many of these co-ops still prosper and we shall look at some of these success stories and explore their strategies for staying in business.

In this chapter, we start with examples of worker-owned retail stores, food services and wholesalers. We then look at examples of the worker co-ops engaged in food processing and conclude with multi-stakeholder food co-ops, which are owned by both workers and consumers.

WORKER-OWNED SHOPS

We start by looking at some examples of the worker co-ops that are retailing food. First, we revisit the Unicorn Co-operative Grocery, the shop that was saved by its customers (**Case Study 5.1**). We then look at Daily Bread, a shop with strong religious roots, which takes seriously the command to *love thy neighbour as thyself* (**Case Study 5.2**). We then visit On the Eighth Day Co-op, a worker-owned foodstore (**Case Study 5.3**), which started life as a clothes boutique and is now running one of Manchester's most popular vegetarian restaurants! What all of these businesses have in common is a commitment to improving the quality and wholesomeness of the food we eat and a determination to provide food excellence at a modest cost to the consumer.

CASE STUDY 5.1: UNICORN GROCERY CO-OPERATIVE[88]: THE SHOP SAVED BY ITS CUSTOMERS

Three friends, who had strong doubts about the quality of the food sold by conventional supermarkets, decided to set up a foodstore of their own in the Manchester suburb of Chorlton. Their shop would feature healthy organic and Fair Trade foods and would be owned and managed by its workers. They registered their co-op under the Industrial and Provident Societies regulations and launched Unicorn in 1996. The funds needed to open the shop were raised by pooling their own modest resources and by persuading other friends to invest in interest-bearing loan stock.

Sales in year one were a modest £40,000 but had risen to £1.4million by 2002, while membership had grown to 15.

As well as a spectacular range of organic foods, Unicorn sells organic wines and beers and specialises in dairy-free, gluten-free and sugar-free products – all at very competitive prices. It also sells fresh organic vegetables sourced from local producers and from its own one-hectare garden located in the nearby town of Sale. Lettuces picked in the morning are on display in the shop by noon. There is a large preparation room next to the shop, where vegetables are carefully washed and bulk foods packaged in smaller sizes.

All was going well at the co-op until, in November 2002, developers decided to bulldoze the building Unicorn was leasing. The co-op members took the brave decision to buy the building, which would also enable them to expand their business. But, even with a mortgage and their own resources, they still needed at least another £100,000 to pull off the deal. They offered their customers the opportunity to buy loan stock in the co-op. This would involve lending money to the co-op for a five-year period. They offered would-be investors the unusual opportunity of choosing their own interest rate, between 0% and 6% annually. Many chose not to receive any interest at all, but the average rate requested was about 3%. To the amazement of the co-operators, they reached the £100,000 target within a week. And by the time the deal to buy the building had gone through, Unicorn's devoted customers had pledged loans amounting to £300,000 to keep the co-op in business.

By summer 2003, renovations to the building had been completed, and Unicorn had expanded into a space about twice the size of its original premises. Now it also has frontage on the main street, which greatly increases the Co-op's visibility.

---

[88] www.unicorn-grocery.co.uk; Lupton (2003).

CASE STUDY 5.2: DAILY BREAD CO-OPERATIVE:
TO EACH ACCORDING TO THEIR NEEDS

Daily Bread is a worker-owned co-operative in Northampton. It has its roots in the religious convictions of nine friends who wanted to operate a business that was compatible with their Christian convictions. They wanted to find answers to the following thorny questions.

How do we pursue profit without being greedy?

How do we create wealth without compromising the teachings of the Gospel?

How do we balance individual freedom and creativity with collective responsibility to care for each other and for the wider community?[89]

They found an answer to these questions by setting up a worker co-op that produces and supplies a wide range of wholefoods (400 of them organic) with a high nutritional value. Products are supplied in a range of sizes to meet the needs of both retailers and shoppers.

The co-operative was registered in 1976 but did not start trading until 1980. It took that long to plan the business and raise the start-up capital. It began with a staff of three and grew steadily until today the co-op employs 25 staff, 12 of them members, and has annual sales of over £1 million.

One consequence of the co-op's nurturing philosophy is that rates of pay are determined on the basis of needs, not on the basis of age or position. As a consequence, a packer with major family commitments may be paid more than a manager with fewer personal responsibilities. The co-operative is also committed to helping others in need and supports people recovering from mental disorders by offering them employment in a caring setting. It also assisted with the development of another Daily Bread Co-op in Cambridge.

Together, the two sister co-ops took over a defunct charity, *Strive Overseas Ltd.*, which they use to channel donations to charitable organisations in the Third World. The donations are funded by committing a percentage of the Co-ops' gross wage bill. They also set up a *Community Fund* to support local charities.

---

[89]   These questions and other information on this co-op came from www.dailybread.co.uk and an article on the co-operative in Woodin (2003).

CASE STUDY 5.3: ON THE EIGHTH DAY CO-OP[90]: FROM BURNED-OUT BOUTIQUE TO VEGETARIAN RESTAURANT

The business that became the Eighth Day Co-op started out in 1970 as an unincorporated partnership of friends trading in clothes and crafts located upstairs above a boutique. After the boutique burnt down, the business moved to a ground floor location, registered as a co-operative in 1976 (with 10 worker-members) and dramatically changed the direction of its activities from a clothes shop to a wholefood shop that also sells clothes. The business continued to mutate and is now described as a *vegetarian café and shop*. Its current activities are described on the Eighth Day website:

> The co-op provides "excellent vegetarian and vegan cuisine, a huge range of vegetarian foods, vitamins, supplements, herbal remedies, organic wines, cruelty-free cosmetics, homeopathic remedies, eco-friendly cleaning products and much more".

The business is handily located on a main street next door to the Students Union Building of Manchester Metropolitan University, which can't be bad for business!

You might wonder where this co-op's strange name comes from? This is the explanation given on the website:

> "On the seventh day, God rested; on the eighth, he made something better."

WORKER-OWNED WHOLESALERS

In the United States, most of the co-operative wholesalers that supply co-op shops with organic wholefoods are second-level consumer co-operatives, owned and controlled by the multitude of consumer co-ops and buying clubs. Things happened differently in the UK, where the wholesalers in this specialised field of health foods tended to be worker co-ops, as were most of the natural foods retail co-ops. In **Case Studies 5.4** and **5.5**, we tell the stories of two of the largest and most successful worker-owned food wholesalers in the UK.

---

[90]   www.eighth-day.co.uk.

CASE STUDY 5.4: SUMA[91]: NEW WAYS OF WORKING – NO BOSS & EQUAL PAY!

Because they are owned by the workers, co-ops like Suma often adopt working practices that you'd hardly ever find in a conventional organisation, or indeed even in other kinds of co-operatives (such as producer and consumer co-ops). Suma runs its business in ways that fundamentally change the nature of work itself. There is no all-powerful chain of command, with supervisors spying on the workers to ensure they do exactly what they are supposed to be doing. The same wage is paid to everybody, regardless of age, experience or gender. Workers rotate jobs and learn a wide range of skills, thereby relieving boredom, building the capacity of workers and increasing organisational flexibility. And they all share in the management of the business. This might sound like a recipe for chaos, but Suma has evolved a system of self-management that really works.

If there is any boss in this co-op, it is the General Meeting (GM) where all members meet, six times a year, to agree on strategies, business plans and major policies. The GM also elects six of its members to form a Management Committee (MC), which meets weekly to implement the GM's decisions. The MC then appoints Company Officers (COs) to advise the MC and co-ordinate the implementation of the decisions and programmes already agreed by the membership. COs take part in the MC's deliberations but, to ensure they don't try to run the business for their own benefit, they have no vote at the MC. This system of management has evolved over years of trial and error – we shall revisit some of these ideas in **Chapter 9**.

Suma describes itself as:

> "The UK's largest independent wholesaler and distributor of quality vegetarian, fairly traded, organic and natural foods. A multi-million pound company, supplying 2,500 customers across the UK and abroad. 100 employees. 25 year history. Powerful brand. Uninterrupted growth. Happy customers and suppliers."

Co-operation between worker and consumer co-ops

Suma was registered as a common-ownership worker co-op in 1977. At that time, worker co-ops (even those in the food industry) had almost no contact with the consumer-owned mainstream co-operatives that had grown out of the Rochdale tradition. In 2000, however, Suma played an important part in the initiative to bring worker co-operatives and consumer co-ops together: the merger of the Co-operative Union (an apex federal body representing the traditional co-op movement) and ICOM (the Industrial Common Ownership Movement, which

---

[91] Most of this information was sourced in August 2003 from www.suma.co.uk.

represented the majority of the new-wave worker co-ops). The resulting organisation was renamed Co-operatives UK, and one of Suma's pioneers sits on its Board of Directors.

CASE STUDY 5.5: ESSENTIAL TRADING CO-OPERATIVE[92]: THE CO-OP STRUCTURE MAKES IT POSSIBLE TO DO THINGS DIFFERENTLY

Essential Trading is another co-operative wholesaler, similar to Suma. Like Suma, it is owned and controlled by its worker-members. It has also devised innovative ways of working and sees its members as co-directors, each with an equal say in the running and development of the business.

Essential Trading was formed in 1991 out of a merger of two existing wholesale co-ops, which were operating in the same region of the UK: Harvest Foods, based in Bath, and Nova Wholefoods, based in Bristol. The merged co-op has a membership of 59 and a total workforce of 72.[93] It has annual sales of over £6 million, and sells 6,000 product lines to 1,500 active customer accounts.

The philosophy and rationale of Essential Trading is summed up on its website:

> "It is the fact that we are a workers' co-operative that allows us to operate based on the ethics we believe in, and it is those ethics that make us function as a workers' co-operative. This is why we are a successful business, with a reputation for friendly, honest, reliable and informed service."

Clearly, it sees its ethical stance as a competitive advantage.

WORKER-OWNED PRODUCTION

Food production is a popular business area for people who want to set up worker co-ops. Usually, the people setting up worker co-ops don't have a great deal of spare cash to invest. Because of this, they look for business opportunities that do not require a huge amount of capital and which serve tiny niche markets, while serving real needs. Small-scale food preparation and production can often fit this bill. In **Case Study 5.6**, we look at a case study of a tiny home-based bakery business, Heron Quality Foods, which grew much faster than anyone expected.

---

[92]   www.essential-trading.co.uk.

[93]   All permanent employees who work at least 24 hours a week are eligible for membership of the co-op.

CASE STUDY 5.6: HERON QUALITY FOODS[94]: FROM HOME COOKING TO INTERNATIONAL MARKETING

From humble beginnings in 1997, Heron Quality Foods, an Irish worker co-operative, now exports its bakery products to Europe and the Middle East. It was launched in 1997 by a retired couple, John and Elizabeth Dawson, who started it as an informal small business in their home in Kinsale, County Cork. The business grew out of Elizabeth's hobby and produced a range of high quality savoury breads and confectionery, which were sold locally.

Elizabeth was in charge of the baking and continued to research and develop new products, while John managed the business. Demand grew rapidly and, by 2000, the business employed 26 people: 14 full-time and 12 part-time employees. This rapid expansion forced them to relocate the business twice, eventually to Knockbrown, Bandon, County Cork, where it is currently located.

This was a bigger business than they had expected, and the Dawsons decided in 2000 to retire again. They began to explore exit options for themselves that would ensure the future of the bakery and the jobs of the experienced and very loyal workforce.

At this time, the Co-operative Development Unit (CDU)[95] was promoting the idea of adopting the worker co-operative structure as a vehicle for owner managers who wished to retire or exit from their business. The manager of the CDU had developed an innovative way of funding worker participation.[96] He proposed that the business be split into two companies, with the *assets* held in one company (owned and controlled by the original owners) and leased to the other company, which owned the *trading part* of the business. This latter company would be structured as a worker co-operative with the shares and democratic voting rights belonging to both the original owners and the participating employees. This worker co-operative company would also have an option to buy the assets at some agreed future date.

Splitting the company in this way gave the owners some security, as they continued to own the assets, while making it easier for the employees to buy-in, as they did not have to purchase the assets outright. The model locked in the original owners for an agreed period

---

94 Written by Colm Hughes, manager of the CDU when Heron Foods adopted a worker co-operative structure. It was Hughes who devised the innovative financing plan above, which has enabled a number of family businesses to convert themselves into worker co-ops.

95 The CDU was originally established in FÁS (the national training and employment agency) to promote worker co-operatives. Later, its terms of reference were extended to include "the design and implementation of other forms of employee involvement where this can contribute to the development of viable enterprises".

96 One of Colm Hughes' many articles on this approach is Hughes (1998).

of time. It guaranteed their continued expertise to the business to help employees to manage the business successfully. Another advantage is that owners, now freed up from the day-to-day running and problems of the business, could further strengthen the business by putting more time into developing its customer base.

After discussions with the CDU, the Dawsons wrote to all employees, advising them of their current thinking and inviting those interested to get involved. Five staff expressed an interest and a meeting was held with all concerned. At that meeting, it was agreed that a detailed strategic plan, examining all aspects of the business, would be drawn up by the owners and the participating employees. The plan identified organic and gluten-free products as a natural progression and complementary to the existing range of products.

The plan also included a new management structure to reflect the additional responsibilities of employees who purchased shares in the business. It closely examined what the company hoped to achieve over the next three to five years and came up with a list of implications that would have to be overcome in order to achieve the strategic objectives (for example, taxation, pension planning, patents, training, funding expansion, etc). One by one, each of the problems was eliminated, the final hurdle being the amount and cost of funding required to develop the business and to begin to produce the newly identified area of gluten-free products.

Substantial funding was raised from a number of 'social' funders, who were willing to assist this worker co-operative venture, to ensure the continuation of a business that provided scarce employment opportunities to small rural communities in the area – the fear being that if the business was bought by another bakery, the recipes would be taken and manufactured elsewhere, and the Knockbrown operation closed.

The Dawsons had always maintained that there was a high potential for gluten-free exports and, with the key employees now running the day-to-day business, they had the time to embark on a marketing and sales mission, first in the UK and later throughout continental Europe. The company's first export order came from Sainsbury's in the UK. Currently, Heron Quality Foods Limited is the largest gluten-free producer in Ireland. It exports to the UK, mainland Europe, Scandinavia and the Middle East, and continues to develop and expand its export base with plans to export to the USA. It has developed a website to promote its products and to attract a world-wide base of customers. In the meantime, John and Elizabeth are still very much involved in the development of the business and appear to have postponed retirement for a little while yet.

WORKERS & CONSUMERS TOGETHER

For a long time, people feared that a co-operative owned by more than one group of stakeholders (such as *workers* and *consumers*) would tear itself to pieces because of the conflicting demands of rival groups. This fear was born out very early in the history of co-operatives, when the Rochdale pioneers decided to set up a worker-owned factory.

Because the workers didn't have enough capital to finance the factory themselves, it was decided to allow sympathetic outside investors to buy shares as well. The factory prospered at first with its highly motivated workers, excited about working for themselves and sharing the profits (according to an agreed formula) between themselves and the altruistic non-worker investors. Things went well, until it was decided that the factory was doing *so* well that it should be expanded. More capital needed to be raised and so more outside investors were invited to buy shares. The factory was now so profitable that the outside investors, who now outnumbered the workers, were finding altruism less attractive than it had been. They outvoted the workers at a general meeting, removed the workers' profit-sharing rights and transformed the co-op into a conventional investor-owned company.

Nowadays, more and more commentators are likely to point to the competitive *advantages* of multi-stakeholder co-ops, rather than their disadvantages. The argument is that, if a number of key stakeholders are brought into the decision-making processes of a co-op, far from damaging the organisation, they are much more likely to give it a distinctive competitive edge. A co-operative owned co-operatively by customers *and* workers is more likely to give a better deal to both groups, thereby creating customers and workers who are both highly motivated to ensure that the business succeeds – and that can't be bad for business.

In this section, we shall look at two very different examples of multi-stakeholder food co-ops, both of which *do* seem to have a competitive advantage. The first example is a relatively small retail co-op, mentioned at the beginning of this chapter: Weaver Street Market (WSM) in Carrboro, North Carolina (**Case Study 5.7**). The second is a massive retailing co-operative, Eroski, which started life modestly in the Basque region of Spain but is now the major player in a co-operative consortium that dominates Spanish food retailing (**Case Study 5.8**).

CASE STUDY 5.7: WEAVER STREET MARKET (WSM): "THIS CO-OPERATIVE IS OWNED BY THE WHOLE COMMUNITY"[97]

WSM is a retail co-operative, owned jointly by its workers and its customers and is managed by a Board of seven directors. Consumer-members and worker-members vote for two representatives each, the Board itself appoints two more and the General Manager is the seventh.

WSM opened its doors in June 1988. The funds to set it up came from a loan from a local business development fund, the shares invested by its members and a Community Development Block Grant from the town of Carrboro. The business started with a terrifying debt to equity ratio of 70:1 but, within four years, its financial situation had improved so much that its debt/equity ratio was a very sound figure of 1:1. By 2004, its membership had grown to nearly 8,000 households (a 45% increase over the 2002 figure), in a town with a total population of only 12,000. WSM is now opening a second store in the neighbouring town of Chapel Hill, a project funded entirely by investments from Chapel Hill, and premises have been purchased for a future store in downtown Hillsborough.

One of the reasons WSM has grown steadily is that it provides significant discounts to members. Consumer members get a 5% discount on their purchases, but can earn even greater discounts (an additional 15%) by volunteering to work at the co-op for three hours a week. Staff members enjoy a 20% discount on their purchases. In order to enjoy these benefits, members must invest in a refundable share. The worker's share cost US$400 (which may be paid for on easy payment terms). Consumers pay according to the number of members in their family: a full share for one adult costs US$75, for two adults, US$135 and for three adults, US$175. Consumer-member shares may also be purchased in instalments.

Discounts are attractive, but perhaps an even more important factor in WSM's growth is the fact that it does a great job of livening up the downtown area and showing real concern for the well-being of the community. WSM has become a vibrant social hub of Carrboro, by offering a wide range of businesses and services in the centre of the town – ventures such as its innovative foodstore, coffee shop, restaurant, and bakery. WSM also stages open-air social events in the summer, such as a Jazz Brunch featuring local bands, and puppet shows for kids. It also teams up with local charitable groups to provide picnic foods for weekly outdoor fund-raising events. It also sees one of its key roles as providing education "to fill in the things we don't know about our food". WSM informs its members about the same kinds of issues as those raised by the UK's Co-op Group in its booklet on *Food Crimes*.

---

[97]   For more on WSM, see www.weaverstreetmarket.com, the source of this summary.

The fact that WSM does things very differently from most conventional retailers is probably a factor in building customer loyalty.

One of the reasons given for opening membership to workers, as well as to consumers, was the desire to ensure that the *co-op was owned by the whole community*. WSM reaches out to the community in all kinds of ways and searches for opportunities to empower people in the solution of their own problems. It sources foodstuffs as far as possible from local producers and builds a mutually beneficial relationship with its suppliers. It also seeks out opportunities for opening new co-operative businesses in its community (the latest prospect is a co-op bookstore) but will not endanger existing locally-owned businesses by entering into direct competition with them. Indeed, it attempts to work with local businesses in building and enriching the community.

It's even involved in solving the community's housing problems by sponsoring the development of housing co-ops, and helps boost the local economy by accepting a local currency in part payment for its goods and services.

WSM is a relatively small retail co-op (like hundreds of others in North America) which thrives in a small community. At the other end of the size spectrum is Eroski, a worker/consumer multi-stakeholder co-op that has an appetite for rapid growth. It attempts to express its co-operative character in ways that are very different from the strategies of Weaver Street Market.

CASE STUDY 5.8: THE EROSKI GROUP: "A CO-OPERATIVE MULTINATIONAL – CAN BIG BE BEAUTIFUL?"

The Eroski Group (EG) is the distribution division of the Mondragon Co-operative Corporation (MCC). MCC is a diversified and highly successful network of self-managing worker co-operatives, with its roots in the Basque region of Spain. The first Mondragon co-op was launched in 1956 with 25 worker-owners. At the end of 2003, MCC had a workforce of 68,260, nearly 28% more than in 2000. We'll be revisiting MCC, with a great deal more detail, in **Chapter 9**.

EG is a major player in Spain's retail industry, with 69 hypermarkets, 516 Eroski centre supermarkets, 243 Eroski city supermarkets, 305 franchise outlets, 28 cash and carry outlets, 176 travel agency branches, 48 petrol stations, 23 Forum sports stores, 148 perfume stores and 19 goods depots. In 2003, Eroski's sales reached nearly €5.4 billion, an 85% increase over 2000, its consolidated profits increased by 21% to a total of €108 million, 4,731 new jobs were created, with full worker participation in ownership, profits and management, with a year-end total employment level of 29,192.

Another achievement in 2003 was the award of SA8000 Certification of Social Responsibility, an award that recognises sustained commitment to social action and management methods that respect the basic rights of shoppers, workers, suppliers and the community as a whole. EG is the first retailer in Spain, and only the second in Europe, to win this award.[98]

How did it get to be so big so quickly?
By listening to the customers. Unlike most of MCC's other co-ops, Eroski didn't start out as a simple worker-owned co-op. Membership was open to consumers as well as workers. Eroski's founders considered that involving consumers would strengthen the co-op by making it more responsive to the needs and problems of its customers. To make sure that consumers are listened to, they elect half of Eroski's Board of Directors; the workers elect the other half. To make doubly sure that shoppers will be heard, the role of the Chairperson, who wields a casting vote, is always filled by one of the consumer-members. In 2003, consumer membership was close to half a million, and 17,778 consumer members participated in information meetings and a General Assembly, which was held in 11 different centres in Spain. The General Assembly agreed to allocate nearly €7 million in profits to support the activities of the Eroski Foundation, which works in the fields of consumer information, sustainable development and the environment.

Motivating workers
Another key factor in Eroski's success is the motivation of its worker-members. As co-owners of the business, they are required to make a substantial investment when they join the co-op. In return, they are eligible to receive a major share of the profits, which are added each year to their individual share accounts. In 2003, Eroski shared €52 million[99] of its profits with its 13,079 worker-owners. With a significant and growing stake in the business, workers are keen to see the co-op succeed. Consumer-members do not have to make a major investment nor do they receive a share of the profits, but their commitment is built by having a say in the design of the co-op and its range of services. Eroski also builds consumer trust by being conspicuous as a supporter of good causes and sponsoring events such as Spain's Fair Trade fortnight.

Mergers and acquisitions
Business growth really took off when Eroski entered into a partnership with Consum, a worker-owned supermarket chain, based in Valencia.

98   www.mcc.coop/ing/noticias/gdistribucion/n_0001.asp?id=479.
99   Profits shared in 2003 were 30% above the 2002 figure.

The Eroski/Consum partnership grew by investing heavily in new hypermarkets and supermarkets, as well as merging with established consumer-owned co-operatives operating in other regions of Spain.

International joint ventures
As well as its business activities in Spain, Eroski also operates three hypermarkets and 19 supermarkets in the South of France. In 2002, it signed an agreement with Les Mosquetaires-Intermarché Group (MIG) and set up a company, Alidis, jointly-owned 50/50 by Eroski and Les Mosquetaires. MIG is a voluntary chain of independent retail companies owned by 2,800 working managers in eight different European countries. Together, MIG and Eroski have combined sales of €41.5 billion, making them the third largest retailer in Europe. The purpose of Alidis is to purchase for the two groups, co-operate in the development of own brand goods and develop new businesses. Other retailers with similar values have been invited to join the consortium.

Innovative financing
Eroski has taken an unusual step to raise finance for its rapid growth, a step that would be frowned upon by many, if not most, co-operators. It has raised investment capital by issuing a financial instrument called *Eroski Contributions* (ECs). These contributions enable it to raise funds in conventional money markets, without giving up ownership rights to outside investors. The market value of ECs will fluctuate according to the comparative profitability and stability of the Eroski Group. Investors were so eager to buy the first issue of ECs in 2002 that it was oversubscribed by €60 million. The first issue raised €90 million for the expansion of the Eroski Group. The second issue of ECs has not been offered on the open market but is being given to the Mercat retail chain in the Balearic Islands in exchange for Mercat shares, which will give Eroski a majority holding in the Mercat chain. There is an agreed plan for Eroski to eventually acquire 100% of Mercat shares.

Responsible retailing or selling its soul to the devil?
In co-op circles, there has been a horrible tendency to look askance at co-operatives that are spectacularly successful. Many co-op enthusiasts will shudder when reading the story of Eroski. They will wonder how a co-op owned by ordinary people can do so well and will assume that they must be doing something immoral! "What sort of a co-op is this," they will ask, "that grows at a breakneck pace, collaborates with conventional businesses and sells bits of itself to stock exchange speculators?"

Others will say, "Hold on, now. This is a courageous and enterprising co-operative business that is not content to hide itself away in a tiny community, but is trying to change the face of European retailing. It is bringing co-operative ownership and ethical behaviour into an industry not renowned for showing any great concern for the food crimes on which it is built, or for paying its workers well. And look at all the other things Eroski is doing to underline its co-operative difference." See **Case Study 5.9**.

CASE STUDY 5.9: EROSKI'S CO-OPERATIVE DIFFERENCE[100]

Eroski is working with UNICEF to support the right to education in Bolivia and has collected 150,000 school packs, of which one-third were donated by Eroski and the rest by its customers and workers.

More than 5,000 Eroski group workers are co-operating with a Medicins sans Frontieres project to fight a tropical disease in Bolivia that threatens 25% of the population, in particular children and pregnant women.

The Eroski group is collaborating once again with the Spanish Food Bank Federation to promote the XIV national food collection campaign, whereby Eroski donates food (for people in need) to match the donations of its customers.

Eroski launches the "Healthy Idea" campaign, a continuous information campaign and is hiring and training 300 university graduates to teach a range of food courses in its hypermarkets and supermarkets, as well as supplying educational materials and running a "Idea San" website.

Eroski introduced a new NCR electronic labelling system, which ensures that the price shoppers pay at the checkout always coincides with the price they have seen on the shelves.

In 2004, Eroski won first prize for *International Co-operation in Sustainable Development*, awarded by the European Environment Foundation.

SUMMARY

In this chapter, we have looked at food businesses owned and controlled by the people who work in them. Many of the worker-owned food co-ops built their competitive advantage by specialising in the so-called health food business, concentrating on organic, vegetarian and fairly traded foods.

We started by looking at three worker co-ops that used this approach and have survived and grown in spite of major chain stores entering the

---

[100] See www.mcc.coop/ing/noticias/gdistribucion/n_0001.asp?id=489.

organic foods market. One useful competitive strategy for the co-ops has been to develop direct links with local organic producers, whose output is too small to meet the demands of major supermarkets. Direct relationships between retail co-op and producer has eliminated middlemen and enabled well-managed co-ops to offer competitive prices to consumers, while paying fair prices to farmers. Next, we looked at two major worker-owned wholesalers in the UK, which pioneered the distribution of health foods by creating a market for organic producers and supporting the worker-owned retailers by supplying them with good foods at favourable prices. Both of these co-ops had also developed new ways of working and attributed their success to the people power that has been generated by doing things differently.

Our next port of call was West Cork, where we visited a highly successful and innovative food manufacturing business that had converted from a family business to a worker co-op – a five-year-old business that already dominates the niche market of gluten-free foods and is exporting specialty breads to Europe and the Middle East.

The chapter concluded with the stories of two multi-stakeholder co-ops owned by both workers and consumers. One was the Weaver Street Market, a highly successful and innovative retailer in North Carolina, which focused on building the downtown centre of its own small community and helping neighbouring towns do the same. The other was Eroski, a multinational enterprise, already dominating retailing in Spain and well on its way to developing a major presence in other European countries. We explored some of the factors that had supported its rapid growth and raised the thorny question of whether big can ever be beautiful!

Now for something very different! In the next chapter, we move completely outside of the food industry to look at how co-operatives are able to help us cope with our money problems.

SIX

FINANCING OURSELVES

Olive McCarthy

User-owned financial institutions, such as credit unions, are probably the most common form of co-operative in the world. A 1997 study showed that there are approximately 60,000 credit co-operatives (mostly credit unions) with more than 150 million members worldwide (Zurdo, 1997). There are also many other forms of user-controlled financial institutions, including *Grameen* banks, Local Economic Trading Schemes (LETS) and Time Banks. This chapter explores the range of innovative ways in which users of financial services successfully meet their financial needs by pooling their resources to operate and control their own tailor-made financial institutions.

User-owned financial institutions often emerge in times of economic distress and hardship, where people in local communities agree to get actively involved in doing something about their situation. Since the late 1970s, there have been serious banking crises in 69 countries (Lietaer, 2001), with an annual average of 4,000 mergers and acquisitions in the world financial industry (Béland, 1999), while billions of people continue to live in poverty. So it is not surprising that people continue to find innovative ways of meeting their own financial needs, rather than relying on governments or conventional businesses to do it for them.

Credit unions are set up to create adequate local savings and credit facilities and to free communities from indebtedness to moneylenders. The Grameen bank, established first in Bangladesh, has been replicated all over the world to enable the poorest of the poor to access the credit they need to sustain their livelihoods. Time banks were first developed in Japan to provide an alternative to the sharply rising costs of health-care. User-owned financial institutions thrive in an environment of need, and they work best, as we see throughout this book, when they reinvent themselves continually in innovative ways to meet the changing needs and circumstances of their members.

WHAT MAKES USER-OWNED FINANCIAL INSTITUTIONS DIFFERENT?

User-owned financial institutions are markedly different from conventional financial institutions (see **Figure 6.1**). Instead of promoting profit for the rich, user-owned financial institutions promote service to savers and borrowers. Instead of promoting dependence, they promote self-help. Instead of promoting secrecy, they promote openness and transparency.

FIGURE 6.1: THE MAIN DIFFERENCES BETWEEN USER-OWNED & CONVENTIONAL FINANCIAL INSTITUTIONS[101]

Characteristic	User-owned	Conventional
Ownership	Owned by its members.	Owned by investors and private business people.
Membership	Open membership.	Limited 'membership'.
Control	Democratic control.	Usually depends on shareholding.
Benefits	Equitable distribution of surpluses to all members.	Return for investors and private interests.
Reason for a service	To suit members' needs and requirements.	Solely for profit-making.

User-owned financial institutions are exactly that – financial institutions owned and controlled by the people who use their services. They are formed by groups of people who identify a need for financial services and agree to work together to meet their financial need for themselves. These needs are usually personal, business-oriented, or community-oriented. They agree to pool their savings so that they can lend to each other at reasonable rates of interest. By owning their own financial

---

[101] Browne (1993).

institution, they can *design it for use*. They can decide the type of service that will be provided, how it will be delivered and how it will be governed. This ensures that the service will be relevant to the needs of those involved. Although the notion of ordinary people designing made-to-measure community banks may sound impractical, there are tens of thousands of actual working examples worldwide. **Case Study 6.1** gives examples of different types of user-owned financial institutions.

CASE STUDY 6.1: USER-OWNED FINANCIAL INSTITUTIONS

Self-help Credit Union Ltd, North Carolina, USA[102]

Self-Help's mission is to create ownership and economic opportunities for minorities, women, rural residents and low-wealth families. Self-Help's small business lending helps entrepreneurs who find it difficult or impossible to obtain more conventional financing. Since Self-Help's start in 1980, it has provided over US$1.78 billion in financing to almost 25,800 small businesses, non-profits, and home-buyers.

The Grameen Bank, Bangladesh[103]

The Grameen Bank of Bangladesh was designed to lend to the poorest of the poor, primarily women, who were desperately poor because oppressive and exploitative economic and cultural systems had kept them trapped. They were not able to access capital to create their own jobs, because they did not have any collateral. Employers and money-lenders exploited them.

Access to credit through the Grameen Bank has allowed them to break free from the poverty trap, explore their potential and create enormous wealth: 92% of the Bank is now owned by its borrowers. A borrower becomes an owner when she accumulates sufficient savings and buys one (and only one) share in the Bank, which costs US$3.

User-owned financial institutions focus on providing benefits to individual members, first and foremost, but also to the wider communities in which they live and work. The main characteristics of user-owned financial institutions are that they:

- Encourage their member/users to build up a habit of savings.
- Give their member/users access to affordable loans.

---

[102] www.self-help.org.
[103] www.action.org.

- Take their member/users out of the clutches of moneylenders.
- Provide banking services to people not normally served by banks.
- Provide a means to enable people to sustain a living.
- Educate their member/users in the wise use of money and in their well-being as members of a community.
- Often help their members to identify new ways of doing business.

They are run on a democratic basis, in that every member is an equal owner of the business and has one vote in decision-making and elections. All members benefit equally from their membership in proportion to their use of the business.

In 1992, the Secretary-General of the United Nations recognised that such financial institutions:[104]

> ... have a strong potential for mobilising local savings and providing credit to members, and are particularly important in apparently capital-scarce conditions, thereby encouraging thrift and entrepreneurial activity and hence stimulating local multipliers.

This is echoed by Douthwaite (1996, p.125), who highlights the ability of user-owned financial institutions to short-circuit local finances and to recycle local money locally and at local prices:

> Once our savings have been passed over the mahogany counter of the bank, they will not return to our communities except at interest rates determined on the world markets.

Local savings can be employed to finance and stimulate local job creation, provide products and services, and sustain local populations. Every €1 of savings collected by a local, user-owned financial institution gives financial leverage to the local borrowing member, creates employment for the local community, sustains the local population, stimulates the supply and demand of local products and services, enhances profitability of local entrepreneurs, gives a financial return to the local savings member, and so on. Thus, this circle of local finances causes a local multiplier effect (a simple example of which is depicted in **Figure 6.2**).

---

[104]   United Nations (1992).

FIGURE 6.2: THE SHORT-CIRCUIT/MULTIPLIER EFFECT OF USER-OWNED FINANCIAL INSTITUTIONS: A SIMPLE EXAMPLE

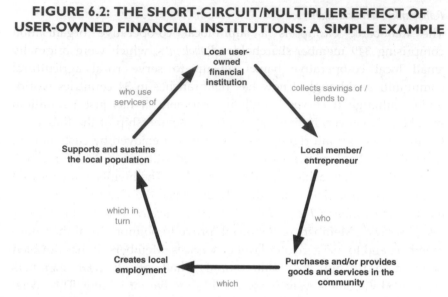

TYPES OF USER-OWNED FINANCIAL INSTITUTION

Financial co-operatives are by far the most popular form of user-owned financial institution. However, other forms of user-owned financial innovations also exist and will be considered in this chapter, including Grameen Banks, Time Banks, and Local Economic Trading Schemes (LETS).

Financial co-operatives

Community-based financial co-operatives are known by various names throughout the world – for example, *Raiffeisenbanken* and *Volksbanken* in Germany, *Rabobank* in the Netherlands, *Credit Agricole Mutuel* in France, Savings and Credit Co-operatives (or SACCOs) in African countries, *Caisses Populaires* in francophone Canada, Building Societies in Ireland and the UK, and of course, probably best known of all, Credit Unions, which can be found all over the world. Co-operative banks are financial co-operatives owned by other co-operatives or groups of co-operatives, for example, the Co-operative Bank in the UK and the Norinchukin Bank in Japan. We will consider a selection of these institutions.

Rabobank, Netherlands[105]

The Rabobank Group is a supra-local co-operative organisation comprising 349 member-shareholder *Rabobanks*, which were originally small local co-operative banks set up to serve rural agricultural communities, although it now has 169 branches in 34 countries world-wide. Although it serves 9 million customers, it has just 1.1 million members. However, individual and bank membership of the Rabobank Group confers certain rights and privileges not enjoyed by customers in general. The bank views its co-operative identity as a vital force that enables the bank to achieve market leadership. The members are viewed as the bank's *true capital* and directly influence the Group's strategy to ensure *"innovation of the products and services offered as well as the bank's role in society"*. Members of Rabobank prove to be more loyal than non-members and to use a greater level of services. Membership has doubled between 2001 and 2003: interestingly, half of all new members mentioned Rabobank's social agenda as a motive for joining. This social agenda includes socially-responsible lending that encourages environmentally-friendly production, respect for animal well-being and "green" investments.

Rabobank has been hugely successful in The Netherlands, serving over half of the Dutch population and over half of all Dutch businesses. It is the market leader for mortgages (24%), private savings (40%), small and medium enterprises (39%) and agriculture (83%). In 1995, the co-operative status of Rabobank came under intense review, and it was concluded that the co-operative ethos of the bank had contributed enormously to its success and needed to be revitalised. This resulted in the issue of investment certificates to members and employees only, which gave a return greater than 10-year Dutch government bonds. Demand was double what had been anticipated and has led to substantial membership growth. The chairperson of the bank said:

> Our co-operative background is not a barrier even though some people occasionally try to convince us otherwise. On the contrary, it is an asset, a major competitive advantage. (Béland, 1999)

Credit Agricole Mutuel, France[106]

The Credit Agricole Mutuel system is made up of about 2,000 local credit co-operative societies, with approximately 3,600 branches throughout

---

[105] Rabobank (2003).
[106] Much of this discussion is drawn from www.wisc.edu/uwcc/icic/orgs.

France, and a total membership of 5 million. It is one of the top five banking institutions in the country. Each local society adopts co-operative principles and is an autonomous unit, offering a range of services to its members. One of the most interesting aspects of the system is the extent to which it involves members in strategic planning and decision-making: over 30,000 members are elected, by the membership, as board members in local societies.

The societies offer a range of services, including personal and corporate savings and lending, insurance, leasing, and card payments. The social role of the local co-operative societies is also clearly recognised – they are involved in initiatives, such as job creation schemes for young people, sponsorship, social housing, and special funds for people in difficulty or collective investments of an ethical nature.

Caisses Populaire – Mouvement des Caisses Desjardins[107]
The Desjardins Movement consists of 671 local *caisses* with a total membership of 5.16 million. There are almost 8,000 voluntary officers, working alongside over 37,000 employees within the movement. Total assets of the movement reach almost CAN$90 billion.

The Desjardins Group is motivated by the desire to provide its members with high-quality financial services and support to community development projects. It has considerable market share in deposits (43.6%), personal lending (26.9%), residential mortgages (37.7%), loans to industry and business (23.5%), and agricultural loans (41.8%) (Annual Report 2003).

One of the most interesting facts about the Desjardins movement is its extensive involvement in community initiatives. It also has a keen sense of social responsibility and produces a Community Involvement Report annually. Examples of its activities include:
- **Promoting Fair Trade:** In 2002, the Desjardins group purchased over 6,000 pounds of Fair Trade coffee, directly supporting the livelihoods of coffee producers in third world countries.
- **Financial guidebook:** Caisse Populaire Desjardins de Saint-Dominique has designed a guidebook to raise awareness among seniors and their loved ones about financial abuse, so they can recognise it and prevent it.
- **Desjardins movement helps youths enter labour market:** The Fédération des Caisses Desjardins has received CAN$3,000,775 in

---

[107] Group Desjardins (2003).

federal funding through the Youth Employment Strategy to implement the Releve Externe Desjardins programme. The programme will give work experience in the financial sector to 80 young college and university graduates (mostly from rural areas of Quebec). They will participate in various practical and in-class training workshops and be twinned with a mentor before receiving on-the-job training (Source: CCA Co-op News Briefs, 21.8.2003).

The Desjardins Group has also set up a subsidiary, Développement International Desjardins (DID), which has provided support for over 30 years to co-operative financial institutions in some 20 countries in Africa, Latin America, the Caribbean, Asia and Eastern Europe. Specialising in technical assistance and investment in the field of community finance, DID works in partnership with the Government of Quebec, the World Bank and other multilateral organisations. An example of its work is given in **Case Study 6.2**.

CASE STUDY 6.2: DESJARDINS HELPS COMPUTERISE AFRICAN CREDIT & SAVINGS CO-OPERATIVES[108]

In Africa a large segment of the population remains completely ignored by the traditional banking sector. Fortunately, support provided by the Desjardins Group and its subsidiary, Développement International Desjardins (DID), through programmes financed by the Canadian International Development Agency (CIDA), has resulted in the creation and expansion of savings and credit co-operatives in many African countries.

"In Africa, credit unions provide the poorest with a safe way to save and obtain loans and other financial products to improve their way of life and participate in the economy ... since local money should serve local interests," says DID President and CEO, Anne Gaboury. "But since most of these credit unions are run manually and their volume of transactions is rising so fast, they need to computerise their operations. The North-South Partnership programme is intended to provide a tangible response to this need."

The Desjardins credit unions' contribution to this innovative programme will help African credit unions to purchase the computer equipment needed. The African credit unions will then assume full control for equipment maintenance and upgrades.

---

[108] www.desjardins.com.

Over the next four years, DID intends to support the computerisation of nearly 300 African credit unions within its partner networks. This is an ambitious goal, but the expected impact is worth the effort, resulting in confident credit unions that will be run in a satisfactory and autonomous manner due to their new ability to access a high level of financial services.

For Oumou Sidibé, the Director General of the Nyèsigiso credit union network in Mali, Desjardins assistance is highly valuable:

> It is truly encouraging to see how well the co-operative model developed by Desjardins produces results and especially how well it can be adapted to a country like Mali! Our network is ready to take on the challenge of modernisation. Computerisation is the step we needed to take for success.

Credit unions

Figures from the World Council of Credit Unions suggest that there are over 40,000 credit unions in existence, with a total membership of 118 million people, across as many as 79 countries. In Ireland, there are approximately 600 credit unions with a membership of about 2 million, representing a population penetration of 50%.

Credit unions take many forms, and have varying purposes, but all have the same basic operating principles relating to their democratic structure, the provision of a good service to members and the implementation of social goals. One of the essential differences between credit unions and other financial co-operatives is that credit unions tend to serve members only, whereas financial co-operatives often serve non-members as well. In fact, in Ireland, and in other countries, legislation specifically prohibits credit unions from providing any financial services to non-members. Here, as well as considering credit unions in general, we will also refer to two specific types of credit union: Savings and Credit Co-operatives (SACCOs) in developing countries and Community Development Credit Unions in more developed countries.

Most credit unions are community-based, in that they serve only those members who live or work in the local community. Credit unions provide personal financial services such as savings facilities, lending facilities, group insurance services, foreign exchange, and electronic funds transfers. They also provide some services to business and are often viewed as an ideal vehicle for the provision of finance to micro-enterprises because credit unions rely almost entirely on social collateral, rather than physical collateral, when granting loans. **Case Study 6.3** presents an example of how a credit union assesses lending.

CASE STUDY 6.3: CCEC, CANADA[109]

CCEC Credit Union in Canada provides loans to small businesses and community organisations that would otherwise be deemed unworthy by conventional banks. Peer group character assessment is used to assess loan applications. Social collateral is also an important lending tool for some members of the credit union, who do not have access to traditional forms of collateral.

Not all credit unions or credit union movements are committed to business or micro-enterprise lending and there are sharp contrasts between different countries. In Ireland, for example, less than 10% of total lending by credit unions is for business purposes. This is partly as a result of legislative restrictions. In Canada, the picture is very different: Bruce (2003), in a survey of the small and medium enterprise (SME) lending market in Canada, concluded that "credit unions rank first in terms of servicing the small business market". The survey of 9,565 SMEs took nine indicators into consideration: willingness to lend, lending terms, information requirements for financing, service charges, understanding of the client's business, treatment by the accounts manager, travel distance to full-service branch, branch hours of operation, and on-line banking. Credit unions ranked first in seven of these criteria and second in the remaining two. Access to local full-service branches was viewed by SMEs as being particularly important. And although credit unions, among all of the financial institutions surveyed, provided among the lowest average size loans, Bruce (2003) concludes that:

> This [survey] provides further evidence that these locally based and managed institutions have an edge servicing their small business clientele.

Another interesting aspect of credit unions is their commitment to social responsibility, particularly towards their members and the communities in which their members reside and are employed. There are many different and innovative ways in which credit unions demonstrate this responsibility. **Case Studies 6.4** and **6.5** show some of the range of initiatives.

---

[109] Coll (2002).

CASE STUDY 6.4: MALLOW CREDIT UNION LTD, CORK

In response to local unemployment, Mallow Credit Union commissioned an in-depth report of employment and training opportunities within the local community. As a result of the survey, the credit union decided to co-operate with the local Sisters of Mercy in the organisation of a resource centre for the community. In 1995, the centre was opened as a meeting and recreational facility. The credit union gave financial resources, accountancy services and a large clerical input into the administration of the centre.

CASE STUDY 6.5: VANCITY CREDIT UNION, CANADA[110]

VanCity Credit Union in Vancouver is an example of a financially and socially successful credit union with a board of nine members and a staff of 1,770. It provides a comprehensive service, including telebanking, to its membership of over 275,000. Members receive a 4.8% share dividend and a 0.6% rebate on loan interest paid. In 2003, VanCity had a balance of CAN$12.7 million given out in community investment loans, including micro-credit, social housing and clean air car loans.

A donations policy commits in excess of 4% of net earnings to community programmes, and the CAN$1 million VanCity award, which began in 2001, supports projects that improve the social, environmental and economic well-being of the community. VanCity VISA contributes to an EnviroFund for community environmental initiatives. The Living by Water programme provides low interest loans for the restoration and protection of community shorelines. The Conservation Finance Programme provides access to credit for small and medium sized organisations that have beneficial impacts on the environment. Specific deposit funds such as the Community Investment Deposits provide loans for local sustainable economic development initiatives.

VanCity produces an annual Social Report to report its activities to the members and to help evaluate and improve its social, community and environmental performance.

We will now look at two specific forms of credit union: Savings and Credit Co-operatives (SACCOs) and Community Development Credit Unions, in developing and developed countries respectively.

---

[110] Coll (2002); www.vancity.com.

Savings and Credit Co-operatives (SACCOs)

SACCOs are to be found primarily in rural parts of developing countries, where the emphasis is on the mobilisation of local savings and the provision of small loans and micro-finance for businesses. They are structured in the same way as credit unions, but the name has been changed to reduce possible confusion with trade unions. SACCOs are generally very small organisations, set up and run by members of the local community. This gives them a sense of ownership of their institution and therefore contributes to effective operations, reducing any risks associated with lending or, indeed, with saving. SACCOs are also extremely important in that they are often the only form of financial institution available in small rural communities in developing countries.

The success of SACCOs has been mixed. Harmful practices such as corruption, embezzlement of funds, unfavourable legislation, nepotism in lending, and patriarchical structures have been well documented[111]. Nonetheless, there are thousands of good working examples of SACCOs throughout the developing world, some examples of which are contained in **Case Study 6.6**.

CASE STUDY 6.6: SACCOS IN THE DEVELOPING WORLD

Thananga SACCO, Kenya[112]

The Thananga SACCO, a savings and credit co-operative for tea farmers in Kenya, is implementing a solar homes revolving finance project in association with Energy Alternatives Africa Ltd., SolarNet, and the UNDP/GEF small grant programme.

The project will provide a revolving fund for 5,000 members of the Michimukuru Tea Farmers Association to install solar energy systems to enhance the sustainability of their livelihoods.

Reaching Women in the Philippines

Credit co-ops in the Philippines are collaborating, with help from the World Council of Credit Unions, to extend both micro-finance services and nutritional education to women and men on Mindanao, the southernmost island of the Philippines.

Part of the programme works with poor women in remote areas. The programme and partner co-operatives select and hire a key representative from each village. Called *field agents*, these women

---

[111]   See, for example, Fitzgibbon (1999).
[112]   SolarNet (2001).

receive training in basic personal finance and health issues: how to save, how to start, run and grow a small business, as well as information on nutrition, infant care and child-care. After training, the field agents go back to their communities and organise small solidarity groups of five to six women who meet weekly to receive training on the same topics.

Once enough solidarity groups are formed, four to six groups form a savings and credit association, which becomes responsible for granting loans and collecting savings deposits and loan payments. The solidarity groups assume joint liability for each woman's individual loan. Each savings and credit association maintains an account at a local credit co-operative, which also provides capital for their credit needs. Currently these micro-enterprise loans range in size from US$13 to US$232, usually for a craft-based service, such as basket weaving, sewing or selling produce.

Source: WOCCU Spotlights on Development: Philippines; www.woccu.org.

Kilimanjaro Co-operative Bank (KCB) and its affiliated SACCOs[113]

The KCB-SACCOs model has managed to contend with difficulties that previously led to failure of a number of rural financial institutions. The SACCOs in the region have grown in number from 16 in 1986 to 104 in 1997. Members increased from 713 to 73,629 in the same period, while member deposits have grown at a rate of 130% per annum. In addition, the SACCOs, together with coffee marketing primary co-operatives and their unions, formed a bank (the KCB) in 1995 by buying the majority shares, hence the KCB-SACCOs rural finance institution model. In this manner, KCB caters for an owner-client market niche.

Deposits at KCB have grown from Tsh311m (US$478,450) in 1996 to Tsh1,352m (US$2m) in 1998. The loan portfolio has grown from Tsh16m (US$24,000) in 1996 to 771m (US$118,600) in 1997, with minimal signs of default. KCB provides training, capacity building services and support to the SACCOs, which in turn act as business conduits to reach a wider client base at a low cost. The bank is making a profit and is set to remit dividends to its shareholders.

The successes of the KCB-SACCOs model of a rural financial institution are attributed to the way it was set up and its key operational features. It is an organisation that originated from the grassroots, resulting in a strong sense of ownership by the client-owner, democratic leadership at the individual SACCOs and at the KCB policy body via elected representatives from each of the SACCOs. The simplicity of its banking facilities has also contributed to its sustainability. The KCB-SACCO

---

[113] Temu (undated).

model has also been tailored to the coffee economy and provides farmers with a facility for the direct deposit of their proceeds from coffee sales.

Community Development Credit Unions[114]

Community development credit unions (CDCUs) are set up to serve people on low or very low incomes *exclusively*. They are structured in the same way as any other credit union but have a strong commitment to serving their communities. They are located primarily in the US, where they demonstrate their community commitment through community outreach, participation in government programmes, partnerships with the private-sector in community revitalisation efforts and collaboration with other CDCUs.[115]

They are based on the premises:

- That low income communities can be developed through self help.

- That this development effort can be self-sustaining.[116]

According to Tansey (2001), CDCUs vary in size but are usually small. As of 1999, over 64% of CDCUs had total assets of under US$5 million, and over half of these had total assets of under US$1 million. By the end of 1999, there were approximately 538 CDCUs in the US.

CDCUs offer conventional financial services such as savings and loans, as well as specifically targeted products such as micro-lending and affordable housing lending. The main aim of their services is to promote local economic development. **Case Study 6.7** provides examples.

CASE STUDY 6.7: COMMUNITY DEVELOPMENT CREDIT UNIONS

Self-help Credit Union[117]

Self-help Credit Union is based in North Carolina, US. Its mission is to create ownership and economic opportunities for minorities, women, rural residents, and low-wealth families. Since 1980, it has provided over US$1.78 billion in financing to 25,800 small businesses, nonprofits, and homebuyers.

---

[114] Drawn from McCarthy, O. (2002).
[115] www.natfed.org.
[116] www.alternatives.org.
[117] www.self-help.org.

Alternatives Credit Union[118]

Alternatives Credit Union in Ithaca, New York was started by a group of small businesses that were financially sound and successful but unable to access loans or respect from conventional banks. These businesses also recognised areas where people on low incomes were not treated well, such as in housing loans.

Alternatives Credit Union was formed to design new lending standards that fit low-income members but that did not expose it to a higher risk of default. Alternatives Credit Union offers financial services to start-ups, family businesses, worker-managed businesses, co-operatives and home-based businesses.

It also provides education and support services to micro-entrepreneurs. The Community Enterprise Opportunities programme provides individuals with opportunities to develop skills, acquire knowledge and create the networks needed to start and expand successful small businesses. The overall aim of the programme is to enable individuals to improve their business plans and to prepare the documents needed to increase their chances of receiving financing. The credit union also offers business loans, and looks for detailed information from applicants. In particular it looks for:

- Steady income sufficient to repay the loan.
- Good past credit history.
- Sufficient collateral.
- Owner equity in the business.

The personal guarantee of the business owner is also essential to ensure that the borrower is committed to seeing their business succeed.

Businesses that cannot provide this level of information are not precluded from applying and an emphasis is placed on encouraging applicants to attend the Community Enterprise Opportunities educational programme, or on assisting them to find alternative sources of finance.

Loans are granted at different rates and to different limits, depending on the security taken and the term of the loan. Loans that are secured by personal guarantees only are limited to US$10,000.

---

[118] www.alternatives.org.

Co-operative Banks

Co-operative bank, UK[119]

The UK Co-operative Bank is not a co-operative, as such, but is a subsidiary of the Co-operative Group, a co-operative body owned by a large number of co-operative retail societies. About 10% of its total business is conducted with its co-operative-member-owners while the remainder serves non-co-operative customers. However, it does attempt to incorporate co-operative values and principles into its activities and decision-making, primarily as a means of positioning itself uniquely in an extremely competitive marketplace (Davis & Worthington, 1993). As a result, it promotes itself to its customers as a bank with a heart: one that has a strong social purpose and dedicated to providing high standards of service to its customers.

The Co-operative Bank currently serves about 1.5 million customers and has 160 branches/outlets, staffed by 3,800 people. It has launched the banking industry's first ethical policy statement, outlining its ethical stance on investments, the environment, customers, staff, charities, and social enterprises. In terms of investments, it seeks to support the Universal Declaration of Human Rights as shown in **Case Study 6.8**. The Co-operative Bank has also led the way in terms of free banking, interest-bearing current accounts and by refusing to provide credit references without the customer's permission.

CASE STUDY 6.8: CO-OPERATIVE BANK'S ETHICAL INVESTMENT POLICY

Through our investments, we seek to support the principles of the Universal Declaration of Human Rights. In line with this, we will not invest in:

* Any government or business which fails to uphold basic human rights within its sphere of influence.
* Any business with links to the state in an oppressive regime where its presence is a continuing cause for concern.

We will seek to support charities and the broad range of organisations which make up the Social Enterprise sector, including:

* Co-operatives.
* Credit unions.
* Community finance initiatives.

---

[119] www.co-operativebank.coop.

In line with the principles of our Ecological Mission Statement, we will not invest in any business whose core activity contributes to:

- Global climate change, through the extraction or production of fossil fuels.
- The manufacture of chemicals which are persistent in the environment and linked to long-term health concerns.
- The unsustainable harvest of natural resources, including timber and fish.

Norinchuken Bank, Japan[120]

The Norinchuken Bank is the central bank for Japanese agricultural, forestry, and fishery co-operative systems. The co-operatives own the bank, which extends loans to and receives the majority of its funds from the co-ops. The bank provides a low-interest co-operative rate fund called the Agriculture, Forestry and Fishery Promotion Fund.

The bank also acts as an intermediary, making adjustments to the supply and demand for funds within the co-operative system. Profits from its activities are passed on to the members in the form of dividends. It also has a social agenda: it sponsors and collaborates with various public and non-profit organisations to educate people about maintaining and preserving natural marine resources. It also makes contributions of flower seeds, bulbs and other gardening items to schools, parks and other public facilities.

As of 2004, Norinchuken Bank had deposits of US$389 billion and loans of US$168 billion.

ALTERNATIVE USER-OWNED FINANCIAL INSTITUTIONS & INNOVATION[121]

Grameen Banks and social collateral

The Grameen Bank has turned conventional banking practice on its head by removing the need for traditional collateral and creating a banking system based on mutual trust, accountability, participation and creativity.[122] It provides credit *only* to the very poorest of the poor in developing countries, primarily women, who are so impoverished that

[120] www.nochubank.or.jp.
[121] This section draws heavily on McCarthy, O. (2002).
[122] www.grameen-info.org.

they have often resorted to begging on the streets. Its loans are not secured by traditional collateral but by a form of *social collateral* (see below for details) and, although it has disbursed billions of US dollars worth of loans, the Grameen Bank has experienced less than 0.5% in bad debts and receives 98% of loan repayments on time.

Bangladesh is one of the world's poorest and most densely populated countries, despite billions of dollars of aid, provided annually from both domestic and international sources. Two thirds of the people who live in Bangladesh are employed in agriculture.

A Bangladeshi rural economics professor, Mohammad Yunus, having become so frustrated with the growing cycle of poverty in Bangladesh and the failure of modern economic principles in reducing this poverty, set about designing a credit system in 1976 that would be aimed at the rural poor.

Yunus claims to have learnt "real-life economics" by "unlearning" all he had been taught and identifying what he calls *poor people's economics*. His first experience in this village was of a woman who worked hard making valuable, high quality bamboo stools and chairs and yet lived in abject poverty because the price she received only barely covered the costs of the raw materials. This was because she had to sell her products to a moneylender, who in turn provided her with the credit she needed to buy materials. Yunus calculated that she was paying more than 3,000% interest a year to the moneylender, almost 10% per day! She did not have the cheaper alternative of institutional credit because, in the eyes of conventional banks, she did not have collateral. Many rural poor were in similar situations, trapped in a cycle of debt, poverty and exploitation.

The Grameen Bank is an independent bank, owned by the rural poor it serves. Borrowers of the bank own 90% of its shares, while 10% is owned by the government. The underlying assumption of the Grameen Bank is that the very poor need access to credit if they are to escape the clutches of moneylenders and emerge from poverty, much the same assumption on which the credit union idea was originally based. The fact that the poor do not have conventional collateral, to ensure they repay their loans, does not make lending to the poor an impossibility. Rather, lending to the poor gives them the factors of production they need, such as tools and raw materials, to earn the money to repay their loans and end the vicious cycle of debt in which they find themselves. See **Case Study 6.9** for an example of someone who borrowed from the Grameen Bank.

CASE STUDY 6.9: A REAL-LIFE GRAMEEN BANK BORROWER[123]

Oirsahi Dhor is a peddler in Bangladesh, supporting herself and her two daughters since her husband died 25 years ago. With cash from the bank in hand, she finds herself in a stronger position. She can haggle with vendors over price, stock higher-quality merchandise, and take advantage of volume discounts.

Before the Grameen Bank came along, Oirsahi borrowed from moneylenders, whose interest rates ranged from 10% to 20% a month. Now she can always buy with cash. "I do my business for profit", she says.

Grameen banking provides finance exclusively to landless, or near-landless, individuals to undertake a wide variety of farming and non-farming activities, including rice-husking, dairy-farming, pottery, weaving, and sewing (Padmanabhan, 1996). It is based on the voluntary formation of groups of five people who provide mutual, morally-binding group guarantees of repayment rather than the type of collateral normally required by conventional banks. This is also known as *peer-group lending* and results in substantial group pressure to keep up repayments so that others in the group may also avail of loans. Therefore, the collective responsibility of the group, as well as the motivation of the borrowers, is the collateral for the loan. This is a form of social collateral.

The Grameen Bank also operates a simultaneous social development agenda. According to Fuglesang & Chandler (ND), the essence of Grameen banking is social development, while the actual catalyst in the social development process is credit. From the earliest stages of Grameen banking in the 1970s, the field workers discussed issues such as health, nutrition and education with the members of the credit groups. This became more formalised over time, with the help of outside funding, to provide workshop training for women. Care for the environment, planting of trees, building and use of latrines and consumption of safe water are all encouraged. Even regular exercise by members is encouraged and facilitated at weekly meetings.

The loan portfolio has also been expanded to encourage members to meet their growing social and domestic needs, such as credit for sanitation facilities and tube-wells that supply drinking water and

---

123   Bornstein (1995).

irrigation, credit for joint enterprises by the group and centre, and credit for seasonal cultivation.

In Yunus' own words:

> Lending money does not help the poor individual unless, at the same time, you help to bring out inner potentials that help the individual overcome seemingly insuperable odds.[124]

The Grameen Bank has also created various non-profit institutions to continue what it terms as its "assault on poverty". An example is provided in **Case Study 6.10**.

CASE STUDY 6.10: THE GRAMEEN AGRICULTURAL FOUNDATION[125]

The Grameen Agricultural Foundation (GAF) encourages small farmers to pool their land and work together in a primary farm of 50 acres. Then GAF provides the capital needed to irrigate the land, as well as fertilisers, seeds, pesticides and farm machinery. A share of the annual crop is taken and sold by the foundation to cover all costs. GAF is a non-profit company so all profits generated are returned to the shareholders (land-owners).

GAF also invests in crop diversification, bio-technology, storage, transportation and marketing.

GAF has taken much of the risk away from small farmers for whom a single failed crop meant losing all they had. In the past, farmers had no choice but to sell their crop as soon as they finished harvesting. With GAF, grain can be stored until there is a demand and transported to markets previously beyond reach. With the security of GAF behind them, farmers are also more willing to experiment with unfamiliar crops.

Grameen Bank members are encouraged to save, and women have proved to be enthusiastic savers. However, considering that the average national annual income in Bangladesh is about US$400, the bulk of the bank's finances have come from government and central bank funding, capital markets, and from bilateral and multilateral aid organisations.

---

[124] For more on the Grameen Bank's approach to development, see www.action.org/summaryp.html.
[125] Source: www.rdc.com.au/grameen.

At first, the bank relied on funding from commercial and agricultural banks. External money began to flow to the bank in 1982 from the UN International Fund for Agricultural Development through the government of Bangladesh, which lent the money to the Grameen Bank at 3%. The Grameen Bank also began to receive grant aid from aid organisations in Norway, Sweden, Japan, Canada and other countries, as well as from private foundations. In 1995, it took the decision not to negotiate any new grants or soft loans and to rely on raising finance through lending and issuing bonds. This is because it wants to be seen as a serious enterprise rather than as a charitable or aid organisation.

By 2003, it had disbursed a total of US$3.9 billion in loans since it started and had a total of US$183 million in savings, paying an interest rate to savers of about 8%. Loan velocity,[126] already an average of six times a year, has been important in recycling the available funds to ensure that access to loans reaches a large number of people (www.grameen-info.org/bank).

Once known as the "barefoot banks", in much the same way as credit unions were once known as "poor people's banks", Grameen banks, like credit unions, can no longer be described in such terms. **Figure 6.3** shows the extent of Grameen banking in Bangladesh today.

FIGURE 6.3: THE EXTENT OF GRAMEEN BANKING IN BANGLADESH (JULY 2004)[127]

Number of members Female Male	3,698,082 3,536,347 161,735
Number of groups	643,952
Number of centres	78,558
Number of villages	46,279

Hashemi & Morshed (1996, p.224) point out that observers of the Grameen Bank:

> ... believe that it is bringing about fundamental changes in the lives of the women it serves, improving their self-perceptions,

---

[126] The rate at which lent money returns to the bank for lending to someone else.
[127] Source: www.grameen-info.org/bank.

their positions within the family and community...They become, in most cases for the first time in their lives, involved in financial transactions and are encouraged and enabled to conduct independent economic activities and acquire assets in their own names.

The Grameen Banking model is easily transferable to developed countries also. **Case Studies 6.11** and **6.12** demonstrate examples of Grameen-type banks/social collateral lending strategies that attempt to replicate the Grameen banking system in developed countries.

CASE STUDY 6.11: GRAMEEN BANKING FOR WOMEN IN THE US[128]

A large number of micro-enterprise programmes in the US have adopted the social collateral technique of the Grameen Bank. These programmes, mainly aimed at helping low-income women become micro-enterprise owners in cities, in rural areas and on Native American reservations, have demonstrated that some concepts imported from the Third World are transferable.

Accion International, based in Massachusetts, aims to create employment opportunities and a better quality of life, particularly through income enhancement for low-income families in the Americas. It works to promote self-help economic development for small businesses in urban and rural areas and has set up micro-loan programmes in 14 countries. It started providing loans in the US in 1987, working mainly with Hispanics and has initiated micro-enterprise lending schemes in a number of areas.

Accion works with micro-enterprises in "solidarity groups" of four people, similar to the Grameen peer group system. However, unlike Grameen, every person within the solidarity group receives an equal loan. Each group member is responsible for ensuring that all the loans are repaid before anyone in the group can get a further loan.

---

[128] *Humberstone Newsletter*, June/July 1995.

CASE STUDY 6.12: FULL CIRCLE, UK[129]

A support scheme for female entrepreneurs in Norwich has taken its inspiration from the Grameen banking formula of Bangladesh: Full Circle, run by the Women's Employment, Enterprise and Training Unit (WEETU) in Norwich, has been providing peer support for women setting up businesses since 1998.

Full Circle complements the business training offered by WEETU by creating lending circles of four to six women, who offer each other advice and support when developing their business. Typically, a new member will discuss her business plan with the others until the whole group thinks it is workable. Then she can apply for an initial loan of up to £1,000 from WEETU. Once that is repaid, a further loan of up to £2,000 can be made.

Loans are made to individuals - usually women - who have no track record of credit and would find it difficult to find the finance elsewhere. The circle has no responsibility for repaying loans in the event of default, but uses its collective knowledge, skills, contacts and equipment to help a struggling member get back on track.

Most of the circles have a wide range of businesses that have no common link, except the women's desire to succeed by helping one another. Participants range from graduates to women with little formal education, and include many who have spent years bringing up children or caring for a family member.

To date, WEETU has trained about 250 women, 120 of whom have formed lending circles. There are 24 lending circles up and running. Forty loans have been made and there has been a 100% repayment rate.

Creating Your Own Currency: the Story of LETS

A local economic trading system (LETS) is a system whereby people in a local community can trade with one another, but without the need for conventional money. In a LETS, members of a local community agree to offer goods and services of their choice to others in the community in return for an agreement from the others to do the same for them (Pam, 1992). Functions such as compiling a trade directory of goods and services on offer, recording transactions between members, and issuing statements are carried out by an administrative group.

It is not equivalent to direct barter, as members of the LETS pay each other in units of their own local currency. Instead, it is a mutual credit

---

[129] *Humberstone Newsletter*, June/July 2001.

system, meaning that currency is only created at *the moment of each transaction* and the amount in debit will always equal the amount in credit (Lietaer, 2001).

The first LETS was established in Canada by Michael Linton, in the early 1980s. It is based on the idea that people interact with society, both through production and consumption. Some people produce more than they consume, while others consume more than they produce. Most people are net consumers. Linton noted that the level of production and consumption in any community was directly dependent on the flow of national currency through the local economy. Scarcity in the availability of money led to business decline, unemployment and hence poverty. However, he also concluded that *willingness* to trade was *not* dependent on the availability of money, and that many people had goods and services to trade but did not have a *means* of exchange (Seron, 1995). He devised the LETS, whereby people could continue producing and consuming without having to use the social lubricant of money, as long as their word was good, thereby allowing the local economy to keep moving even when money is scarce (Pam, 1992). Almost any goods or services can be traded in a LETS, from carpentry to home-baking, to toys and clothes.

LETS groups now exist all over the world, in Australia, UK, US, Norway, Senegal, Thailand, Japan, Belgium, France, Argentina and Canada (see **Case Study 6.13** for an example). Estimates of the number of LETS worldwide vary, depending on the source of information used, but it is reasonably safe to say that there are between 1,500 to 2,000 operating throughout the world, ranging in size from about 50 members in Guelph, Canada, to over 2,000 members in Blue Mountain, Australia (Mendez & Salverda, 1999). About half of all LETS are in North America and Europe.

CASE STUDY 6.13: LETS IN MEXICO[130]

Three years ago, La Otra Bolsa de Valores launched a community currency system, known as *Tianguis Tlaloc* (in Aztec, *Tianguis* means "market", while *Tlaloc* is taken from the name of one of the highest divinities in the Aztec cosmology, related to water, rain, thunder and life). In this system, products and services are exchanged using an alternative currency called tlaloc, alongside the national currency.

---

[130]   More information is available on www.appropriate-economics.org/materials/Towards_An_Economy_in_the_hands_of_the_People.pdf.

The tlaloc bill is equivalent to 30 pesos (approximately US$3). There are several denominations: ½ tlaloc, 1, 2, 3, 4 and 5 tlalocs. Every member of the network of producers, servers and consumers signs a letter of agreement and receives 15½ tlalocs to start trading products and services with other members of the Tianguis (social market and network). He or she also receives 50 *tequios* (tokens) (*tequio* is an Aztec word meaning "communal effort"). One tequio is equivalent to one peso. While the tlaloc plays the role of bills, the tequio plays that of coins. It is recommended that members accept at least 30% of the price of a transaction in tlalocs and tequios. Pesos are accepted, but the policy is to increase the use of tlalocs as much as possible.

Every member of the network is given space in a quarterly directory, where offers and demands for goods and services are publicised. People living in Mexico City and its surroundings are eligible to become members; the intention is to bridge urban and rural people. There are approximately 150 registered units (micro-enterprises) as members, which can consist of several individuals.

Perhaps more important than the economic benefits are the opportunities to strengthen the local social fabric. Monthly fairs are organised to allow producers and consumers to meet face-to-face, and to create solidarity through a new spirit of exchange - not just goods and services but also cultural and ecological values, like spiritual traditions, art, music, entertainment, bio-energetics, health and a sort of intergenerational party. Children take centre stage.

There are an estimated 20 LETS groups throughout Ireland, including groups in Cork (see **Case Study 6.14**), Dublin, Mayo, Clare, Galway and Belfast, although the number has been reducing over the past few years. Douthwaite (1996) maintains that LETS groups will only thrive when there is underemployment and a shortage of national currency. This may go some way towards explaining why the number of LETS groups in Ireland has declined in recent years.

CASE STUDY 6.14: BANTRY AREA TRADING SYSTEM, CORK[131]

The Bantry Area Trading System has been set up to facilitate the fair exchange of goods and services between members, who receive payment in units of local currency known as *Bats*. Each transaction is recorded by the administration.

---

[131] www.gmlets.u-net.com.

It is an unincorporated members' club, which aims to develop and encourage the experience of "community" in the Bantry area and to stimulate the creation of social and economic benefits by, and for, its members. Membership is open to any individual or organisation sympathetic to the aims of the system. At the AGM, members elect a committee to act on their behalf. Every member has one vote.

The committee maintains an up-to-date list of all members, publishes directories of goods and services available and records member transactions. Every member receives a statement of transactions every three months. A quarterly newsletter is issued to members to keep them up-to-date on events and administrative news. Two Bats are deducted from each member's account per mailing to pay people to produce the newsletter and to do other administrative tasks.

There are many obvious benefits accruing to local communities from running a LETS:

- **Money stays in the local economy:** Through a LETS, it is impossible for local currency to leave its community of origin because trade can only take place within a finite group or community.
- **Boosts the local economy:** Local currency can only be spent locally, therefore local businesses that are members of the LETS will experience an increase in customers. Members won't always need national currency to spend so, even if they cannot afford the price of various goods and services in national currency, they will be able to pay at least part, if not all, of the price in local currency[132]. The use of local businesses also saves members in travelling and telecommunications costs.
- **Friendly atmosphere:** Experience of LETS suggests that the members of the system share a strong community ethos and are often friendlier to deal with than non-members, because they are working towards the same community-based goals.
- **Equal opportunities:** Anyone in a community can join, regardless of race, religion, sexual orientation, income and so on. It is also open to people whether they are employed or unemployed and may even generate employment for the unemployed.
- **Less pollution:** Local communities become more self-sufficient through having a LETS, which reduces the need for transport of

---

[132] Local businesses often have to charge a proportion of their price in conventional currency because they need it to pay for stock.

goods and people, thereby reducing pollution. Furthermore, local currencies cannot be used for speculative investment either within or outside the community, investment that may have negative ecological or social consequences.

LETS challenge conventional economic thinking, particularly in a world that is becoming increasingly globalised. A LETS is an unusual way to trade, given a world where the multinational or global business is king.

Time dollars & time banks

Time dollars and time banks are similar to LETS in promoting social inclusion, mutuality and self-help within local communities. They operate as mutual credit systems, whereby people can "deposit" hourly units of their time in terms of practical support and assistance and "withdraw" these hours when they need someone to give them support or assistance.[133] One hour spent helping another person earns one time dollar, regardless of whether it is the time of an expert or a novice. Everyone's time and effort is valued the same.

Time dollars schemes enable neighbours to help neighbours on a voluntary basis, the only payment being in terms of hourly units of time. Anyone in a local community can participate, from the very young to the very old, enabling people of all ages to contribute their talents to a community and to receive assistance in return. It is similar to the traditional *meitheal* system in Ireland, whereby neighbours helped each other during the busy harvest season for no payment other than similar assistance in return. Unlike the *meitheal*, a time dollar or time bank scheme formally records the hours deposited and spent by all members. It is "elegantly simplistic" (Lietaer, 2001) and virtually cost-free to establish. A time-keeping software programme can be downloaded free from the Internet to record transactions (www.timedollar.org). **Case Studies 6.15** and **6.16** give examples of the benefits of a time dollars scheme.

---

[133] www.timebanks.co.uk.

CASE STUDY 6.15: PEOPLELINK, DENVER, COLORADO[134]

PeopleLink in Denver, Colorado is a collaboration between Catholic charities, Lutheran Family Services of Colorado and Jewish Family Services of Colorado. It serves people of all ages, but is especially dedicated to supporting the independence of older adults and individuals with disabilities through the mutual exchange of services.

PeopleLink began recruiting participants in January 1999 and, during its first year, facilitated the exchange of nearly 700 hours of services to support the independence of older adults and people with disabilities. The services most requested were transportation for doctors' visits and errands, home management tasks, light yard work, window washing and minor household repair.

CASE STUDY 6.16: A REAL-LIFE EXAMPLE OF TIME BANKING[135]

For 15 years, he was pastor of a Baptist church in Washington, D.C. People relied on him as someone they could turn to 24 hours a day for guidance, comfort, and conversation. Then the Reverend, who suffers from diabetes, lost his right leg to an infection and was forced to retire.

For a long time, he lived almost as a recluse, refusing to leave his apartment, but when a local Time Dollar programme was created, the Reverend signed up to earn time dollars by conducting prayer services for his fellow tenants. He spent them to have his meals prepared by another volunteer. The Reverend's isolation and sense of powerlessness came to an end through the new contributions he was now able to make. Time dollars had made possible a new community involvement for the Reverend that otherwise would probably never have happened.

There are now about 250 time dollars schemes across the US, involving people of all ages in a variety of activities. There are 33 time banks in the UK, involving over 700 people who have earned over 47,000 hours to date (www.timebanks.co.uk). There are also a number of schemes in Japan (see **Case Study 6.17**), but only one in Ireland (see **Case Study 6.18**).

---

[134] www.timedollar.org.
[135] www.timedollar.org.

CASE STUDY 6.17: JAPANESE HEALTH-CARE CURRENCY[136]

The Japanese population is the second-fastest ageing population in the world. To face the rapidly rising problem of health-care, the Japanese have implemented a new type of Health-care Currency. In this system, the hours that a volunteer spends helping older people in their daily routine is credited to that volunteer's "time account". This time account is managed exactly like a savings account, except that the unit of account is hours of service instead of yen. Different values apply to different kinds of tasks and at different times of the day. For example, household chores and shopping have a lower credit value than personal body-care.

These health-care time credits are guaranteed to be available to the volunteers themselves, or to someone else of their choice, within or outside the family, whenever they need similar help. Some private services ensure that, if someone can provide help in Tokyo, the time credits become available to his or her parents anywhere else in the country. Many people just volunteer the work and hope they will never need it. Others not only just volunteer, but also give their time credits away to people who they think need them. To them, it amounts to doubling their time. It works like a matching grant: for every credit hour of service, the amount of care provided to society is two hours.

The Japanese also report a significant increase in volunteer help, even by people who do not bother to open their own time accounts. The reason may be that with this system, all volunteers feel more acknowledged. As of the end of 1998, there were over 300 health-care time credit systems in Japan.

CASE STUDY 6.18: GLOUNTHAUNE TIME BANK, CORK

Following discussions in the local community association regarding diminishing levels of community participation, especially among young people, a Time Bank was established in Glounthaune, County Cork in 2002 to encourage local people to give (and receive) time locally. There are over 600 members from across the community.

The Time Bank has one staff member, who co-ordinates membership and activities across two local centres. It is financed through a number of different sources, including support from East Cork Area Development.

The Time Bank engages in two main types of activity:

- **Flagship projects:** These are large projects for the benefit of the community, in which a large number of local people get involved.

---

[136] Lietar (2001), pp.201-202.

One example is a project to build a playground: 10 people were involved and, in less than 6 months, they acquired the necessary land, planning permission and half of the capital needed. Another example is a group of local people who donate their time and expertise to work together to develop a website for the Time Bank.

- **Personal activities:** These activities are based on voluntary assistance to individuals within the community. An example is an individual who donated time to caring for the elderly in the community. In return, she receives gardening advice from a local gardening expert.

There are four core values associated with time dollars or time bank schemes:

- **Social capital:** Time dollars or time bank schemes link people together for mutual advantage and provide a way for people to support themselves, each other and their communities, thereby generating valuable social capital in a community.
- **Assets:** We normal associate community assets with tangible, fixed assets, such as premises, vehicles or leisure facilities. The assets of a time bank or time dollars scheme are intangible, but recognise that everyone in the community is a potential asset to the scheme in terms of the contribution they can make to the community.
- **Equality:** In a time dollars or time bank scheme, everyone is equal. The currency used – hours – is equal for everybody.
- **Reciprocity:** This value recognises that everyone can give and receive. One-way transactions are replaced with two-way transactions. Just as in co-operatives and other forms of mutual business, "you need me" becomes "we need each other" (www.timedollar.org).

Case Study 6.19 gives more examples of the type of benefits that can accrue.

CASE STUDY 6.19: THE BENEFITS OF TIME DOLLAR SCHEMES

Time Dollars are good for your health![137]

A comparative survey was made of retirement homes: those with a time dollars' scheme and those without. In those with time dollars schemes, it was found that using this type of currency knits the group together. People look out for each other. In short, a community has been created. People feel valued. Participants became healthier!

One health insurance company decided to accept 25% of the premiums for its senior health policies in time dollars. The time dollars scheme started as a home repair service through which potential household problems are fixed *before* they cause accidents. Their motto is: *a broken towel rail is a broken hip waiting to happen*. The insurance company noticed that seniors participating in time dollars schemes were experiencing fewer health problems. The bottom line is that health-care for seniors is less expensive.

Benefits to communities[138]

As many as 55 struggling schools in Chicago have been pioneering time banks, paying time credits to pupils as peer tutors, which they cash in for refurbished computers. Academic results go up and bullying goes down.

Teenagers in Washington earn time credits serving on teen juries, which try non-violent first offences in the city, and cash them in for recycled computers.

In each of these cases, time banks are rebuilding community, local trust and the sense of self-worth among those taking part. They are also revitalising their host institutions - be they schools or courts - by involving clients as equal partners in the business of regeneration.

SUMMARY

It is clear that user-owned financial institutions can be, and have been, enormously successful in providing financial services to individuals and businesses. Much of their success can be attributed to their structures. That they are *owned and controlled* by the people who use their services helps to ensure that they remain relevant to members' needs. This means that the organisation must serve its members and not *vice versa*. Of equal

---

[137]   Lietaer (2001), pp.190-191.
[138]   www.londontimebank.org.uk.

importance is the generation and maintenance of *social collateral*, which is not only useful as loan security but also builds relationships based on trust and solidarity.

Education of members is also critical. In many of the examples presented in this chapter, there have been instances of user-owned financial institutions educating their members in areas as diverse as financial management, entrepreneurial skills, agricultural technology, youth training, and nutrition.

It is also true to say that user-owned financial institutions face their fair share of difficulties in an environment of intense competition from highly-resourced conventional banking institutions. Many of the difficulties faced can be culture-specific, country-specific, or institution-specific, making it next to impossible to generalise across the range of user-owned financial institutions discussed in this chapter. However, it is reasonably safe to say that the issue of raising finance to expand operations is high on the agenda of many of the user-owned financial institutions discussed in this chapter. Demutualisation, merger, consolidation or, sometimes, even collapse are just some of the possible threats being faced. And, despite the obvious competitive advantages of institutions that are owned by their users, many find themselves preoccupied with competing with mainstream banking institutions, rather than communicating their unique character more effectively, a character that is essential to survival in their current form.

SEVEN

SERVING OURSELVES

Mary O'Shaughnessy & Robert Briscoe

A growing trend in Europe is for co-operatives and other social enterprises to take-over and improve the quality of services previously provided directly by the state, by religious institutions or by investor-driven businesses, as well as to provide services that are not readily available in local communities.

In Scandinavia, for example, there has been a rapid growth in the number of co-operatives engaged in providing high-quality child-care services. Sometimes these co-ops are consumer-controlled (owned and managed by parents); often they are worker co-ops (owned and controlled by the care workers), and sometimes, they are multi-stakeholder co-ops (owned by a partnership of workers and parents).

This chapter explores strategies for meeting neglected needs, such as creating jobs for disadvantaged people, providing care for people with disabilities and for the elderly, and organising rural transportation to improve access to remote areas. We start by looking at some examples of Ireland's *Work Integration Social Enterprises*, not-for-profit organisations, which have a good track record for combating social exclusion. We then look at how co-operatives of many different kinds provide new kinds of services for their constituencies. A key emphasis in the co-operative approach is the involvement of both users and providers of services in the design of more appropriate and higher quality services.

WORK INTEGRATION SOCIAL ENTERPRISES IN IRELAND

Consider a local organisation delivering a daily hot meal to elderly bachelor farmers living in remote rural locations, or a group of local women providing laundry and child-care services, which, in turn, facilitate other local women to enter paid employment outside of the home. Or a local community radio that not only gives a voice to persons with intellectual and physical disabilities but also trains them to produce their own radio programmes. Now consider the fact that volunteers and paid workers come together to provide these services and, in the process, contribute to the regeneration of the rural communities and provide employment and training opportunities for the long-term unemployed and other local groups at risk of social and economic exclusion. This takes place through a particular type of social enterprise that has evolved across the Irish landscape: the *Work Integration Social Enterprise* (WISE).[139]

This section focuses on four rural WISE engaged in distinctive sectors of community-based activity: elder-care, community radio, child-care and housing refurbishment for the elderly. However, let's begin by improving our understanding of what a WISE actually is.

What is a Work Integration Social Enterprise?

WISE are not-for-profit organisations, evolved to serve disadvantaged communities, that combine the efforts and expertise of voluntary and paid workers. They deliver a range of goods and services and, in the process, create training and employment opportunities for the long-term unemployed and other marginalised groups. WISE generate trading income through the sale of goods and services and combine this with significant statutory funding and, to lesser extent, private and public donations, to sustain their activities. They also generate a range of individual and collective benefits. The organisational structure of these socio-economic initiatives, generally encompassing a local voluntary board with a focus on addressing local needs, decreases dependence on external service providers and increases self-sufficiency within the local community. People's needs are met as a WISE manages to bring the sites of production and consumption closer together.

---

[139] For further information, see www.emes.net. O'Hara has described the different types of Irish social enterprises in O'Hara, P. (2001).

Irish WISE pursue the multiple goals of community support provision and job creation; certain individual benefits accrue to those working within the organisation. Benefits include access to training, work experience, and a social setting that facilitates interaction with other individuals, which can aid personal development. WISE offer a flexible work place that can be conductive to enhancing self-confidence and improving interpersonal skills, in particular, for those experiencing difficulty accessing the wider labour market due to physical and/or intellectual difficulties and/or other social problems.

WISE can be found in both urban and rural locations. Those located in peripheral rural locations deliver a range of essential community services, including transport, rural house refurbishment, elder- and child-care – in fact, a range of goods and services that, in many instances, would not be available to the rural community were it not for these specific types of socio-economic initiatives.

Common to the following examples of social enterprises is their commitment to create local employment opportunities in addition to providing essential local services in innovative ways.

CASE STUDY 7.1: DUBLIN COMMUNITY COMMUNICATIONS CO-OPERATIVE (DCCC)[140]

DCCC is a registered not-for-profit co-operative society that runs *North East Access Radio* (NEARfm 101.6), a community radio station for the North-East of Dublin. The station is part of the Independent Radio and Television Commission's pilot programme in Community Radio.

The co-operative is managed by a Board of Directors, which is elected at the Annual General Meeting of members. Shareholding is open to anyone subscribing to the aims of the Co-op and investing in a single share of €5.

The process of securing a licence to broadcast took 10 years of active campaigning. The co-op was eventually granted a licence in 1995 (for an 18-month pilot project), but is now on a firmer footing with a five-year licence.

The station currently broadcasts Monday to Sunday, from 8am to midnight, with the help of more than 130 volunteers. These include interested individuals, as well as organised groups from the catchment area. Training is provided to enable members to produce their own radio programmes.

---

140 www.nearfm.ie/aboutus.html.

CASE STUDY 7.2: TULSK PARISH SERVICES

Tulsk Parish Services (TPS) is located in the small village of Tulsk, in north Roscommon. It is a not-for-profit company, limited by guarantee and operates a one person, one vote principle. It evolved in 1994 from a voluntary group called Tulsk Action Group (TAG), which included a core group of five female volunteers, and has three primary objectives:

• The creation of sustainable employment opportunities, especially for local women.

• The development of training opportunities for those involved in the project and the wider community.

• The provision of accessible and affordable services and facilities for the elderly and young families.

TPS began by offering a range of home-care and transport services to the local community. These included elder-care, child-care, respite for the ill, a private taxi for those with hospital appointments, and a pension collection service for the elderly.[141]

In 1995, TPS played a part in establishing the Tulsk Voluntary Housing Association Ltd. With the assistance of the Department of Environment and Roscommon County Council, six houses for the elderly and four family homes were built. In the mid-1990s, the group was awarded close to €125,000 through an EU-funded initiative under Measure B206, aimed at assisting women over 35 to re-enter the labour market. These funds were used to provide training and employment opportunities to 14 local women, and to build an office, laundry, meeting rooms and kitchen area. In 1997, financial resources from a regional third sector organisation were used to equip the laundry, office and kitchen. A project manager was also appointed that same year.

This WISE addresses local needs and generates commercial revenue in a number of different ways. It continuously reacts to market conditions and demonstrates flexibility in responding to needs as they arise. It has been very successful in attracting public subsidies, in turn enabling it to develop new services. It has also been market-led, having diversified into new, more profitable services. The surplus generated is used to meet the running costs of its less viable services, enabling it to undertake a redistributive role within this rural community and provide services to those less able to pay. Although this WISE has evolved from a wholly voluntary organisation to one that is increasingly dominated by paid employees, it still relies extensively on volunteers to manage its strategic development.

---

[141] See O'Hara, P. (1988).

CASE STUDY 7.3: WEST LIMERICK RURAL REFURBISHMENT LTD.

West Limerick Rural Refurbishment Ltd. (WLRR) emerged as part of a pilot caring initiative called the Rural Community Care Network (RCCN)[142]. Its main objectives are:

- To refurbish the housing stock to a reasonable level of comfort.
- To delay the onset of the demand for residential care.
- To create training and employment opportunities for the long-term unemployed.

WLRR is a not-for-profit company, limited by shares, with charitable status. It has a full-time manager and a voluntary board of directors, made up of representatives of a local development company, statutory agencies and a number of community activists. In 1997, the company called a public meeting for the purpose of (a) identifying potential services users and (b) potential employees. The company began negotiating with the local authorities and the health board to tackle jointly the problem of poor housing conditions amongst elderly residents in the area.

This relationship has evolved into a contractual one; the WISE is regularly contracted to undertake a number of jobs in the provision of repairs and refurbishment works in the area. Initially, 14 full-time job equivalents were created. The employees were predominantly male and in the late 30s age bracket. All were taken from the long-term unemployed register, in general had no recognised qualifications or formal training, limited access to training courses because of complicated domestic circumstances, low self-esteem and learning difficulties. Each employee availed of training in minor housing maintenance and repairs and participated in a Manual Handling, Health & Safety at Work course. This was delivered by County Limerick VEC and funded under Article 6 ESF programme.

By 1999, there were 17 workers (16 semi-skilled and one supervisor) employed on a part-time basis, supported by the Community Employment (CE) scheme, granted by the National Training Authority (FÁS). By 2000, more than 60 houses had been repaired by the WISE. Two on-the-job training courses had also been organised, in conjunction with skills development under the CE scheme.

One of the most innovative aspects of this project has been the development of strong linkages between many of the key stakeholders. These include the manager of the WISE, staff members of the Housing

---

[142] RCCN has a voluntary management board, representative of the statutory, community and voluntary sectors. It was established with funds from an EU Initiative under Article 10 of the ERDF, and is a company limited by guarantee, formed in 1997.

Section of the local authority (Limerick County Council) and the Housing Aid for the Elderly programme operated by the Mid-Western Health Board (the regional health authority).

By 2001, WLRR had successfully applied for funding from the national Social Economy Programme. This provided it with almost 95% of its labour costs. It now employs a manager and four full-time employees drawn from the long-term unemployed register. The WISE continues to provide rural house maintenance and refurbishment services serving a rural elderly client base who cannot afford to pay for the service.

CASE STUDY 7.4: EIRÍ COMMUNITY RADIO

EIRÍ Community Radio evolved from a relatively *ad hoc* organisation, which grew out of the collaborative action of two local development companies and a voluntary unemployment action group. The action group saw community radio as a means of addressing unemployment in this peripheral rural coastal location of West Clare and a way of providing a "voice" for the local community.

The first stage in the development of the WISE was the formation of a voluntary management committee and the adoption of a not-for-profit legal structure – a company limited by guarantee. This company then secured a temporary radio licence from the National Broadcasting Commission and the community radio station went on air for the first time in early 1999, and was awarded a full licence later that same year.

Around this time, the radio station was also successful in its application for a Community Employment scheme, which provided the resources to employ 15 workers. This proved to be a significant turning point in the evolution of the organisation, enabling it to extend its broadcasting hours and meet its "work integration" objectives.

EIRÍ Community Radio has now developed its own studio in a local community hall, and provides access to the airwaves for specific interest groups, such as people with disabilities, the elderly and non-nationals.

(For more on community radio, see **Case Study 7.1** for information about NEARfm, a co-operative radio station serving North-East Dublin.)

CASE STUDY 7.5: KILLUCAN CARE LTD.

Killucan Care Ltd was established in 1998 in the rural village of Killucan, in County Westmeath. It evolved from a local development process, originally initiated by the FÁS[143] Community Response training programme for women in the early 1990s. The social entrepreneurs who secured the funding for the programme were three local women. Their participation in a university community development course involved the conduct of a local survey, which highlighted the need for elder- and child-care services.

Another finding that emerged from the survey was the existence of 16 independent development groups active in the locality. They all shared the similar objective of meeting local needs, but worked independently. To get them co-operating, a community festival called *Get Together* was initiated. This required each group to organise an event for the festival, and encouraged them to co-ordinate their activities, all of which eventually culminated in the establishment of an umbrella organisation called *Golden Years*.

The umbrella group then applied for public funding to refurbish a local community centre and to develop elder- and child-care services. This was made possible with funding from a number of statutory training programmes, such as the Community Youth Training Programme (targeting early school leavers), and the FÁS Community Employment measure. They were also able to lease a local derelict site (owned by a local religious order). The labour market programmes provided the financial assistance needed to refurbish the community hall and staff the child-care service.

In 1998, with the assistance of an external facilitator, the group established itself as a legal entity with charitable status, incorporating a voluntary management board comprising local interest groups. It became a not-for-profit company, signalling a major transition for the group, with some of its members now formally occupying a "directorship" in the newly-established company. Thus it evolved from a voluntary community organisation into a work integration social enterprise, combining the goals of providing community services and work integration opportunities for disadvantaged persons.

The WISE has been successful in establishing itself as a recognised FETAC (further education) training provider in child-care, enabling it to offer a recognised quality child-care certification.

---

[143] FÁS is the national training and employment authority in Ireland.

DEVELOPING CO-OPERATIVE SERVICES

Co-operative Action Foundation

So far, we have looked at examples of community-owned organisations that provide a wide range of services designed to address the special problems of local communities. In the rest of this chapter, we look at some of the ways in which co-operative businesses provide services. Let's look first at a foundation, which is managed and funded by UK retail co-operatives. The Co-operative Action Foundation (CAF) assists the development of new kinds of co-operatives, many of which are in the business of providing services.

CAF was launched by Tony Blair, the UK's prime minister, in April 2002. In its first 16 months, the Foundation had awarded £1.2 million in grants and loans to 29 innovative co-operative projects, from funding donated by nine UK co-operatives.[144]

One of the beneficiaries of a CAF loan is Wood'n'Stuff, a co-operative day-care centre, "where everyone is equal and disability doesn't count". **Case Study 7.6** tells Wood-n-Stuff's story.

CASE STUDY 7.6: WOOD'N'STUFF – THE WORKSHOP WHERE DREAMS ARE MADE[145]

This is a sheltered workshop co-operative day-care centre in Bury St Edmonds that combines a day-care centre for disabled people with community education, training, production and sales. It was set up in 1995 and General Manager John Morley quit his job as an insurance underwriter to join his parents "who have always worked in the care field. It's in the blood".

Wood'n'Stuff offers training, rehabilitation and social therapy for its 110 members, who regularly attend from up to 25 miles away. They are people with mental health problems, learning difficulties, sensory and physical disability, including stroke and accident victims – all with different reasons for wanting to rebuild their lives. Some want to return to work but most are unlikely ever to work again.

---

[144] The nine co-ops are: The Co-operative Group; Chelmsford Star Co-op; Lincoln Co-operative Society; Oxford, Swindon & Gloucester Co-op Society; Raunds Co-operative Society; United Co-op; West Midlands Co-operative Society; the Co-operative Bank and the Co-operative Insurance Society.

[145] Reprinted, with permission, from a CAF press release. The Co-operative Action website that published this press release is www.co-op.co.uk/ext_1/Development.nsf/.

"The youngest is 19, the oldest is 93, and they all have goals and targets", says John Morley. "For our part, we have absolutely no barriers – the only criterion is that they want to come here". Twelve carers, with volunteer help, teach them to develop skills – whether arts and crafts or woodworking, horticulture and computers.

Together, they produce 25 core products, including wooden garden furniture – from bird-tables and Wendy houses to planted wheelbarrows and Welsh dressers. Their commissioned items have included purpose-built two-tier garden decking, a wishing well, medieval stocks, a Russian gun carriage for a local theatre group, and flat-packed fire engine toys for Romanian orphans.

Their shop and garden centre sells the work, and produce from four large greenhouses "to help the running expenses", says John, "but sales are not what we're about. We've evolved around the people who come to us and we're here to encourage them to achieve their goals".

Now these achievements will continue on two sites – with the help of the Co-operative Action loan, which meets nearly half the start-up cost of refurbishing and refitting the Haverhill premises 15 miles away in Rookwood.

Among the other innovative co-operative projects that have been able to grow rapidly, thanks to support from CAF, are two of the successful businesses discussed earlier in this book: Cambrian Organics, the co-op of organic farmers who sell meat via the internet (see **Chapter 4**); and Unicorn Grocery, the worker-owned organic supermarket, loved by its customers (see **Chapter 5**). CAF has also invested in a number of promising service delivery projects that are in the early stages of development. These include a project sponsored by the OSG consumer co-op (which we visited in **Chapter 3**), to develop a network of stakeholder-governed child-care co-ops, and another major project to provide co-operatively-owned broadband Internet services to rural communities that are being neglected by the mainstream providers.

YOUTH CO-OPS

In Western Canada, an innovative co-operative has developed strategies for involving young people in the development of their own business projects (see **Case Study 7.7**).

CASE STUDY 7.7: SASKATOON'S YOUTH CO-OP

Using the philosophy of the co-operative movement, a youth organisation is making a real difference in the lives of kids in the underprivileged core neighbourhoods of the city of Saskatoon in the prairie provinces of Canada.[146]

The Core Neighbourhoods Youth Co-op (CNYC) began in 1996, when community activists were looking for ways of helping young people who were growing up in under-privileged areas of the city. It has three main objectives:

• To develop a youth programme that would show young people how to use co-op principles to meet their needs.

• To give young people the chance to earn spending money.

• To achieve these objectives in environmentally-friendly ways.

Income-generating projects include making compost bins, benches and plant shelves from recycled materials, repairing donated bikes, growing organic foods and delivering fliers.

Nearly 200 young people are currently participating in CNYC's programmes and it is they themselves who choose the co-op's projects and take responsibility for the maintenance of their building. In return, about 80% of the money generated by projects is returned to the young people. The balance is used to contribute to the co-op's expenses. The revenue of the co-op has increased from CAN$9,800 in 2001 to CAN$19,000 in 2002 and an expected CAN$34,000 in 2003.

Because most of the young people involved are too young to enter into the legal arrangements needed to incorporate a co-operative, the whole operation is overseen by the Saskatoon Environmenters' Co-operative Limited, which was set up to provide a stable administrative and funding structure for the Youth Co-op.[147]

---

[146] www.coopscanada.coop/newsletter/intersector/autumn2003/#item5.

[147] The University of Victoria in British Columbia features a website for young people interested in co-ops: http://bcics.uvic.ca/youthzone/.

INVOLVING THE COMMUNITY IN HEALTH-CARE

In **Chapter 1**, we learned about the Group Health Co-operative (GHC),[148] a consumer-governed care delivery system based in Seattle. **Case Study 7.8** expands on its role in community health-care.

CASE STUDY 7.8: THE GROUP HEALTH CO-OPERATIVE

Much of GHC's success has stemmed from the active involvement of its members. In addition to attendance at AGMs and standing for election to the board, members have many opportunities for active involvement in the governance of the co-op and the design of its services. All GHC medical centres have councils made up of volunteer members. The medical centre councils (MCCs) and the staff of each medical centre work together to improve the care and well-being of members and their communities, meeting at least four times a year.

There are also special support groups, such as GHC's Senior Caucus. All members aged 65 and above are automatically members of the Caucus and there are local chapters throughout the Puget Sound area. The Caucus campaigns for seniors' needs, working on care delivery, health-care coverage and legislative issues, as well as convening local meetings to address health-related issues. The Caucus contributes to many programmes, including a senior peer counselling programme, the Resource Line, and the Senior Outlook newsletter.

GHC has also established a Group Health Community Foundation, which engages in outreach, programmes, partnerships and community sponsorships as well as support for charitable, non-profit organisations. The foundation also co-ordinates volunteer opportunities for co-op members. Members can enquire via GHC's website for information about volunteer opportunities in their area.

American health-care co-ops have not been content merely to serve their own immediate backyards. A dramatic example of international co-operation between co-operatives is the development of a national health co-operative in Uganda (see **Case Study 7.9**).

---

[148] See www.ghc.org.

CASE STUDY 7.9: THE UGANDA HEALTH CO-OPERATIVE[149]

It all started when an American dairy co-op, Land O' Lakes, asked Health Partners, a group of consumer-governed health-care organisations in Minnesota,[150] to help set up community-based prepaid health-care schemes in Uganda.

The project, which has received funding from USAID, started by working with Ugandan dairy farmers, helping producers boost their incomes by pooling resources and encouraging them to put money aside to prepay health-care and provide preventive care. This meant that medical emergencies would be less likely to force farmers into selling their cattle. The Uganda Health Co-operative team has worked hard to expand membership across the country and now works with providers in most regions, including in Kampala, the capital city.[151]

Like PSGHC and the Uganda Health Co-op, effective co-operatives of all kinds usually put a good deal of emphasis on involving their members in the governance and design of co-op services. One of the benign consequences of organising services on a co-operative basis is that the users of the service have opportunities to participate actively in governance issues such as the design of the services they are receiving. A classic study of the value of participation suggests that user-involvement might be particularly important in the management of services for elderly people[152] (see **Case Study 7.10**).

CASE STUDY 7.10: THE IMPORTANCE OF PARTICIPATION

This study involved an experiment, which was conducted in a top quality residential home with two groups of elderly residents. The perceived control exercised by one of these groups was increased, but remained unchanged in the other. The following measures were taken in each group before, and after, the intervention:

---

149   For more on the international development work of Land O' Lakes, see
      www.landolakesinc.com/corp_function/int_dev.asp.
150   www.healthpartners.com (click on "About Us") for more information on HealthPartners
      and its related organisations, which provide health-care services, insurance and HMO
      coverage to nearly 660,000 members in Minnesota.
151   www.managedcaremag.com/archives/0006/0006.uganda.html; Aebischer (2000).
152   Langer & Rodin (1976). (*Authors' note:* Our thanks and appreciation to Charles Musselwhite
      for telling us about this thought-provoking study and to Co-opNet – www.co-opnet.coop –
      for providing the communication link with Charles.)

- Self-ratings of happiness and activity
- Nurse ratings of sociability, fitness and well-being
- Records of attendance at events and
- Mortality rates.

After three weeks, 93% of the *increased control* group were rated as improved, the majority of the others were rated as more debilitated.

Most surprising of all were the results over the next 18 months. The mortality rates experienced during that time were 15% in the *increased control* group and 30% in the other group, where no change had been experienced.

CHANGING THE NATURE OF HOME-CARE

Co-operatives have proved effective in many parts of the world at offering quality home-care to people with disabilities and to the elderly. Such services make it possible for housebound people to enjoy independent living in their own homes, at a fraction of the cost of a nursing home.

One of the most famous home-care co-ops is to be found in the South Bronx district of New York. Co-operative Home-Care Associates (CHCA) is a worker co-op that has been replicated successfully, notably in Boston and Philadelphia, and inspired the establishment of Co-operative Care in Wautoma, Wisconsin (a semi-finalist for the prestigious 2002 Innovation in American Government Award, sponsored by Harvard's Kennedy School of Government).[153] In 2002, the Bronx CHCA employed more than 300 workers, mostly from minority groups, and another 120 worked for the Philadelphia and Boston offshoots.

CASE STUDY 7.11: CO-OPERATIVE HOME-CARE ASSOCIATES

CHCA was set up in 1985 as a welfare-to-work project, providing health-related and personal hygiene services, as well as housekeeping and shopping for housebound people. The co-op provides home-health-care aides under contract to major health-care providers.

---

[153] For details of the Wautoma story, see Diane Harrington's case study *Cooperative Care, Wautoma, Wisconsin* (November 2002) available on www.wisc.edu/uwcc/ .

CHCA set out with the ambition of changing the very nature of the home-health-care industry. The industry had the dubious reputation of employing unskilled, temporary workers who provide poor quality services. CHCA aimed to replace the *low-investment, temporary worker* strategy by emphasising careful recruitment, substantial up-front training (through its own training institute), reasonable wages and fringe benefits, and on-going support. CHCA has also developed career progression programmes, which have created a career path for care workers.

Investment in the workers has improved the quality of both the jobs and the care services. CHCA workers now enjoy higher wages than the industry norm plus health insurance and holiday pay. More than two thirds of them are employed full-time and staff turnover has dropped to less than half the industry average.

FUNERAL CO-OPS

In the early 1960s, Jessica Mitford wrote *The American Way of Death*[154], a best-seller that lambasted the American funeral industry for manipulative selling practices, which took advantage of the grieving relatives of the deceased. This was followed shortly by a movie version of Evelyn Waugh's novel *The Loved One*,[155] a satirical diatribe against American morticians. Funeral co-ops were already growing in popularity in the USA but Mitford and Waugh gave the co-operative option a shot in the arm. A number of American retail co-ops successfully launched their own funeral divisions in the late 1950s and 1960s, promising gentle considerate treatment at a time when people felt at their most vulnerable and advocating that people pre-planned their own funerals to protect their heirs from the hard-sell tactics of unscrupulous undertakers.

In the UK, retail co-operatives have long provided funeral services and are now the largest funeral directors in the country, building their businesses with a hard-to-beat prepayment plan. See **Case Study 7.12** for an example of the services offered by the Plymouth and South West Co-operative Society, similar to most major retail co-ops in the country.

---

[154] Mitford (1964).
[155] Waugh (1948).

CASE STUDY 7.12: CO-OPERATIVE FUNERAL SERVICES IN PLYMOUTH[156]

The Funeral Service of Plymouth and South West Co-operative Society is the largest Funeral Director in the South West of England, with 26 branches throughout Devon and Cornwall.

Prepaid funerals
On the death of a co-op member, or the spouse of a member, a funeral grant of £100 is payable toward the cost of a co-op funeral. The Co-op also offers pre-paid funeral bonds, which enable funerals to be prearranged and paid for at today's prices with a guarantee that there will be no extras charged at a later date. The money a member spends on a funeral bond is safe because it is invested in individual whole life insurance policies between Plymouth Co-op and the national Co-operative Insurance Society. The cost of the funeral bond includes all disbursements, such as cemetery/crematorium fees, newspaper notices, etc. and there is nothing further to pay at the time of the funeral.

Bereavement support services
Plymouth & South West Co-op offers services that go beyond the usual scope of undertakers. The co-op employs *bereavement support group co-ordinators,* who provide services free of charge in centres throughout the co-op's area of operations. The aim is to establish friendly places where people who have suffered a loss can benefit from having a chat in the company of others with similar experiences. For example, drop-in coffee mornings are provided free of charge every Wednesday morning in the co-op's central department store. The co-op also organises relevant presentations and can put members in contact with other support agencies.

SUMMARY

In this chapter, we have looked at examples of a variety of the ways in which co-ops and other kinds of social enterprises offer services to meet neglected needs. We started by reviewing the work of four work integration social enterprises (WISE) in Ireland, organisations designed to create employment by providing a multiplicity of services for neglected groups in peripheral rural communities. The WISE are not-for-profit, community-owned enterprises, managed by broad cross-sections of local stakeholders, and do an excellent job of meeting a wide range of local needs. Though they have much in common with co-

---

[156] Source: www.plymco.co.uk/funeralsites/funerals.

operatives, most of them are not legally incorporated as co-ops and have a strong charity focus. Most are heavily subsidised by the state, but all generate income from their trading activities. They make a major contribution to combating social exclusion (particularly in the form of active labour market programmes), but could do more to involve the users of the services in the management and design of those services. It is probable that the WISE and the co-ops could learn from each other.

The rest of the chapter gave examples of how co-operative businesses manage the provision of services, starting with the UK's Co-operative Action Foundation and its support of new, innovating co-operatives, such as Wood'n'Stuff. We then visited the Saskatoon Youth Co-op, a creative strategy for involving young people in the selection and operation of a range of business projects. The chapter concluded with the work of health-care co-ops in America and Uganda, and a successful home-care co-op in New York, which redesigned the whole industry to the benefit of both workers and clients.

In the next chapter, we focus on a network of community development co-operatives in the West of Ireland. Community co-ops take the concept of the WISE a step further, by opening membership to all in the community and encouraging widespread involvement in the design and implementation of development plans for the locality. We then explore the ways in which many other kinds of co-operatives have a powerful and often surprising impact on the well-being of local communities.

EIGHT

DEVELOPING OURSELVES

Robert Briscoe, Olive McCarthy,
Michael Ward & Bernard Thompson

When we talk about developing a community, exactly what type of development do we have in mind? Are we merely looking for an influx of jobs, any old jobs, or is there more to development than that? In his classic text, *The Economic Pursuit of Quality*,[157] the economist Thomas Power proposes a challenging list of objectives for local economic development – one that would probably please most of those who are striving to develop co-operatives. According to Power, the primary objectives of development are to secure the following benefits:

- The availability of useful and satisfying work for members of the community.
- Security for members of the community in their access to biological and social necessities.
- Stability in the community.
- Access to the qualities that make life varied, stimulating and satisfying.
- A thriving, vital community.

Power goes on to argue that conventional approaches to developing communities (such as trying to tempt a multinational to come in and set up a call centre) will be less effective at providing these benefits than a community-based approach to development. When he talks about jobs, he doesn't mean any old job or any old source of income. He's talking about *useful and satisfying* jobs. And when he talks about *the security of a*

---

157 Power (1988).

community, he's talking about safety nets that provide durable solutions to problems as well as temporary relief from distress. He is arguing that we should place our trust in those organisations that are rooted in the community, instead of pinning all our hopes and dreams on nomadic multinationals.

And *community stability* is not just about the availability of lots of jobs and high pay:

> If the ready availability of jobs and high pay were the major objectives of economic development policy, then the mining and construction camps of the [American] West would be our models. But those boomtowns are hardly anyone's idea of what a community should be.[158]

Community stability is also about the creation of complex social and support networks within the community, those networks that create social capital and are key elements in Power's final two objectives (providing access to the qualities that make life varied, stimulating and satisfying and creating a thriving, vital economy).

What can co-ops do to reinvigorate an ailing community? What can they do to achieve Power's goals? This chapter explores a wide variety of ways in which we can work together to improve the environment and the quality of life in our local communities. Let's start by visiting the West of Ireland to see how remote communities have used co-operatives to build their economies, retain and attract public services and improve the quality of life. We then explore the co-operative contribution to a range of issues, which can provide pathways to more vibrant communities, affordable housing, a sustainable environment, appropriate tourism, and enjoyable, stimulating leisure activities.

WHEN ALL ELSE FAILS, START A CO-OP!

The Irish-speaking communities of Western Ireland are battling for survival on the Atlantic periphery of Europe. The main weapon in their struggle is a scattered network of community-owned co-operatives. Most of these co-ops came into being in the 1970s and 1980s, but the oldest of them dates back to 1907. In their efforts to keep communities alive, these co-ops engage in a mind-boggling variety of business, social

---

[158] *Ibid.*, p.172.

and cultural activities. This section explores the range of strategies employed by 23 of these co-ops, as well as the services they provide.[159]

There is a common tendency to invoke the co-operative approach in exceptional circumstances, when more conventional approaches to meeting needs have broken down. In a prosperous, thriving locality, we expect needs to be met through the activities of entrepreneurs, supplemented by public services from government. It is only when the marketplace is not working well that we attempt to *develop the community*. The Gaeltacht[160] co-ops evolved in just such unfavourable circumstances. These community co-ops have had the unenviable tasks of providing basic public services where government found the costs too high to justify; and running businesses in situations where conventional firms were closing down. So you usually find these co-ops in regions remote from the main population areas, where land is less fertile and markets are often too small for sustained business development. The islands have particularly costly access problems but, in one sense, most of the co-operatives are operating on islands. Access is costly for most of them, with inflated prices for inputs and tortuous distribution chains for their outputs.

The co-ops are also seen as the guardians of the language and culture, not just of their own small communities, but of the nation as a whole. Through their activities, the Irish language has developed as a living language of commerce and government. It is a tribute to the community co-operatives that they have been able to perform these difficult tasks and provide cost-effective services in situations that had defeated conventional business and government alike.

The range of co-operative services

The most comprehensive packages of services are offered by co-operatives on the offshore islands. These island co-ops provide services usually associated with local authorities and public utility companies. They have brought piped water and electricity supplies to their communities; they upgrade and maintain roads; and operate local airstrips (providing land transportation for passengers as well as basic airport fire services). Other activities include: land reclamation; importing bulky commodities (such as building supplies and coal);

---

[159]   The study summarised here was funded by Údarás na Gaeltachta, the State body responsible for fostering economic development in the Gaeltacht (the areas of Ireland where Irish is the main language in use).

[160]   The Gaeltacht is the name of those areas of Ireland where Irish is the main language of use.

helping to upgrade the quality of housing; operating community centres and pubs; providing and promoting tourist attractions; building and operating tourist complexes; marketing local produce; providing facilities for medical and other public services; and promoting small business development.

The value of co-operatives as defenders of rural communities and the Irish language is recognised by Údarás na Gaeltachta, the body charged by government with the economic and social development of Irish-speaking communities. Údarás makes government subsidies available to communities that have prepared viable development plans for their area. The grant covers the basic administrative overhead costs of a community co-operative.

HOW COMMUNITY CO-OPS GET THINGS DONE: A TYPOLOGY OF STRATEGIES

Let's look at some of the commonest strategies used by the co-operatives to serve their communities. Most rely predominantly on *one* of the following strategies; but many use combinations of *two or more*.

Sectoral co-ops

In this approach, the co-ops adopt a strategy similar to conventional user-owned and controlled co-operatives. They provide services mainly for one identifiable group of users (consumers, builders, farmers, and fishermen, etc.) even, on occasion, effectively limiting shareholding to that particular grouping. The core business provides a nucleus and source of funding for all the other developmental activities of the co-op (social, cultural and economic) (see **Case Study 8.1** for examples of this type of co-op).

The key advantages of this approach include:

- The co-operative is built around a single central business, with services designed to meet the needs of one specific group of stakeholders. This makes the business simpler to manage, compared with co-ops that try to do everything for all major groupings in the community.
- Properly managed, this kind of co-operative can be very motivating for members, providing them with a stream of tangible benefits.

These might include better-designed products and services and bonuses based on their usage of the business.

• In this context, *properly managed* means that the business, while being open to all who can make use of it, is designed to provide shareholders with some unique benefits not available to non-shareholders (see the Retail Co-op item in **Case Study 8.1** for an example of what happens when this is not done). This gives users an incentive to become shareholders and to get involved in the running of the co-op. It also has the marketing plus of making the co-op more clearly distinguishable from its competitors.

CASE STUDY 8.1: EXAMPLES OF SECTORAL CO-OPS

The Knitting Co-op
A community co-op in Donegal builds its activities around a core business that provides marketing and purchasing services for local producers of knitwear. The co-op bulk-buys the inputs they need and markets their products in a small roadside shop and internationally through a mail order catalogue.

The Fishing Co-op
A community co-op in Mayo runs a core business that provides collection and marketing services to local fisherman, enabling their fish to be transported to major urban centres, instead of being sold at rock-bottom prices on the quay. The co-op also co-ordinates a successful environmental programme that is replenishing the stock of lobsters in the area.

The Retail Co-op
A community co-op in Donegal operates a substantial retailing business, featuring a comprehensive range of goods including groceries, clothing, hardware and farm and building supplies, as well as two small branch stores in nearby villages. It rewards its customers by giving them discounts on many of the goods they purchase, but gives these discounts to *all* customers, members and non-members alike, instead of reserving discounts as one of the privileges of membership. It is perhaps not surprising that this co-op is starved of equity capital, as there is little incentive for customers to subscribe for membership shares.

Spin-off generators

This strategy, like the sectoral co-op, starts with a core business and uses profits from this business to generate new businesses. But instead of trying to run a varied portfolio of enterprises, the co-op sells off viable enterprises to individuals or co-operative groupings. This makes the business activities of the co-operative easier to manage and generates additional, major inflows of capital for continued development. The really sensible co-ops retain an interest in the spun-off business, which entitles the co-op to receive a continuing share of the spin-off's profits (see **Case Study 8.2**).

CASE STUDY 8.2: A SPIN-OFF GENERATOR

A community co-op in Mayo runs a supply store for farmers and builders. In the first floor of the retail building, it houses a branch of a credit union as well as providing meeting spaces for local groups. One of its major ventures was the setting up of a sawmill, which was then sold off to a local consortium (including a farmer-owned co-op). Additional funds were also raised by selling off its delivery trucks to the drivers. This enabled the drivers to run their own haulier businesses, with the co-op as a major customer. The co-op also bulk-buys petroleum products to help reduce the costs of the haulier businesses and the sawmill.

Closely linked with this approach is the notion of *downsizing*, where specific non-core activities of the co-op, such as transportation, are sold off to employees, who may set themselves up as independent business operators or worker-owned co-operatives (as in **Case Study 8.2**). The co-operative may also provide services to the spin-off businesses, such as buying petroleum products in bulk, or providing office or accounting services. Sometimes this is done as a deliberate strategy, but often the businesses are sold off reluctantly to overcome financial difficulties. In the latter case, the capital inflow is used to keep the main business alive rather than as finance for a new venture.

The spin-off generator has advantages in that it simplifies the management process, by keeping the focus narrowed on a core business. It also disperses ownership and control of businesses throughout the community. The spin-off businesses are often more likely to prosper, because they harness the motivation of individual entrepreneurs and groups of worker-owners.

Infrastructure co-ops

Several co-ops have focussed mainly on developing infrastructure, improving access, and providing services in areas where the usual providers are reluctant to get involved because of exorbitant costs or inadequate profits. A closely-related strategy is the *provision of premises*, which can be used to attract and retain vital services within the community, such as medical services, advisory services, sports facilities, etc.

The provision of important infrastructures is of inestimable value to a community, radically improving the quality of life and earning considerable appreciation from local inhabitants. Because the activities of the co-op are important for residents' well-being, this approach also encourages active participation by members. See **Case Study 8.3** for more on Irish infrastructure co-ops and **Case Study 8.4** for examples of other co-operative approaches to running utilities.

CASE STUDY 8.3: INFRASTRUCTURE CO-OPS

Many of the island co-ops started out as providers of infrastructure. They ran ferry services to the mainland, introduced mains electricity and water supplies, and bulk-bought heavy goods such as coal and building supplies and shipped them over to the islands.

Several community co-ops still provide some of these services, but are now paid to manage electricity supply systems on behalf of the national utility (see **Case Study 8.4** for examples of co-operative approaches to running public utilities). Some of them still have contracts with county councils to ensure the upkeep of island roads, others are venturing into sustainable sources of energy such as wind farms. Many provide premises, the infrastructure for the provision of necessary services, such as surgeries for doctors and dentists.

Increasingly, they are diversifying into activities such as tourism development, seaweed and fish farming, and renewable sources of energy.

CASE STUDY 8.4: A BETTER WAY OF RUNNING PUBLIC UTILITIES?

Glas Cymru: Welsh Water for the Welsh

Glas Cymru is a not-for-profit social enterprise (incorporated as a company limited by guarantee)[161], which was set up with the explicit purpose of buying the privately-owned company Welsh Water and operating it for the benefit of its customers. A year after the take-over in 2001, Glas Cymru has set its charges at £11.5 million below the regulator's price cap and plans to invest £1.2 billion by 2005 in improved services.[162]

Electric Utilities

In the United States, about 25 million people get their electric power from co-operative utilities, which serve mostly rural populations in areas that have been of little interest to privately-owned utilities, because of the high costs of serving sparsely populated areas.

Promoter co-ops

A promoter co-op acts as a catalyst for local development. Rather than running enterprises itself, this kind of co-op assists local entrepreneurs to access resources (such as information, workspace, grants and sources of funding). It also attempts to identify opportunities for new business development and lobby for resources on behalf of the local community.

The capital needs of such a strategy are modest, though the opportunities to generate enough income to ensure self-sufficiency are more restricted. This strategy can, however, have a major impact on local economic development and can multiply many times over the cost of subsidising its activities. This type of co-op may also be used to represent and mobilise other special interest groups, which can co-ordinate their purchasing, fund-raising and lobbying activities through the co-operative (see **Case Study 8.5**).

The effectiveness of such co-ops cannot be judged in terms of profitability alone. More appropriate indicators of success are criteria such as *costs per job created* or *persons taken off benefit*. See **Case Study 8.5** for an example of an Irish promoter co-op, and **Case Study 8.6** for an example of a promoter co-op in an inner city area of Bradford, in England.

---

[161] This is a company that has no shares and no shareholders. It is a structure that can use its profits to improve the quality of services and reduce costs to consumers.

[162] www.dwrcymru.com/English/Results/Report_E.pdf.

CASE STUDY 8.5: AN IRISH PROMOTER CO-OP

An island co-op, which had brought mains electricity and water to the community, sought another role after its electricity supply service was taken over by the national Electricity Supply Board. It decided to focus mainly on helping to promote small, locally-owned businesses to identify new business opportunities and to lobby on their behalf. Among its other activities was the construction of an incubator mall, which provided affordable space to small businesses and generated a continuing income for the co-op.

CASE STUDY 8.6: ACTION FOR BUSINESS (BRADFORD) LTD.

Action for Business, known as ABL, is a community-based economic and social regeneration organisation started in 1992 by people living or working in a district of Bradford, where over 70% of the population is from black and minority ethnic groups. Its aim is to improve the economic and social prospects of the local people.

In partnership with Bradford City Council, ABL converted a redundant site in Manningham, by developing it into a business centre with 89 offices, workshop and storage units with conference and meeting rooms for hire. There is well-lit parking for 120 cars, monitored by close circuit TV and night-time security. The centre is fully accessible by disabled people.

One of ABL's activities is to organise a monthly community lunch, the aim of which is to develop a network of local people and to encourage them to get involved in the regeneration of the area.

Heritage business co-ops

A number of co-ops concentrate almost exclusively on preserving and developing the Irish language, and increasing awareness of the local heritage and culture. This is done by developing businesses activities and services based on local resources, culture and heritage. See **Case Study 8.7** for examples of these kinds of businesses.

CASE STUDY 8.7: THE BUSINESS ACTIVITIES OF HERITAGE CO-OPS

Businesses and services of co-ops using this strategy include:

- Operating *Coláistí Samhraidh*, summer schools to help children improve their Irish.
- Providing Irish language training to non-Irish-speaking residents.
- Providing resource rooms and heritage centres, often featuring crafts and souvenirs for sale, and coffee shops.
- Identifying and documenting local archaeological sites and marketing these as cultural tourism attractions.
- Marking and publicising local walks.
- Producing pamphlets on local fauna and flora.
- Fostering the preservation of local craft skills.
- Teaching computing skills to ensure community access to information and to facilitate low-cost networking.

The business activities in this type of co-op are closely linked with the specific social and cultural goals of the co-operative, making this an attractive strategy. They also often provide spin-off boosts to the local tourist industry. All those summer school students (at the Irish Colleges) and their visiting parents have to stay somewhere, bringing additional income to the community, which should be taken into account when assessing the development impact and viability of this strategy.

Single cause advocacy co-ops

New co-operatives, in their early days, may focus all their efforts on one major issue of burning interest to the whole community, such as improving access to the community by provision of a pier, a ferry, a plane service, or cable car, etc.

Social economy business co-ops

This is an ingenious strategy that enables co-ops (even when starved of capital) to improve living conditions of residents, while building the skill-base of the community and creating local employment. It involves using government social welfare provisions as the basis for business activities for the co-op. This may be done, for example, by alerting pensioners to their home improvement entitlements, helping them apply for grant aid and using those grants to employ people to install those home improvements. The workers employed to do the home improvements will probably have been trained in a government-funded Community Employment scheme.

An island co-op also built an award-winning tourism complex, while helping locals acquire construction skills and developing the capacity of the community to maintain its own infrastructure (see **Case Study 8.8**).

CASE STUDY 8.8: A SOCIAL ECONOMY BUSINESS CO-OP

One island co-op built on the strategy of using government home improvement grants and community employment and training programmes, by using the skills learned by participants in these programmes to contribute toward the construction of an award-winning development of tourist cottages.

The design for a superb tourism complex was acquired free of charge! This was achieved by inviting a national architects association to hold a competition for the best design by a newly-graduated architect. The winning design was featured in a national journal and built, cottage by cottage, by local people who had been trained and or were being trained on government-subsidised community employment programmes. This tourist facility is now in great demand and generates a steady stream of funds for community development.

HOW OTHER CO-OPS DEVELOP COMMUNITIES

Community co-ops on the Irish model are not the only viable strategy for developing communities. In earlier chapters, we have seen how other kinds of co-ops, consumer, producer and worker co-ops can create meaningful jobs in the food industry and enhance the quality of community life. Weaver Street Market, for example, helped reinvigorate the downtown centre by developing innovative businesses, supporting local producers and other downtown businesses and sponsoring activities that brought a festival atmosphere to the central business district. It also tackled local problems by assisting housing co-ops, as well as by recognising a local currency, which helped to stimulate local businesses, to create jobs and to increase the self-sufficiency of the community.

In the UK, many of the larger consumer co-ops have earmarked substantial development funds to promote community-based development in their own areas. The effectiveness of co-operatives as vehicles for local development has been recognised by the UK's Small Business Service, which, through its Development Fund for Rural Renewal has funded a Rural Co-operation project led by Co-operatives UK (the UK's Union of Co-operative Enterprises).

In the rest of this chapter, we shall explore examples of how other kinds of co-ops and social enterprises make major contributions to their communities. In particular, we'll look at examples of co-ops and other social enterprises in the fields of housing, tourism, leisure and entertainment, and the environment.

CO-OPERATIVES & HOUSING[163]

Although Ireland has been a leader in the development of community co-ops generally, in the field of housing, it has lagged behind its colleagues in Northern Europe and North America. Irish housing co-ops had their origin in the efforts of local self-help societies formed to provide dwellings for home-ownership, often using the direct labour of the members themselves. The projects usually consisted of up to 10 or 20 family houses, financed with mortgage loans raised by the individual members.

The process of urbanisation in Ireland during the 1960s and 1970s led to an expansion of co-operative house-building, mainly in the rural towns and the expanding urban and suburban areas.

Having obtained suitable building sites from the local authorities (town councils and county councils) at a reasonable cost, the co-operatives then engaged architects to prepare plans for group schemes of affordable houses. As fewer and fewer of the members have the relevant building skills or free-time to engage in construction work themselves, the use of building contractors has become the normal means by which the houses are built. The size of many, but not all, of the co-operative housing projects has also expanded up to 40 dwellings or more.

The National Association of Building Co-operatives (NABCo) was formed in 1973 by representatives of local housing co-operatives. NABCo is a federated co-operative society, mutually owned by its affiliated housing co-operatives. NABCo acts as the representative, promotion, information, and training and development organisation serving the co-operative housing movement in Ireland.

---

[163] This section was contributed by Bernard Thompson, General Secretary of the National Association of Building Co-operatives Society Ltd. (NABCo), www.nabco.ie.

A key aim of NABCo is to promote the relief of housing needs through mutual aid, based on the co-operative principles. During the past decade, there has been a substantial improvement in economic conditions in Ireland but this has led to a rising demand for houses, particularly as the demographic trend shows an increase in population size due to the end of outward migration. This, in turn, has led to a rise in house prices and rents. The role of the expanding co-operative housing movement has been to offer more housing options or choices and to help in the amelioration of affordability problems facing those with modest, but limited, incomes seeking housing accommodation.

The diversification of government housing policy, begun in the 1980s, has facilitated more capital funding support for non-profit housing organisations. This has enabled NABCo to organise and promote a new network of *rental* housing co-operatives, mainly in the Dublin area, but also in other parts of the country.

These rental housing co-operatives provide a means for people in a lower income group seeking social rented housing to become co-operative members/tenants, as a solution to their housing needs. Over 20 local housing co-operatives are now in operation, providing a new stock of good quality rental houses and apartments, with more projects at planning and design stage.

In order to provide housing management and other common services, including staff support, arrangements have been made to form four district/area co-operative housing societies in the Dublin area, with estate management offices and management boards representing the local housing co-operatives.

Acting as a strategic development agency for more new housing co-operatives, NABCo has started to acquire building sites directly for future projects and has also entered into partnership arrangements with private commercial developers for the inclusion of co-operative housing as part of integrated larger scale mixed urban renewal projects.

To ensure that the movement remains relevant to emerging housing needs, NABCO is helping to develop new types of co-ownership housing co-operatives. These mix co-operative social equity with the members' own capital investment, to provide an affordable ownership stake in their dwellings for those members who cannot afford full market prices. This has resulted in the organisation of pilot projects of apartments, for co-operative co-ownership purchase by members, along with the provision of rental units.

The expansion of co-operative housing provides new options for people in need of housing and willing to accept the responsibilities of co-operative membership. NABCo emphasises the need for training programmes for new members, and has also stressed follow-up information and guidance for novice management committees and officers. The operation of effective information, education and training programmes about co-operative organisation, management and membership responsibilities continues to be a challenge at the core of the successful promotion of the movement.

TOURISM CO-OPS

Most of Ireland's community co-ops are situated in areas of spectacular natural beauty. More and more communities have seen their surroundings as a competitive advantage that can attract visitors and thus improve the livelihoods and levels of service enjoyed by the locals.

In the development of tourism, community co-ops have been supported by producer co-ops, owned and controlled by the owners of Bed & Breakfast guest-houses. (See **Case Study 8.9** for information on Irish Country Holidays, a marketing co-op for smaller co-ops owned by the providers of tourist accommodation and see **Case Study 8.10** for an account of an English tourism co-op, which was set up to boost the income of farmers who had been badly hit by the 2001 outbreak of foot and mouth disease.)

CASE STUDY 8.9: IRISH COUNTRY HOLIDAYS[164]

The Rural Community Tourism Co-operative Society (Ireland) Ltd. (RCTC) operates under the brand name, Irish Country Holidays (ICH). RCTC is a co-operative of local tourism co-ops, which was set up to develop, promote and market rural community tourism in the parts of Ireland that are not so well known to tourists, mostly in the so-called BMW (border, midlands, and western) regions.

Its Board of Management is made up of elected representatives of local tourism co-ops, farming organisations, and the Irish Co-operative Organisation Society, as well as representatives from public bodies such as Fáilte Ireland (the Irish Tourist Board).

---

[164] www.country-holidays.ie/english_index.html.

The ICH website enables potential visitors to search through hundreds of options in 18 different areas and to book on line. The co-op also designs itineraries for activity-based holidays and makes arrangements for farm visits, horse-riding, golfing, etc., tailor-made to suit individual and group needs. Each of the regions offers a range of self-catering and B&B businesses, all approved by Fáilte Ireland.

CASE STUDY 8.10: CARTWHEEL HOLIDAYS[165]

"Quality holiday accommodation, award winning rural attractions and delicious places to eat in Devon, Cornwall, Somerset and Dorset all available through Cartwheel."

Cartwheel is a farmer-led co-op of 200 members that markets rural tourism throughout the SouthWest region. It was set up to mitigate the desperate business situation that existed in the SouthWest of England after the 2001 outbreak of foot and mouth disease.

Any operator of a farm business (regardless of size), who is willing to meet the quality requirements of the Cartwheel brand, is eligible to become a member. The co-op promotes not only holiday accommodation but also farm shops, farm attractions and restaurants. A professionally designed and operated website presents a high quality brand image and markets member businesses nationally and internationally.

CO-OPS IN THE WORLD OF ENTERTAINMENT

Perhaps one of the most successful ways of reinvigorating a community is to make it a more enjoyable and interesting place to live in. From their earliest days, co-operatives and other community-based organisations have played a major role in providing entertainment and enjoyable leisure activities. In **Chapter 5**, we saw how the Weaver Street Market brings a festival atmosphere to the downtown centre of its community. For decades, consumer co-ops in the UK, as well as running retail stores, sponsored a wide range of clubs, events and educational activities, which improved the quality of life in communities throughout the country. In Switzerland, the Migros consumer co-operative network is still the biggest provider of adult education activities in the country.

---

[165] Rural Co-operation (2003); www.cartwheelholidays.co.uk/. Cartwheel Holidays is a project funded by the Small Business Service's Development Fund for Rural Renewal under the Phoenix Fund.

One of the earliest preoccupations of the Rochdale Pioneers was to convert the attic above their shop into a reading room for members, and provide educational programmes to enrich the lives of industrial workers and their families. The education they were keen to get had little to do with running a shop. They had their eyes on less humdrum issues: the first course held in their reading room was taught by an astronomy professor from Manchester University! See **Case Study 8.11** for an example of typical activities that individual consumer co-ops in the UK have funded over the years.

CASE STUDY 8.11: PLYMOUTH & SOUTH WEST CO-OPERATIVE SOCIETY (PCS)[166]

Television was late in coming to the city of Plymouth. The high plain of Dartmoor interrupted television signals relayed from London and, for years, there was strong local opposition to defacing the moors with a transmitter. This pre-TV era was the heyday of Plymouth Co-op's cultural and educational activities. Across the city, there were busy networks of co-op youth clubs and branches of the Co-op Women's Guild. There were choirs for children and adults, and the PCS Girls Choir and the PCS Women's Choir had reached a high enough standard to be featured on radio programmes of the BBC Home Service. The Co-op also organised an annual festival of music and drama, a one act-play competition and a range of evening classes at their Western College Educational Centre. Many of these faded away after the arrival of the TV in the late 1950s.

The most impressive survivor is the co-op's Drama Group, The Western College Players. Its first three-act presentation in the early 1950s was an ambitious production of J.B. Priestley's utopian drama, *They Came to a City*. Western College Players still prospers today, and there remains a branch of the Co-op Women's Guild, but most of the old activities have disappeared.

New leisure ventures have taken their place in this age of television. Most notable of these is the construction of the *Co-operative Way*, a 15-mile sign-posted footpath that links many of the city's nature reserves, parks and green spaces. The project was drawn up to celebrate the Society's 140th anniversary in 2000 and has been left as a legacy to the citizens of Plymouth. The Co-op got support in this project from Plymouth City Council, the Countryside Agency, and nationwide co-operative-owned organisations such as Co-operative Chemists, the Co-op Group, the Co-operative Insurance Society and a number of other

---

[166] www.plymco.co.uk/index.htm.

local sponsors. The environmental charity, Groundwork, along with the Probation Service's young offenders on community service, helped re-develop areas that had been defaced with litter and illegal tipping. The Co-op now organises a programme of popular guided walks along stretches of the Co-operative Way, led by local experts on ornithology, flora and fauna and the history of Plymouth.

Leisure Trusts

In the London borough of Greenwich, a new generation of co-operative leisure enterprises was born when the local authority agreed to turn its leisure facilities over to the workers (see **Case Study 8.12**).

CASE STUDY 8.12: GREENWICH LEISURE LIMITED (GLL)[167]

This is how GLL describes itself on its web-site:

> GLL is an innovative staff-led "Leisure Trust", structured as an Industrial and Provident Society, which manages over 40 public leisure centres within the M25 area, in partnership with five London Boroughs and Epsom & Ewell Council.

The birth of this innovative organisation dates back to 1993, when the Borough of Greenwich faced major budget cuts, which required a 20% cut in the funding of the Borough's leisure centres. This would have meant closing three leisure centres and laying-off 20% of the staff. It was decided instead to set up a non-profit-distributing mutual organisation to operate the Borough's leisure facilities. The new structure would be managed by the staff, who would elect a majority of the Board of Directors from their own ranks. The board would also include representatives of the customers, the borough council and the workers' trade union. All profits would be reinvested in the up-grading and expansion of leisure facilities.

GLL was launched in July 1993 and, instead of having to close down leisure facilities, it has been able to upgrade existing services and open new centres. In fact, GLL has been so successful that it has inspired the development of a whole new wave of leisure trusts around the country.

Today, GLL has over 2,000 staff (full- and part-time) and is one of the largest leisure employers in the capital, as well as the highest paying external leisure provider in the country, with very low sickness and staff turnover levels.

---

[167] www.gll.org.

Famous co-ops in the world of entertainment

Perhaps the most famous co-operative in the world of entertainment is the world-renowned London Symphony Orchestra, which has attracted conductors of the calibre of Hans Richter, Sir Colin Davis and André Previn. Founded in 1904, the LSO was the first British orchestra to be owned and managed by its musicians.[168] It is the players who audition and select new musicians for the orchestra, and it is the players themselves who select and hire their conductor. See **Case Study 8.13** for the story of another worker-owned orchestra, which discovered that the co-op approach was not only a more pleasant way of running their affairs but was also great for business!

CASE STUDY 8.13: THE LOUISIANA PHILHARMONIC ORCHESTRA (THE LPO)

"You need a positive climate to produce good music, and we have that here."[169] So says Klauspeter Seibel, the LPO's musical director and a resident conductor of the Frankfurt and Dresden Operas. The positive climate he is talking about stems from the excellent relationships between the orchestra and their conductor and the loyalty and commitment that is generated by a self-managing organisation.

The LPO grew out of the ruins of the New Orleans Symphony, which, like many other major orchestras, had been accumulating huge deficits. After 60 years of bringing classical music to the city, it couldn't make ends meet and was wound up in 1990.

A group of players revived it as a co-operative and it returned to the stage in 1992 as the Louisiana Philharmonic Orchestra. A decade later, the orchestra had 69 members (as many as 90 for special performances), a budget of US$3.9 million, 1,200 subscribers and a cohort of 500 active volunteers. It has a busy, 36-week concert season, and accompanies local opera and ballet companies and travels throughout the state performing to school children.

Another example of a co-op in the world of entertainment is the Movie Co-op, owned and controlled by some of Canada's most famous movie stars and directors (see **Case Study 8.14**).

---

[168] www.lso.co.uk (Click on "About Us", then "Biography").

[169] Quoted in Kinzer (2002); www.nytimes.com/2002/03/20/arts/music/20LOUI.html

CASE STUDY 8.14: THE MOVIE CO-OP[170]

Mozart Loves Me is the name of the first movie to be released by the recently launched Movie Co-op. The idea for the co-op came from Canadian director George Bloomfield, and the 16 members include some of Canada's best-known actors, such as Gordon Pinsent, Eugene Levy and Saul Rubinek. In exchange for working for free, the members own a share of the production and any profits it makes.

CO-OPS & THE ENVIRONMENT

Washington Electric Co-op serves its consumer members in more than 40 towns in rural Vermont. The Washington Co-op has long been determined to ensure that as much as possible of the power it distributed would come from renewable sources. In 2003, it launched an innovative project to complete its environmentally-friendly portfolio by ensuring that 100% of its power would come from renewable sources. See **Case Study 8.15** for more about the Rural Electric Co-ops of Iowa State and the role utility co-ops can play in community development and service provision.

CASE STUDY 8.15: ELECTRICITY CO-OPS & DEVELOPMENT[171]

Iowa Association of Electric Co-operatives is a service organisation representing rural electric co-operatives (RECs) in Iowa State, and based in Des Moines, Iowa, USA. Iowa's farmers began forming RECs in the 1930s, when large electric companies bypassed rural Iowa because of the widely scattered population. These pioneering men and women borrowed start-up money from the Federal Rural Electrification Administration, created by President Franklin D. Roosevelt.

Today, RECs in Iowa offer more than a reliable electric service: they also work to improve rural living. For example, the co-operative supported the Iowa Area Development Group to bring new industry and new jobs to rural Iowa. Many RECs offer high quality modern satellite television equipment and programmes to rural homes outside the reach of cable TV companies (which are mainly for-profit businesses). Other RECs lease emergency pagers, ideal for elderly people. Still others are involved in unique programmes to improve rural

---

170 CBC's *Art Review*, quoted in *CCA Co-op News Briefs*, 30.10.2003.
171 Extracted from IAEC website: www.iowarec.org/public/about/about.shtml.

housing or help people who want to buy residential houses with low-interest loans.

Iowa's RECs are part of a national network of 1,000 electrical co-operatives. These utilities, which serve 25 million Americans in 46 states, work together through the National Rural Electric Co-operative Association (NRECA), which was formed in 1942, to provide services to electric co-ops throughout the United States.

Co-ops in other parts of the world are also getting actively involved in cleaning up our energy act. After the success of Danish co-operatives in the development of wind farms, more and more co-ops in other parts of the world have become involved in wind power. See **Case Study 8.16** for information about the first UK co-op to own wind turbines and **Case Study 8.17** for the Washington Co-op story.

CASE STUDY 8.16: BAYWIND ENERGY CO-OPERATIVE[172]

Baywind was launched in 1996 to generate energy from renewable sources and promote energy conservation. It now has 1,300 members and has raised £2 million through share offers. So far, it owns six wind turbines in two sites in Cumbria – the home of the Sellafield nuclear re-processing station!

To help Baywind in its efforts to provide an eco-friendly alternative to nuclear power, the Co-operative Action Foundation (see **page 147**) awarded the energy co-op a grant of £50,000.

CASE STUDY 8.17: POWER FROM LANDFILL METHANE[173]

Most co-operative utilities have been interested in developing alternative ways of generating energy. A recent example of this, in central Vermont, is the plan announced in September 2003, by Washington Electric Co-operative and Casella Waste Systems, to turn other people's garbage into electricity. About 40% of Washington Co-op's energy supplies are already generated from renewable sources, plus a further 25% supplied by Hydro Quebec. Now it plans to use the methane gas issuing from a major landfill to generate up to six megawatts of electricity.

---

[172] www.co-operativeaction.coop. See also: www.bwea.com.
[173] www.washingtonelectric.coop; Joy (2003); Smith (2002).

> Benefits to the local communities include a long-term energy source in
> Vermont with predictable costs, unaffected by fluctuations in oil prices,
> the creation of jobs in the construction and maintenance of the facility,
> as well as reduced emissions of greenhouse gas. An added bonus is that
> methane should generate enough energy to free the co-op from having
> to use energy generated by Vermont Yankee, a nuclear power station.

In addition to co-operatives that are overtly involved in cleaning up the
environment – for example, via recycling activities or the generation of
energy from renewable sources, there are many other newly formed co-
ops engaged in activities that also have a positive, if more indirect,
environmental impact. These include many of the different kinds of co-
operatives we have been visiting in this book – for example:

- The CSA partnerships between farmers and consumers, which, by
  encouraging more and more people to eat locally-grown produce,
  reduce the environmental costs of transporting foods over long
  distances.
- The UK's Co-operative Action Foundation, funded by retail co-ops,
  which has financed the Soil Association's campaign to develop more
  CSAs throughout the country.
- The car-sharing co-ops pioneered in Switzerland, which reduce the
  number of cars on the roads and help to build the demand for public
  transportation systems, by negotiating good deals for co-op
  members.
- The host of worker and consumer co-ops (such as Suma, Essential
  Trading, the Dublin Food Co-op, and Unicorn) that pioneered the
  marketing and distribution of organic foods and provided access to
  the market for local producers switching to organic production.
- The efforts of consumer retail co-ops in small communities (the
  Weaver Street Markets of the world) to source locally, and to reduce
  the appeal of out-of town shopping centres by reinvigorating
  downtown centres.
- The community co-operatives that help to retain shops and other
  services within endangered communities
- The environmental and ethical commitments of the UK's Co-
  operative Bank, including its refusal to finance environmentally
  damaging projects and its efforts, in co-operation with Greenpeace, to
  develop a biodegradable credit card!

SUMMARY

After a discussion of Thomas Power's goals of development, much of this chapter has focused on the variety of strategies used by Ireland's community co-ops to reinvigorate remote rural communities in the West. In Ireland, we often think of community co-ops as an Irish invention, but similar strategies have also been used in many other places, including remote communities in Atlantic Canada, the highlands and islands of Scotland, and, more recently, in underprivileged inner-city neighbourhoods. We also saw how co-operatives of all kinds can help communities move toward Power's goals. In particular, we took a brief look at how co-ops can address housing problems, build a local tourism industry, reinvigorate a community by making it a more interesting place to live in, provide locally-controlled, renewal sources of power and generally to help to clean up the environment.

NINE

WORKING FOR OURSELVES

Robert Briscoe, Bridget Carroll & Colm Hughes

If shrewd industrialists with an open credit line ran these companies into bankruptcy, how can worker-controlled co-operatives with no capital and no business experience be thriving during the worst economic slump in Argentina's history?[174]

How would you feel about working in a business where you were a co-owner along with the other employees? Imagine also that your business was run democratically and that you had the same voting rights as everyone else who worked in the firm. When profits were distributed, you would share them fairly with your fellow workers. If the business lost money, it would be up to you and your co-owners to solve the problem.

It sounds good to us, but probably might not suit everybody. It might be nice to work in a world without bosses, to share the profits and feel that you and your friends are working for yourselves. It wouldn't be so nice to have to share the losses. Your family might not like it much either, because there's a good chance you would be so motivated by your job that you would be staying later at work!

---

[174] Reporting on the successful worker take-over of bankrupt factories in Argentina, Reed (2002).

WHEN WORKERS TAKE-OVER

Consider what happened in Argentina in 2002, when workers took over bankrupt factories that were abandoned by owners who couldn't pay their employees. Shopfloor workers, who had never been involved in management, book-keeping, financial planning or marketing, suddenly found themselves having to take an active role in all of those tasks and many more besides.

This was the extraordinary situation reported in the *Sydney Morning Herald*,[175] but strangely neglected by most of the media. In the ruins of the Argentinean economy, workers in dozens of factories had taken charge of the business in the absence of disappearing owners. In other cases, local councils expropriated bankrupt factories, abandoned by their owners, and handed them over to their workers to run. Between 2000 and 2002, in Buenos Aires alone, 17 bankrupt factories, abandoned by their owners, were expropriated. In still other cases, the owners had allowed the workers to take-over production in return for payment of rent or as compensation for unpaid wages. According to a later news story, in March 2003, more than 140 Argentinean factories had been taken over by their workers.[176]

And how did the workers cope? In most cases, they did amazingly well; in many, business had never been so good. An outstanding case is the Union y Fuerza metals plant, which manufactures copper tubes and pipes. Workers there, with no business experience, amazed themselves by being able to run a plant better than the professionals had done. Under their own management, workers earned twice as much as they did as employees and were able to provide new jobs to new members. One of the reasons they gave for their success was that the business was now freed from the burden of high management salaries and exorbitant profit distributions to shareholders. Another reason was that they were themselves highly motivated. They were running their own business and were desperate to make a success of it. Everyone earned the same, but salaries might vary according to the profitability of the business. Major decisions were taken democratically. All of this meant longer working hours and everyone putting their heads together to figure out how the business could be turned around.

Most of these factories now operate as worker co-operatives. In this chapter, we focus in on the worker co-operative, a type of co-op that is

---

[175] *Ibid.*

[176] Hall (2003); also www.bayarea.com/mld/mercury news/business/.

owned and democratically controlled by the people who work in it. In Argentina, worker co-ops were used with dramatic success to save jobs. In many other parts of the world, the worker-owned co-op has also proved itself to be a useful tool for creating new jobs and developing new kinds of community-based businesses.

The Irish experience

In Ireland, worker co-ops are in their infancy. Back in 1980, you could have counted the number of Irish worker co-ops on the fingers of one hand. By 1994, there were at least 66 of them, with 306 full-time and 103 part-time workers; still small in numbers but a significant improvement on past performance. Today there are estimated to be about 100[177]. Most worker co-ops in Ireland (more than 60%) are in the service sector, while most of the rest are involved in manufacturing. More recently, Ireland's Co-operative Development Unit has been successful at identifying a number of promising growth sectors for worker co-ops as:

- A suitable vehicle for the employee buy-out of established family businesses with no heir.

- A vehicle for the employee rescue of all, or part, of a business that has decided to close down.

- Associate companies providing complementary services and/or outsourced services to a major company.

We shall be exploring the first of these in some detail later in this chapter.

Worker co-ops in the UK

Growth of worker co-ops has been more dramatic in Britain. In 1971, there were only about six of them; but, by 1992, there were at least 1,115 worker co-ops employing 11,000 people.[178]

In recent years, growth areas for co-ops in Britain have been:

- **Community care** (providing home-care for the disabled and the elderly).

---

[177] A problem when trying to estimate the numbers of worker co-operatives (in Ireland and the UK) is that worker co-ops may register under at least four different legal structures: as an industrial and provident society; a company limited by guarantee; a company limited by shares; or a partnership. In the last three of these, there is no easy way of identifying from available statistics which of the businesses are worker-owned and operating as co-operatives.

[178] ICOM and Co-operative Research Unit (1993).

- **Social employment co-operatives**, offering employment and training opportunities for people with learning, physical or sensory disabilities and the recovering mentally ill.
- **Employee buyouts and conversions**[179].

One commentator has made the point that worker co-op statistics in Britain do not include conversions to employee-ownership using employee share ownership plans (ESOPs) and structures other than traditional co-operative ones. Nor do the statistics include the John Lewis Partnership, a highly successful retail chain owned by its workers. As well as running department stores, including its flagship department store in London's Oxford Street, the John Lewis Partnership also includes the Waitrose chain of supermarkets.

> If we include, as we should, all democratic employee-ownership structures, then in terms of numbers employed, turnover, and net assets, the sector is enjoying a period of unparalleled growth brought about by the successful conversion of existing businesses in situations of privatisation, contracting-out of services and threatened closure[180].

While the *numbers* of UK co-ops have increased markedly, most of them are very small businesses and the numbers employed are still a tiny proportion of the overall work-force.

Worker co-ops in Spain
The growth of co-ops has been more impressive in Spain. Between 1985 and 1990, over 13,000 new co-ops were launched. Of these, some 9,600 were worker co-ops, providing jobs for over 81,000 people. In 1988, worker co-op sales in Spain had reached US$5.7 billion.[181] By 1996, sales of the worker co-ops in the Mondragon group alone had reached US$6 billion, and their worker members totalled nearly 29,407.[182] By 1999, Mondragon's sales had increased again, by more than 50% and the workforce now totalled 46,861, an increase over 1996 of more than 59%.[183] By the end of 2002, Mondragon's sales had reached €9.2 billion (14% above 2001), consolidated profits amounted to €370 million (10.45%

---

[179] Catell (1996).
[180] Blackley (1995).
[181] Godoy (1990).
[182] MacLeod (1997), p.27.
[183] Mondragon Corporacion Cooperativa (2000).

up) and the workforce totalled 66,558 (10.5% up). We shall be analysing the remarkable success of Mondragon later in this chapter.

THE PROMISE OF WORKER CO-OPS

Over the years, worker co-ops have been touted, often extravagantly, as the answer to an extraordinary range of industrial and societal problems. At first glance, they would seem to have much to recommend them. Many of their strengths are obvious from the experience of the Argentinean co-ops:

> Since workers own their own enterprises, they share directly in the success as well as the failure of the firm. This not only produces strong personal incentives to be productive but also considerable peer pressure on colleagues to do their share. Furthermore, it contributes to low rates of worker turnover and absenteeism.[184]

What could be more motivating for most of us than to know that we are working for ourselves and our work colleagues, and that the profits from our efforts will be shared fairly amongst us all? To add to our satisfaction, we would have the opportunity to get involved in the decision-making of the business, and would have a greater chance to acquire a range of skills and know-how than would be available to the employees of a traditional firm. We would also be in a position to improve the quality of working life, refurbish the working environment and redesign jobs to make them more interesting.

Because members of a worker co-op own the business and share the profits, they'd be much more motivated than the average employee. This should provide a cost advantage to worker co-ops, as they can dispense with the costly armies of supervisors, whose main function is to ensure that the workers do what they are supposed to be doing.

Other related competitive advantages stem from the ability of worker co-ops to harness *social capital*[185] more effectively than conventional firms. Possible benefits of this include:

- Most tasks in a business require effective teamwork among the employees. This should be facilitated in a co-op[186] where the teams

---

[184]   Jackall & Levin (1984).
[185]   Social capital is defined by Fukuyama (1996, p.10) as *"the ability of people to work together for common purposes in groups and organisations."*

own and control the business and are more likely to trust the management they have appointed themselves.

- Moreover, it should be easier in a co-op to harness the initiative and creativity of the work force.
- The quality of the end-products of the business would tend to be more important to worker-owners than to mere employees.

The concept of a worker-owned and managed business seems to fit well with the messages from today's business gurus who stress in their books the importance of activating employees– for example:

- *When Workers Decide: Workplace Democracy Takes Root in North America* (Krimerman & Lindenfeld, 1992).
- *Business without Bosses: How Self-Managing Teams are Building High-Performing Companies* (Manz & Sims, 1993).
- *Managing without Management: A Post-Management Manifesto for Business Simplicity* (Koch & Godden, 1996).
- *The Intelligent Organisation: Engaging the Talent and Initiative of Everyone in the Workplace* (Pinchot, G. & E., 1996).
- *The Age of Participation: New Governance for the Workplace and the World* (McLagan & Nel, 1997).

John Stuart Mill and worker co-ops

More than a century ago, the respected philosopher John Stuart Mill (often referred to as the father of modern-day economics) foreshadowed many of the arguments of present-day management theorists. He talked enthusiastically about the importance and power of worker participation. He was also an ardent advocate of worker co-ops, arguing that changed attitudes to work would result in greater efficiency and productivity. He even went so far as to predict the eventual triumph of worker co-operatives as the predominant form of association in industrial society. Mill argued that, if humanity were to continue to make progress, one form of association would eventually triumph over all the others:

> Not that which can exist between a capitalist as chief, and workpeople without a voice in the management, but the association of the labourers themselves on terms of equality,

---

[186] In this chapter, the words *co-op* or *co-operative* refer to a worker-owned co-operative (unless otherwise stated).

collectively owning the capital with which they carry on their operations and working under managers elected and removable by themselves.[187]

THE PROBLEMS OF WORKER CO-OPS

Mill predicted the triumph of worker co-ops well over a century ago. Obviously, something has gone badly wrong! Either he was mistaken, or he was talking about a distant future yet to come. Apart from isolated examples like Mondragon, worker co-ops have clearly not become the predominant form of industrial association.

So *what* went wrong? Although the concept may sound appealing, conventional economists have identified plenty of potential problems in practice. Some of the more serious problems are:

- Under-capitalisation.

- Management dilemmas.

- Lack of entrepreneurs.

- Equity dilution dilemma.

Let's review these problems that have restricted the growth of worker co-ops in the past. We'll then analyse how successful worker co-ops, such as the Mondragon network in Spain, have found ways of making worker co-ops excel.

Under-capitalisation

As we saw in **Chapter 2**, the *Rochdale Principles* preclude the possibility of paying high returns on capital, which often makes it difficult for co-ops to attract investment capital. This is particularly serious for worker co-ops, which typically require a higher investment of capital per member than do most other kinds of co-op. This is probably one reason why worker co-ops in Northern Europe and the USA have been largely restricted to businesses that require relatively little capital, such as service providers, bookshops, bicycle repair shops, restaurants and health food stores.

---

[187]   Quoted in Pateman (1970), p.34.

Management dilemmas

> Consider a railway managed on the system of the porters choosing
> the station-master, the station-master choosing the traffic
> superintendent, the whole body of employees choosing the board
> of directors![188]

Beatrice Webb, an influential social commentator in the 19th century
used this railway example to ridicule the concept of the worker co-
operative. She had been a strong advocate of *consumer* co-operatives but
argued that the task of management in a *worker* co-op would be an
unusually difficult one. She was sceptical about the feasibility of workers
on boards of directors supervising their own managers. According to
Webb, it would put management in an intolerable position when they
were required to discipline those workers who were also board
members.

Shortage of entrepreneurs

One theory about why worker co-ops have not achieved their potential
in most economies relates to the process of how businesses get started in
the first place.[189] The *entrepreneur* is widely considered to be the engine of
new business development and the source of economic growth. An
entrepreneur setting up a new business would not usually choose to
launch the business as a worker co-operative. It is unlikely that
conventional entrepreneurs, operating by the logic of the marketplace,
would choose to give away their bright ideas, the control of their
business and their investment opportunities to the people they've
employed to work on the shop-floor!

Occasionally, very occasionally, magnanimous entrepreneurs *do* give
away the businesses they've painstakingly built up over the years:

- The British retail multiple, John Lewis (mentioned above), which
  incorporates the Waitrose supermarket chain, was given to its
  employees, now called "partners", and continues to operate as a
  highly successful worker-owned business.
- Similarly, in Ireland, Bewley's coffee shops were gifted to a trust on
  behalf of the workers. Eventually, though, this business was sold off
  to a conventional company.

---

[188] Beatrice Webb, quoted in Young & Rigge (1983).
[189] Abell (1983).

- The British entrepreneur Ernest Bader gave away his prosperous plastics company to his employees, who now run it as a successful worker co-op (Schumacher, 1973, pp.230 *et seq.*).
- Even more impressive was the generosity of Swiss retailer, Gottlieb Duttweiler, who gave away his massive Migros organisation to his employees and his customers.[190] Migros has thrived as a co-operative under worker and consumer ownership and is now the dominant retailer in Switzerland, closely followed by the conventional consumer co-operative movement.

But such philanthropic acts are extremely rare. If it is true, as many would argue (Timmons, 1988), that the primary impetus for new business development comes from the *individual entrepreneur*, then it is hardly surprising that worker co-ops have failed to live up to the exalted expectations of their promoters.[191] Although worker co-ops, once established, can be highly successful businesses, there is less opportunity for them to get started in the first place.

The equity dilution dilemma

The economist Benjamin Wood has argued that the problem of equity dilution has been the most serious impediment to the growth of worker co-ops. According to Wood, there are situations in which worker co-ops will choose not to grow, when a conventional firm, faced with similar circumstances, would find it in its own best interests to choose growth[192].

For example, bringing in a new worker-member of a co-op could be a much more costly option than hiring a new employee in a conventional firm. The new co-op member would not only receive his/her weekly pay, but would also be entitled to a share of the business and a share of the distributed profits. In a conventional firm, new workers will be hired if their expected additional output exceeds the cost of employing them. But, according to this argument, new workers are only likely to be admitted to a worker co-op if their expected additional output exceeds employment costs *plus* the costs of ownership (equity entitlements and share of future profits).

---

190   Briscoe (1971).
191   One of the reasons for the success of the Mondragon Group of worker co-ops, in the Basque region of Spain, was their recognition of the entrepreneurship problem. To counter it, Mondragon developed its own banking system and invested substantial amounts in new co-operative development through the bank's Entrepreneurial Division. See Ellerman (1990).
192   Benjamin Wood, discussed in Lutz & Lux (1988).

It follows from this argument that worker co-ops are less likely than conventional firms to hire additional staff members. It would also seem to follow that when someone leaves the co-op, it will often be in the best financial interests of existing members to refrain from hiring a replacement. If this line of reasoning is correct, it would seem that, compared to conventional firms, worker co-ops are by nature averse to growth. This would certainly explain in part why Mills' enthusiastic predictions have gone awry.

THE DILEMMAS RESOLVED

Perhaps the most famous examples of worker co-operatives that have successfully resolved the gamut of these dilemmas are the more than 150 worker and multi-stakeholder co-operatives of the Mondragon group in the Basque region of Spain. Largely through trial and error, they have developed new versions of worker and multi-user co-ops, resulting in a highly successful network of industrial, retail and educational co-operatives, which has sprung up over the last 45 years in and around the Spanish town of Mondragon.

Mondragon is in the Basque region of northern Spain, remote from the main population centres and in an area that used to be severely depressed and underdeveloped. The first of the Mondragon co-ops was started in 1956, a modest venture assembling Aladdin paraffin stoves under licence. By 2000, the group was providing 46,861 well-paid jobs in some 130 large-scale co-operatives.[193] By 2004, this number had risen to more than 68,000.

Worker co-ops in most parts of the world are labour-intensive, and usually suffer from an acute shortage of investment funds. In Mondragon, things are very different. The typical worker co-op is a capital-intensive factory engaged in the production of consumer durables, refrigeration equipment, or capital goods.

The Mondragon system is serviced by a co-operative bank, with branches throughout the region, a co-op industrial health-care and social benefits centre, a co-op research laboratory, a co-operative technological university and a business school (where one can study for a co-operative MBA). At this unique university, students not only learn the technical know-how and skills they need to be productive members of the Mondragon system, they also operate their own manufacturing co-op

---

[193] Mondragon Corporacion Cooperativa (2000); www.mcc.com.es.

(owned and democratically controlled by students and staff). At this co-op, they not only get valuable on-the-job experience, they also learn how to manage and run a co-operative – and can earn enough to pay their way through college.

Economic studies have shown that the Mondragon group has consistently out-performed conventional Spanish businesses,[194] and the group exports between 25% and 30% of its output.

THE MONDRAGON MODIFICATIONS

Let us examine how the Mondragon workers have modified the concept of the worker co-operative, and how these adaptations have enabled them to overcome most of the dilemmas and problems outlined in this chapter. The following practices of Mondragon's primary manufacturing co-ops seem to be particularly significant:

- All workers must be members.
- Substantial initial investment.
- Individual capital accounts.
- Distribution of profits.
- Equitable salary scales.

All workers must be members

After a short probationary period, all workers are required to join the co-operative. Workers who quit their jobs cease to be members and must withdraw the capital they have accumulated during their employment.

In recent years, however, it has proved difficult to apply this principle fully – particularly in Mondragon's retailing division, Eroski (see **Chapter 5**). Eroski has grown rapidly, by acquiring or entering into partnership with a variety of retail businesses. Many of these have been consumer co-ops, where employees had no ownership rights and where it would be problematic to require long-term workers to invest the capital needed to become a member just to hold on to their job. However, in spite of all these problems, Eroski is converting non-member workers into members at a rate of about 2,000 per year.

---

[194]   See, for example, Bradley & Gelb (1983); Levin, H.M. (1984), pp.16-31; Morrison, R. (1991), pp.167-182.

Substantial initial investment

When workers join, they must subscribe a substantial sum of money. If they join an existing co-op, their initial investment will be something in the order of €3,000 to €6,000. This initial investment does not have to be found all at once. There are usually arrangements for paying the amount in instalments out of earnings (a scheme facilitated by the Caja Laboral Popular, Mondragon's co-operative bank).

Individual capital accounts

Each member has an individual capital account (ICA), into which is paid the initial investment plus the member's share of those profits distributed at the end of each year of his/her employment. Members are not allowed to withdraw money from their ICA until they leave the co-op, and then they must withdraw all their capital. If members retire, leave for health reasons or to work in another Mondragon co-op, the full amount is refundable. If they leave for other reasons, up to 20% of their investment may be retained by the co-op.

Savings bank rates of interest are paid on the amounts in ICAs, and periodic adjustments are made to compensate for inflation, if the financial condition of the co-operative permits.

Distribution of profits

In a Mondragon co-op, distributed profits are allocated to workers in proportion to their wages (one of the *Rochdale Principles*). Distributed profits are paid directly into workers' ICAs and cannot be taken as cash. Withdrawal of money from ICAs is restricted as outlined above. There are also clearly stated restrictions as to how much of the profit can go directly to the workers' accounts. Profits must be divided up as follows:

- No more than 70% of annual net profits may be distributed to the workers' ICAs.
- At least 20% must go to collective reserves, which are not withdrawable.
- At least 10% must be spent on social services to benefit the community as a whole – services such as health, education and recreation projects.

Conversely, if the co-op makes a loss, at least 70% of the loss must be withdrawn from ICAs, and not more than 30% from collective reserves.

The workers are clearly sharing in the risks as well as the benefits of running their own business – another key motivating factor!

Equitable salary scales

To cement the feeling that *we are all in this together*, the range of salaries is deliberately restricted. Originally, the highest paid worker could not normally be paid more than three times the lowest paid. The exception to this was that senior professional staff could earn supplements of up to 50% of their salary for special responsibilities and long hours (resulting in an effective salary range of up to four-and-a-half times the lowest paid). In recent years, since about 1992, this range has increased to six times the lowest. This has been done to ease problems in recruiting professional expertise.

MANAGEMENT DILEMMAS REVISITED

How do these modifications to the co-operative concept address the management problems discussed above?

Managing a democracy

The Mondragon success story demonstrates that democracy is not at odds with efficient business management. Management can be even more efficient within a democratic setting given the following kinds of practices:

- Design of appropriate representative structures to manage the decision-making and evaluation tasks of the organisation.
- Distinguishing carefully between *policy issues* and *implementation issues*.
- Appropriate delegation of management functions.
- Use of suitable styles of decision-making.
- Use of measurable goals, and procedures to enable the Board to monitor and evaluate performance in key result areas.

Raising finance

Whereas most worker co-operatives in Ireland and Britain tend to be labour-intensive and starved of capital, the Mondragon co-ops are technologically sophisticated and relatively capital-intensive. They have found ways of raising adequate equity and debt capital at reasonable cost and without violating co-operative principles – for example:

- · The Mondragon system meets some of its capital needs by requiring a major financial commitment from would-be worker-members. Not only does this bring in a good deal of capital, it also increases the individual worker's determination to ensure that the co-operative succeeds.

- Distributed profits are retained in individual accounts (ICAs) and are therefore also available to meet a co-operative's investment needs.

- There is a requirement to allocate a fixed minimum proportion of profits (20%) to collective reserves.

- The Mondragon co-operatives have developed their own community-based savings bank, which funnels investment funds into the co-op network.

Shortage of entrepreneurs

The American economist David Ellerman[195] maintains that Mondragon has solved this problem by *institutionalising the process of entrepreneurship*. Mondragon's Co-op Bank set up its own Entrepreneurial Division, which nurtures new ideas, invests in them and provides the back-up services needed to turn them into reality. This division was eventually turned into a self-managing co-operative and continues to provide its services to groups wishing to set up new co-operatives.

Surviving success

The Mondragon model resolves the dilemma of equity dilution through the requirement of a substantial initial investment plus the concept of individual capital accounts. In the Mondragon system, a new member does not dilute the individual equity shares of other members, whose shares are carefully preserved in their own ICA. Far from diluting the equity of existing members, the new member brings in additional new capital. Moreover, new members make no claims against the capital accumulated by individuals in the past. Their only claims are on the profits distributed during their own term of employment. Thus Ellerman[196] argues that the Mondragon co-operators have solved the

---

[195] Ellerman is an economist who helped set up the Industrial Co-operative Association in the United States, which promoted and assisted the development of worker co-ops. He also helped to draw up the worker co-operative statute of the State of Massachusetts.

[196] Ellerman, D.P. (1990); see also the discussion in Lutz & Lux (1998).

dilemma by implicitly drawing a distinction between *membership rights* (voting rights + economic profit rights) and *conventional share rights* (membership rights + net book value).

Not only does the Mondragon approach resolve problems of equity dilution, it also addresses another set of problems that has led to the demutualisation of co-ops. Thanks to the concept of the individual capital account and the retention of allocated profits during the working life of a shareholder, the value of shares held by members provides an adequate reflection of the value of the co-operative's assets. As a result, there is little temptation to sell off the co-op in order to realise the full value of members' equity shares.

IRISH STRATEGIES FOR DEVELOPING WORKER CO-OPS

How businesses get started

Ireland has developed its own approaches to resolving the dilemmas of worker co-ops. Recent research by Colm Hughes has identified some of the key problems confronted by worker co-operatives in Ireland (Hughes, 2000). He demonstrated that the whole support system for developing small businesses tends to be centred on the individual entrepreneur (Hughes, 2000, p.54 *et seq.*).

His research has also shown that the key people who give advice to new business start-ups, people like accountants, bankers, and employers' organisations were, for the most part, either ignorant about or hostile towards the concept of the worker co-op. There was a general tendency to see the worker co-operative as a weak business structure, which was used only in futile attempts to create and subsidise marginal jobs for the socially excluded (Hughes, 2000, pp.40-63).

New strategies for developing worker co-ops

From his findings on the small business start-up process and its impact on the development of worker co-ops, Hughes set about developing strategies for altering the process to the advantage of the worker co-operative. In his capacity as manager of Ireland's Co-operative Development Unit, his brief was to promote the worker co-operative sector in Ireland. He hoped to alter the business start-up process by influencing the main actors in the small-business support system. His aim was to change their attitudes toward the worker co-op as a suitable structure for business development. Given their existing negative attitudes toward the co-operative, this was a tall order.

Instead of selling the worker co-op as a structure for empowering the socially excluded, Hughes decided to promote it as a powerful corporate structure for operating highly-successful businesses. He did this, by identifying a number of significant business problems for which the worker co-op appeared to be an ideal solution. The strategy was then to sell the concept of the co-op as a solution to accountants and bankers and the members of employers' associations (Hughes, 2000, pp.64-92).

The problem situations he identified included:

- **Family firms with succession problems:** The worker co-operative could be a vehicle for transferring the business to the employees, thereby providing an exit mechanism for owners of family businesses without a suitable heir.

- **Larger companies with problems of retaining and rewarding excellent employees:** The worker co-operative could provide a structure for setting up *associate companies,* which would develop services, products and/or markets related to the parent company, but would be managed and controlled by a team of workers from the parent company.

Let's look at the first of these problem areas.

Family firms with succession problems

According to a survey by the Chamber of Commerce of Ireland, 90% of all businesses in Ireland are family firms, employing an estimated 50% of the country's workforce. An alarming 70% of these firms do not make it into a second generation of owners, and only 13% survive to the third generation. Moreover, even though 66% of the owners were over 50 years old, 70% of family firms in Ireland have not made any plans for transferring the business.[197]

Even more worrying statistics emerged from a 1994 EU study, which revealed that at least 300,000 jobs disappear each year across the European Union as a result of poorly-managed business transfers.[198]

The failure to transfer a family firm to the next generation typically creates immense problems for the family (perhaps forcing them to wind up the business and sell off the assets). It also creates problems for

---

[197] Reported in the *Irish Independent* (27.11.97) and quoted in Hughes (2000).
[198] Official Journal of the European Commission 94/C 400/01.

employees who often lose their jobs after years of service (a source of grief to the family owners as well). The option, when there is no suitable heir, of transferring ownership to a co-operative of employees appears to be an attractive one, since:

- The employees know the business inside out and have established relationships with the customers and suppliers.
- The employees want to see the business continue and succeed, as the consequences of its closure would be disastrous for them.

The survival of the family firm is also likely to be of great importance to the community as a whole, and particularly to the other businesses and the professionals who deal with the firm.

One of the barriers to an employee take-over is their ability to raise the capital necessary to buy the family business as a going concern. This is one of the oft-quoted management dilemmas of a worker co-operative: how is it possible for a group of ordinary workers to raise the capital necessary to buy or set up a substantial business?

To address this problem, Hughes proposed splitting the business into two parts, as follows.

- A *holding company*, to which would be transferred the main assets of the business, land, buildings and some of the more costly capital equipment. This company would continue to be owned and controlled by the family.
- A *trading company*, which would be structured as a worker co-operative, with the workers owning at least 51% and the family, the remainder. Each working member (including the family and the worker shareholders) would also hold one voting share to ensure democratic control of the business. The trading company would own and run the trading part of the business and would lease the assets from the holding company on a long lease, with an option to buy the assets over time.[199]

---

[199]   Hughes (2000), pp.74-75. Students of Irish co-operative history might notice a similarity between this approach to resolving the financial dilemmas of a worker co-op and the approach used in the 19th century at the Ralahine co-operative in County Clare. At Ralahine, the farm business prospered spectacularly when the workers took it over, but the workers lost their stake in the business when the landowner lost the whole estate in a game of cards. Hopefully, lawyers today are too vigilant to allow this sort of risk to be tolerated!

Advantages for the workers include:

- They now only have to raise sufficient capital to purchase 51% of the trading company.
- The family remains involved in the firm after the transfer and can provide the business and/or technical skills that may be lacking in the workforce.
- The family will have a vested interest in ensuring the business succeeds and will be motivated to transfer skills and know-how to the worker-shareholders.
- Jobs have been safeguarded and the assumption of increased responsibility by the workers should lead to business growth and the creation of more jobs.

Advantages for the family include:

- There is a satisfactory business transfer: the business they have built up survives under a different ownership structure.
- They are able to *withdraw* partially from the business, sharing more responsibility with the worker-shareholders. But they are also able to continue to *participate* in the business to the degree mutually agreeable to family and workers.
- Because they are sharing management responsibilities with the workers, the family members may now have the chance to spend more time specialising in areas such as marketing, with a beneficial impact on the growth of the business.
- The lease provides a continuing flow of income to the family, which can be very important, as many small business owners have inadequate pension provisions

An added advantage for both is that splitting the business in this way is tax-efficient in Ireland; because assets are not sold, the family is not liable to Capital Gains Tax; and because the employees have bought their share of the business at current market price, they are not subject to taxes on Benefit-in-Kind.[200]

---

[200] Hughes (2000), p.77.

IMPLEMENTING THE STRATEGIES

Persuading the influencers

As a first step in the implementation of these strategies, an intensive publicity campaign was directed at accountants, bankers and employer associations, to make them aware of the usefulness of the co-operative as a vehicle for addressing the above problems. Hughes held numerous meetings with professional associations, and carefully targeted accounting firms and banks. He also wrote numerous articles for the Irish business press. The result was numerous requests from accountants on behalf of their clients, as well as direct approaches from family firms with transfer problems.

Family firms to co-ops

In 1996, the first family firm converted to a co-op. It was a small engineering firm that manufactured abattoir equipment. The conversion appears to have been an unqualified success. In the first two years after the transfer, the co-op extended its premises, leased new equipment, expanded into export markets, increased employment, reduced its costs, and increased gross profit percentage and net profit (see **Case Study 9.1**).

CASE STUDY 9.1: P. BARRY LTD & THE FAMILY FIRM TRANSFER MODEL

Based outside the village of Caragh in County Kildare, P. Barry Ltd. manufactures abattoir equipment. Originally set-up in 1969, this firm became a workers' co-op in 1996. It was the first of the *Family Firm Transfer model* initiated by the Co-operative Development Unit (CDU) of FÁS. The co-op has three members and employs four full-time non-member employees, including the wife of the original owner. It has contracts in Ireland and abroad.

The Family Firm Transfer model, as the name implies, is targeted at family owned businesses that have a potential difficulty in transferring the business to the next generation (CDU, 1998). In the case of P. Barry Ltd., the owners, a married couple, had built up the business but neither of their two daughters were interested in taking it over. The owners contacted the CDU and outlined their case. The couple then approached their employees, two of whom decided to take on the idea of running the business as a co-op.

A business plan was prepared outlining the new structure. The process of take-over involved splitting the business into two separate firms, a *holding company*, which owns the fixed assets, and a *trading company*. The holding company is owned and controlled by the family. It leases the fixed assets to the trading company, which owns and controls the business. The trading company carries on the business activities of the original family firm and is owned by the three co-op members (CDU, 1998). Remaining staff decided not to buy into the co-op, which was registered as a limited company, with memorandum and articles of association that incorporate co-operative principles.

Because the business is now a co-op, the former owner is able to spend less time on production and more on marketing, for which he had a considerable flair. As a result, export markets were identified in the UK and Northern Europe and, after the first two years of the co-op's existence, exports accounted for 30% of the co-op's sales. During the seven years since its founding, the co-op has extended the premises and leased new machinery. It has also diversified into a number of areas and has patents pending for innovative production processes developed by the members.

The second business to convert to a co-operative was a family-owned nursing home with 20 employees. Other businesses that have successfully converted to a co-operative include a local newspaper, a pewter manufacturer, a fish processor, a furniture manufacturer, a motor repair firm, a coach operator and Heron Quality Foods, a rapidly-growing speciality foods producer (see **Chapter 5**).

SUMMARY

In this chapter, we've explored the promise and the problems of worker co-ops and have travelled as far afield as Argentina, where we witnessed the worker-led renaissance of abandoned factories, and Spain, where we visited the famous co-ops of Mondragon.

The worker co-operative is an organisational model that has much to recommend it and much of the chapter was spent discussing the problems and barriers that have restricted the growth of this promising way of doing business. We saw how the Mondragon group has successfully resolved the apparent dilemmas of managing worker co-ops and created a network of world-class businesses.

We also explored some of the innovative strategies developed in Ireland for unleashing the potential of worker co-ops. While Ireland has not been famous in the past for its successes in the field of worker co-operatives, this could well be about to change. In the past, there had been a general tendency to see the worker co-operative mainly as a tool that inexperienced people could use to create jobs for themselves, or to rescue jobs in firms that were on the verge of closing down. Many of the co-ops set up in such difficult circumstances did succeed against the odds. Those successes were, in themselves, tributes to the ingenuity and determination of the workers involved and the viability of the co-operative concept. But this approach is unlikely to establish worker co-operatives as major players in the national economy.

The innovative strategies developed in Ireland provide us with some important new ways of thinking about co-operative development. They take into account the nature of the business development process as it exists in most countries, with its reliance on the individual entrepreneur and professional advisors who have little knowledge of or sympathy with the co-operative idea. Starting with this recognition of the facts of business life, the strategy of *saving the family firm* shows us how we can use the existing system to promote new ways of launching and running successful co-operative enterprises.

TEN

THE WAY FORWARD?

Robert Briscoe & Michael Ward

*There is a sedulously fostered idea that an esoteric science called
"economics" is chock-full of inexorable laws which sternly forbid
all monetary reform and even all social improvement. There is the
constant retort: "If you knew political economy, you would not
advocate that". In this country ... the economist is still appealed
to by the well-to-do, who naturally want to retain and to justify a
system which has been good to them.*[201]

*Co-operation is not just a way of doing business in its own right.
It is the only right way of doing business.*[202]

In this book, we have made many claims about the efficacy of co-
operatives. We have argued that they are an effective way of addressing
problems that many have considered intractable – for example, the
dilemmas of worker co-ops covered in the previous chapter. Much of
what is in this book may well be greeted with the retort O'Rahilly refers
to above. But we wouldn't go quite as far as Coady, who maintains that
co-ops are the "only right way of doing business".

In this chapter, we shall discuss some of the questions raised by these
two quotations. Are co-ops demonstrably a better way of doing business,
or are we trying to achieve the impossible by pitting businesses owned
by users against the might of multinational giants driven by investors?
We shall summarise some of the reasons why we think Coady was on
the right track. But we do not want to leave you with the impression that

---

201 O'Rahilly (1942), p.viii.
202 Coady (1939).

all is sweetness and light in the world of co-operatives. In spite of all the success stories in this book, co-operatives, like any other type of business, do not always prosper. So, in this final chapter, we plan to say a bit more about the dilemmas facing co-ops of all types and how the pitfalls can be overcome.

THE RIGHT WAY OF DOING BUSINESS?

Monsignor Coady (1888-1959) taught at St. Francis Xavier University (known locally as St. F.X.), in the rural town of Antigonish, in the Canadian province of Nova Scotia. From the 1920s to the 1950s, he was one of the leaders of an unusual adult education movement, which encouraged people to get active and do something about their own economic plight. This was an unheard-of approach to running university extension courses.

The process usually started with a public meeting in a down-at-heel community, where the audience was confronted with the questions, "What should we study? What can we do?". The meeting would often begin with exasperated cries from the floor of, "What on earth can *we* do? We're only poor people without much education." One of the main purposes of these meetings was to help the ordinary people of Nova Scotia develop what psychologists today call an *internal locus of control* – the confidence that they themselves could exert significant control over their own lives and not be totally dependent on the decisions of powerful elites. In spite of the participants' misgivings, the typical outcome of such meetings would be the formation of one or two small study clubs, which would attempt to come up with detailed, practical answers to the questions.

These ambitious study clubs stimulated all kinds of economic group action. Agricultural and fishery co-ops and networks of credit unions and consumer co-ops sprang up across the province, and transformed the livelihoods of their members, bringing prosperity to neglected communities.

Right for whom?

These new co-operatives demonstrated convincingly that they were the right way of doing business (right, that is, from the point of view of the members who used the co-ops' services). In 1923, for example, the lobster fishermen at Havre Boucher took the ambitious step of building their own co-operative canning plant. This enabled them, in their first season, to earn an average of 12 cents a pound for their lobsters, while those who had remained outside the co-op made barely half that amount, and were quick to join up with their neighbours.[203] Similar developments followed in the marketing of livestock and the processing of milk, in the retailing activities of consumer co-ops and in the establishment of a network of successful credit unions.

Such stories could be duplicated a thousand-fold in every continent, demonstrating the effectiveness of the co-operative model at meeting the needs of people in distress. But, of course, they don't always succeed. There were many attempts to set up consumer co-ops before the Rochdale Pioneers developed a model that worked well. Many of these early efforts failed, because they made the mistake of allowing members to buy on credit that was never repaid. Many more folded, because someone absconded with the funds.

The Rochdale Pioneers succeeded mainly because they learned from the mistakes and the good ideas of others.[204] For example, they sold goods at the going market price rather than selling at cost, and they refused to sell on credit, They also copied the idea of dividend on purchases as a means of distributing profits, which built the business by rewarding members according to their use of the business, and was an incentive for others to join up.

Once the model was shown to work, it spread like wildfire and success became relatively easy for almost a century. But times change and so do members' needs.

PITFALLS & DILEMMAS

Over the years, the grand plans of co-operators have frequently been greeted with the discouraging retorts of so-called experts.

> It won't work. If you knew anything about business, you wouldn't even attempt it!

---

[203] Coady, *op. cit.*, pp.50-52.

[204] One good idea, which might have been borrowed by the Rochdale Pioneers from an earlier co-op, was the key concept of *distributing profits according to use of the business*. The Lennoxtown Co-operative Society in Scotland, founded in 1812, "is reputed to have adopted the method of dividend on purchases long before Rochdale was heard of" (Cole, 1944, p.14).

There is often an element of truth in what the detractors say. There are major pitfalls to be avoided, and new ways of doing things have to be carefully devised to fit the special goals and processes of co-ops (as we saw in the case of worker-owned co-ops in **Chapter 9**). Promoters of co-operatives have been aware that starting something radically different is not an easy matter. Here are some examples of their warnings:

> The pursuit of viability, combined with the pursuit of higher social aims, produces many dilemmas, many seeming contradictions, and imposes heavy burdens on managers.[205]

> Beware of co-operatives which believe that enthusiasm is a substitute for adequate capitalisation, technology and planning.[206]

So let's look at some of the problems and dilemmas that can raise their ugly heads when we are trying to manage businesses of all kinds, conventional firms as well as co-operatives.

Dilemmas of management

It has been argued that the whole job of management is about managing dilemmas.[207] But what exactly is a dilemma? According to one dictionary definition, a dilemma is:

> ... a situation in which you must choose between two or more courses of action, both (or all) equally undesirable.[208]

"To be or not to be", was the dilemma Shakespeare put into Hamlet's mouth. Should the Prince of Denmark live on in an intolerable situation, or should he escape from it all by killing himself – both very undesirable options? In organisations, managers are constantly confronted with dilemmas, though usually somewhat less drastic than Hamlet's. Here is a classic example from the world of business: Centralise or decentralise?

Should we centralise the business, keep decision-making powers at the centre and make the business more orderly and predictable (but at the risk of stifling initiative and flexibility). On the other hand, should we decentralise and encourage entrepreneurship and creativity at the

---

[205] Schumacher (1973), p.212.
[206] Jose Maria Arizmendi-Arrieta, the priest whose ideas and advice inspired and shaped the Mondragon network.
[207] Hampden-Turner (1991).
[208] Chambers (1999).

local level (at the possible expense of disorder and lack of overall control)?

In **Chapter 9**, we looked in some detail at the management dilemmas confronting worker-owned co-ops, which are brilliantly dealt with by the Mondragon group. In the rest of this chapter, we shall explore both the dilemmas confronting conventional firms and those experienced by other kinds of co-ops, in particular, producer and consumer co-ops.

Dilemmas of conventional businesses

Before we look at the management dilemmas more commonly found in co-ops, let's look first at some of the dilemmas afflicting conventional business. Consider the following problems:

- **Cut costs *vs* maintain ethical standards?** Should we keep costs as low as possible to remain competitive, while providing a good return on investment to our shareholders? Should we do this, even though it may mean cutting our workforce, moving toward part-time workforces, even relocating to lower wage areas where child labour can be employed and governments are less fussy about environmental impact? Should we cut costs, even if it means ignoring environmental and health needs and undermining the viability of small-scale producers and local communities?

- **Short-term focus *vs* concern for the future?** Should we focus single-mindedly on short-term profits to keep our shareholders happy? Should we do this, even if it means producing what is profitable, regardless of the impact on society, and/or disposing of toxic by-products, etc., as cheaply as possible? Should we do this, even though the consequences might include severe environmental degradation, unsustainable production, and or increasing inequality?

Competitive pressures to serve rich investors ahead of other more needy stakeholders are at the root of the dilemmas experienced by conventional businesses. Former Harvard Business School professor David C. Korten summarises the issue:

> Modern capitalism involves a concentration of wealth by the few to the exclusion of the many; it is more than a system of rule by human elites. It has evolved into a system of autonomous rule by money for money that functions on autopilot beyond the control of any human actor or responsiveness to any human sensibility. ...[It] is about using money to make money for people who already have more of it than they need. Its institutions breed

inequality,   exclusion,   environmental   destruction,   social
irresponsibility and economic instability while homogenising
cultures, weakening institutions of democracy and eroding the
moral and social fabric of society. [209]

Resolving the dilemmas of conventional businesses

As a strategy for resolving the dilemmas of conventional business,
Korten recommends an economic system that appears to have much in
common with the concept of the co-operative.

> The challenge is to replace the global capitalist economy with a
> properly-regulated and locally-rooted market economy that
> invests in the regeneration of living capital, increases net beneficial
> economic output, distributes that output justly and equitably to
> meet the basic needs of everyone, strengthens the institutions of
> democracy and the market, and returns money to its proper role as
> the servant of productive activity.[210]

The co-operative form of organisation is one approach to resolving the
dilemmas of conventional businesses. Because their main aim is to meet
the needs of users rather than the needs of rich investors, co-ops often
have a degree of freedom to do things very differently. In many of the
stories told in this book, we have shown how co-ops provide a business
structure and a process that often enable us to meet our economic and
social needs with fewer of the negative side-effects inherent in
conventional approaches to business (as outlined by Korten above).

Design for use instead of *design for profit* can enable co-ops to pursue
creative strategies that differentiate them from conventional businesses,
building trust and addressing local and global problems in innovative
ways. For example, CSA co-ops build the local economy, increase the
viability of small farmers, improve the quality of food for consumers,
and help the environment by reducing the miles travelled by our food.
Retail co-ops can build a competitive advantage by identifying and
combating *food crimes*, while energy co-ops are often in the forefront of
energy conservation and identifying renewable sources. However, we
need to remember that co-ops have dilemmas of their own.

---

[209]   Korten (1998).
[210]   *Ibid*.

Dilemmas of co-operative management

There are a number of business management problems that might be particularly troublesome to managers trying to abide by the *Rochdale Principles*, including:

- **Credit:** Even before their co-op shop had opened its doors, the Rochdale Pioneers were faced with a massive dilemma: what was to be done about credit? Should they allow members to buy on credit, which invites them to get into debt and will destroy the business when debtors can't pay what they owe? Or should they refuse all credit, which will make it impossible to meet the needs of the poorest who are unemployed or temporarily without work?

  > The choice was hard, for the refusal of credit tended to limit the appeal of Co-operation to those whose lives were relatively secure, either because they were in the steadier jobs or because, even if not, their earnings when they were employed were enough to enable them to put something aside against adversity.[211]

  When deciding what to do, the Pioneers had the benefit of the prior experience of many would-be co-ops, which had started out with high hopes but had been wrecked because many of their members had bought on credit and couldn't pay their bills. The Pioneers could find no easy resolution of this problem and decided to ban all credit in order to safeguard the co-op. (With hindsight, one might argue that they should have thought about the possibility of starting up a credit union, but it was not until 1862, nearly 20 years after the launch of Rochdale Stores, that *Raiffeisen* set up the first co-operative credit banks in Germany, and even *they* didn't serve people who had no money to save.)

- **Financing the co-op:** Another serious dilemma has been how to raise adequate business finance, while observing co-operative principles. The *Principles* stipulate that *only a limited rate of return can be paid on capital* and that *profits should be distributed according to use of the business* (rather than on the amount of capital invested). This makes co-operatives less attractive to people with money to invest. As a result, co-ops are likely to have problems raising adequate capital and are more dependent than conventional businesses on *debt* than on share capital (*equity*). This increases the riskiness of the co-op,

---

[211] Cole (1944), p.9.

because of the costs of servicing this additional debt and the necessity to repay it to the lender.

- **Principal-Agent problems:** When a co-op's board of directors hires a manager to manage the organisation on behalf of the membership, it is entering into a necessary relationship that is often fraught with danger! The members of the co-op are the *principals* of the business (they own it). They have elected a board of directors to act as *agents* to oversee the management of the co-op on their behalf, and the manager is another *agent* appointed by the board. Inevitably, the interests of principals and their agents are somewhat different. Even though the board is elected by and from the membership, there are still some divergences. The board may not be totally representative of the membership – for example, in many co-ops, boards are dominated by men, many of whom may be getting on in years. In such a case, women and younger members will be under-represented and may find that their special needs and interests are not addressed in the board's plans and programmes. The gaps between the interests of members and managers are likely to be even more significant than those between members and boards.

Consider the following dilemma confronting the board of directors of a long-established retail food co-operative:

> The directors were having great difficulty replacing their manager who had retired a year earlier. In the meantime, they ran the co-op by a committee consisting of the co-op's president and section managers, none of whom felt up to the top job. They considered all the external job applicants to be unsatisfactory: they either lacked relevant business skills and experience or, if they had those skills, they were totally ignorant about the nature of a co-operative business and didn't share the co-operative values, considered essential by the board.

This is a dilemma that has haunted many co-ops. It is often resolved unsatisfactorily by hiring a manager who knows how to run a business but is ignorant of the fact that a co-operative is different from an ordinary firm and has a different set of objectives. This lack of understanding can have a disastrous impact on the co-op if members and their elected representatives do not do a good job of *re-educating* the manager, and do not keep a careful eye on what is happening.

Consider Race Mathews' comments on the issue of principal-agent problems in Australia:

> [I]n the absence of adequate member involvement and scrutiny, complacent, incompetent or opportunistic management can cause once thriving co-operatives and co-operative movements to vanish virtually overnight, and be forgotten as completely as if they had never existed. Alternatively, where co-operatives are successful in commercial terms, there may be attempts to demutualise them by their boards or managements or external corporate raiders. Where members have lost the habit of seeing themselves as having property rights in it or otherwise actively looking after their interests, a determined takeover bid may well be successful.[212]

Perhaps this is why the successful worker co-ops in Mondragon put so much effort into setting up their own technical university and graduate business school, which enables them to train their own managers from scratch.

There are a number of other problems that confront highly successful co-operatives. For example, when a co-operative prospers as a business, a high proportion of profits are often reinvested in the business, thus allowing the real value of the co-op to increase much more rapidly than the value of the members' shares. This means that members may become unhappy at the gap between the value of their shareholding and the value of their thriving business. As a result, they will be increasingly inclined to sell up all, or part, of the business or to convert it to a conventional company in order to realise the full market value of their shareholding. This has been a factor in the setting up of public limited companies (PLCs) by some of the major Irish dairy co-operatives.[213]

In a similar vein, some of the longer-established mutual businesses (like building societies and mutual insurance societies) have been transformed into PLCs, simply because their members were unaware of the fact that they were co-owners of these businesses. As a result, they signed away their ownership rights (as well as the more favourable terms they enjoyed as owners) in return for a once-off windfall.

The windfalls appeared good at the time, but were usually far less than the real value of the business. Selling off a successful mutual business at a fraction of its real worth is like selling off the family silver to pay for a night out on the town. It gives you some cash in your pocket,

---

[212] Mathews (1999).
[213] How to resolve this set of dilemmas is explained in Jacobson & O'Leary (1990).

but denies future generations the use of resources that have been painstakingly accumulated. And the morning after your night on the town, when your money is spent, you'll realise with regret that the sell-off can't be reversed!

Resolving dilemmas of co-operative management

The economist, E.F. Schumacher, has some advice on how to go about resolving dilemmas:

> Whenever one encounters such opposites [as **centralisation** and **decentralisation**], each of them with persuasive arguments in its favour, it is worth looking into the depth of the problem for something more than compromise, more than a half-and-half solution. Maybe what we really need is not **either-or** but **the-one-and-the-other-at-the-same-time**. [214] [emphasis added]

So, when it comes to managing the dilemmas of co-operatives, as discussed above, we need to follow Schumacher's advice and to seek out "the-one-and-the-other-at-the-same-time."

Let's revisit some of the dilemmas outlined above and see how co-ops have often managed to get the best of both worlds:

- **Resolving credit dilemmas:** The existence of credit unions and other co-operatively-controlled financial institutions has greatly reduced the seriousness of the credit dilemmas that confronted the early consumer co-ops. Credit unions and other financial institutions such as the Grameen Bank (see **Chapter 6**) have redesigned banking to provide credit to people who do not have significant collateral by i) recognising the value of social collateral and ii) by finding ways of dramatically reducing transaction costs.

  In many cases, co-ops have also introduced a competitive element into the financial services industry, which made big players bring their prices down. In the UK, the Co-op Bank was first to pay interest on current accounts and to eliminate current account transaction costs. It also radically reduced interest rates on credit cards, causing other banks to follow suit.

  However, there remains much to be done. Moneylenders, who charge exorbitant interest rates, still prosper, and more and more people are getting into financial difficulties by using their credit cards to borrow huge amounts of money at high interest rates. To remedy such

214 Schumacher, *op. cit.*, p.202.

problems, financial co-ops need to figure out why they are happening and how they can be addressed.

- **Resolving financial dilemmas:** Perhaps the most troublesome dilemmas confronting co-operatives have involved financial problems. In particular, how can a co-op raise the funds needed to expand its business, when it can pay only a limited return to investors? Why should anyone choose to invest money in a co-op when profits are distributed, not on the basis of capital invested, but according to use of the co-op's services? If we look at this problem as an *either-or* dilemma, we have only two choices, suffer the consequences of inadequate funds or convert the co-operative into a conventional business, a PLC. Both responses are self-defeating. The former remains true to co-operative principles, but ends up with an inferior business that offers inadequate services and gives co-ops a bad name. The latter throws the baby out with the bath water: to raise funds, it loses the opportunity to serve more needy stakeholders rather than rich investors, and the business becomes subject to the dilemmas confronting conventional businesses (outlined above). However, many successful co-operatives have found ways of resolving these dilemmas, including:

  - **Design for use:** Make sure that the co-op is designed to provide services in great demand and provide tangible benefits for members only (such as services and refunds available only to members). Unique services and tangible benefits will help to motivate members to invest adequate funds.

  - **Co-operate with other co-ops:** Some co-ops have raised finance by co-operating with the credit union sector – for example, the Desjardins credit union movement in Quebec has been particularly active in co-operative development. In Ireland, to address the country's severe shortage of affordable housing, a number of credit unions are working with housing co-operative organisations to explore the possibility of investing credit union funds in co-operative housing developments.

  - **Set up joint ventures:** In order to finance new developments, some co-ops have set up joint ventures as subsidiaries. Such ventures may be jointly owned by co-ops or may involve non-co-operative partners.

  - **Distribute profits as bonus shares:** Distributing profits in the form of bonus shares, which have to be retained within the co-operative for a period of time – agreed at an AGM, and varying from 10 years or until the member leaves the co-operative – enables the co-operative to reward members for using the co-op, while the co-op continues to use the capital to develop its services. This tactic also lessens the gap between the value of the business and the value of members' share-holdings, thereby eliminating one of the main causes of demutualisation.

- **Require realistic member investments:** Many co-ops raise adequate capital by requiring a more substantial investment from members, sometimes in proportion to the member's use of the business. New Generation Co-ops (NGCs) in the American Mid-West, have been very successful at raising money from farmers. These co-ops are designed to process farmers' produce and to earn for their members a larger slice of the consumer dollar. NGCs link member shareholdings to the amount of produce a member can supply to the co-op. Each share entitles, and requires, a farmer-member to supply one unit of production to the co-op and members must buy at least a set minimum number of shares in order to become a member. Although this means that a substantial investment is required from new members, farmers are happy to invest because of the profit potential of the business.

  Some worker co-ops (such as those in the Mondragon group) also require a substantial initial investment from new members, but help the worker find the money by guaranteeing a loan, which is repaid in instalments from wages earned at the co-op.

- **Create co-operative banking systems:** To ensure adequate financing, some co-ops have set up their own banking system – for example, the Mondragon Co-operative Corporation (see **Chapter 9**) and the substantial co-operative banks that operate in Europe and the USA.

- **Sell shares to *bona fide* users at current market prices:** More controversially, some New Generation agricultural co-operatives (mentioned above) allow members to sell their shares in the business at current market value to other member-users of the business. This allows for a degree of capital growth, which makes the investment more attractive to the member.

- **Facilitate conversion through innovative capital structures:** In **Chapter 9**, we discussed strategies used in Ireland of converting endangered family businesses into worker co-ops. The capital needed for the worker takeover was drastically reduced by splitting the business into a *holding company* and a *trading company*.

- **Invent financial instruments to attract ethical investment funds:** In **Chapter 4**, we saw that Eroski, the Spanish consumer group, has been able to expand rapidly with the help of innovative financial instruments that raise substantial capital without endangering the co-operative ownership of the business. More co-operatives need to explore ways of accessing ethical investment funds with carefully designed, non-voting financial instruments that enable the investor to enjoy capital growth, while protecting the co-operative organisation of the business.

- **Resolving principal-agent dilemmas:** Earlier, we quoted Race Mathews, who suggested that agency problems are much more likely to occur in situations "where members have lost the habit of seeing themselves as having property rights in [the co-op] or otherwise actively looking after their interests." This suggests that the co-op should offer services to the members that are important and significant enough to ensure that members keep a close watch on what is happening in the organisation. Ways of ensuring this happens include:

    - **Design for use & the co-operative process:** Continuing design for use is the key to resolving this dilemma. The restless search for new ways of *meeting more of the members' needs more effectively* is vital for the long-term survival and growth of co-operatives. And the process of design for use is likely to be more effective if members are encouraged to be active in working together with other members to identify new ways of meeting their needs (see **Chapter 2** for more detail on the co-operative process). When an organisation is important to its members, they are more likely to be actively involved in design for use, to ensure that competent people are elected to the board of directors, and to hold directors and managers accountable for effective performance. If the co-op is only of minor interest to its members, and if it is almost indistinguishable from a conventional business, then members will not bother to ensure competent and honest management and will be only too ready to grab a cash windfall when it is offered.

    - **Moving into new kinds of business:** When it works well, *design for use* alerts co-ops to the fact that members' urgent needs may have changed. To meet the changed needs may require the co-op to give up its old business and do something entirely different or, more usually, to set up a new division to operate a new set of services.

      An example of the first strategy is the Oak Street Co-op in Michigan, which started out as a consumer food co-op. Then, with the influx of low-cost multiple retailers, it recognised that the co-op could do more for the community by providing reasonably-priced spectacles, so it opened a successful optician service that became its main business. It later identified the urgent need for affordable housing for senior citizens and currently operates a network of housing co-ops for seniors in four states.

      The Kobe Consumer Co-op is another example of the readiness to rethink radically the role of a co-op. One of the largest retail co-ops in Japan, the Kobe Co-op played a key role in getting food supplies to residents during the disastrous earthquake that devastated the city. As a result of the destruction and trauma caused by the earthquake, the co-op saw an urgent need to move into health services and elder-care.

A less recent example is the strategy of the Swedish second-level consumer co-op, Koopertiva Forbundet (KF), which, in the early half of the 20th century, decided to intervene in industries that overcharged consumers or produced goods of poor quality. As a result of this strategy, it set up successful manufacturing plants to produce consumer goods such as galoshes and light bulbs!

- **Co-operation between co-operatives:** The results of *design for use* can be greatly enhanced when co-operatives co-operate with one another. Co-ops have often been very effective at co-operating *within* their individual sectors – for example, consumer co-ops have set up second level co-ops to provide processing, wholesaling and purchasing services; credit unions have set up jointly-owned insurance societies to meet their common needs; and agricultural co-ops have co-operated to market their produce, provide services and buy inputs to the mutual benefit of all. But, arguably, even greater benefits could be gained by co-operating between sectors. Because people's problems and needs cross the boundaries of individual sectors, there is an even greater potential for creative *design for use* when co-ops from different sectors work together. Innovative strategies for meeting housing needs can be developed when housing co-ops work together with credit unions and even consumer and producer co-ops (in **Chapter 4**, we saw the example of the Weaver Street consumer/worker co-op helping to set up a housing co-op). Also, consumer co-ops are beginning to explore participating in power generation by establishing relationships with wind power co-ops. The possibilities are only limited by our imagination: the co-operative process of *activating members* to engage in *design for use* is a powerful way of stimulating creativity and imagining radically different ways of getting things done.

- **Co-operation between key stakeholders:** Another way of enjoying the benefits of co-operation between co-ops is to create an organisation that brings together the insights and concerns of more than one set of stakeholders. Multi-stakeholder co-operatives, owned by two or more sets of stakeholders, have been able to build competitive advantage by involving complementary strategic interests in the governance of a co-op. In Eroski, for example, consumers and workers together have managed to build a dynamic, rapidly growing retailing organisation, which has outperformed most of its conventional competitors. Arguably, much of this success derives from the fact that the structure motivates the workers and ensures that they pay very close attention to consumer needs.[215]

Many of the other co-operatives in the Mondragon Group also benefit from a multi-stakeholder structure. On various boards of directors, pig farmers work together with the providers of agricultural services and

---

[215] See Turnbull (2001).

with consumers (as represented by Eroski); university students collaborate with teaching staff and the industrial co-ops that help fund the university and employ its graduates; bankers work together with the co-ops that are the bank's principal borrowers. On a much smaller scale, the Weaver Street Market (see **Chapter 5**) owes much of its success to the creativity, motivation and mutual concern that derive from a multi-stakeholder structure owned and controlled jointly by workers and consumers.

WHERE DO WE GO FROM HERE?

This book has given an introductory overview of the range of co-operative businesses and the main kinds of contributions they make toward meeting peoples' needs and solving their problems in an innovative way. We have seen that co-ops can feed us, finance us, serve us, develop us and work for us. The importance of the co-operative lies in the fact that it represents the only viable alternative to the conventional way of doing business. Co-ops working together can provide a significant counterbalance to the power of investor-driven multinationals and can alleviate some of the problems that are created by conventional businesses, but there is much more to be done if co-operatives are to fulfil their potential. This book is a small contribution to the development of a co-operative alternative.

However, if we are to be fully convinced of the merits of co-operatives and the appropriateness of the co-operative process, deeper analysis is needed of each of the main sectors summarised in this book. To provide a more detailed and analytical examination of co-operative development and potential, five more books – *Feeding Ourselves*; *Financing Ourselves*; *Serving Ourselves*; *Developing Ourselves*; *Working for Ourselves* – will soon be published as companions to this volume. Each book will be based on a chapter in this "cornerstone book" and will explore and develop the subject of that chapter.

APPENDIX

A DISCUSSION OF CO-OPERATIVE PRINCIPLES, UPDATED BY THE INTERNATIONAL CO-OPERATIVE ALLIANCE, 1995

Co-operatives in most parts of the world are required by co-operative legislation to abide by a number of so-called **'principles of co-operation'**. These principles are sometimes called **the Rochdale Principles**, so named after the successful consumer co-operative discussed in Chapter 1. The Rochdale Principles have become the most popular basis for defining the concept of the co-operative. They are summarised below. The first three are the ones most commonly incorporated into legislation to provide a legal definition of the essential characteristics of the co-operative.

1. Voluntary & Open Membership
Membership in a co-op is open. Anyone who can make use of a co-op's services should be free to join. In a consumer co-op, for example, any customer is entitled to become a member and enjoy the benefits of the co-op. In a worker co-op, any permanent employee in the co-op is entitled to become a member.

2. Democratic Member Control
The co-op should be democratically controlled and administered. All members have an equal say in the co-op's annual general meeting and in elections for the board of directors. The Board in turn appoints the manager and oversees the running of the co-op. Voting rights go with membership, not with the size of capital invested or number of shares owned (as would happen in a conventional company). The rule is **one member one vote.** In other words, you can't buy more votes in a co-op by investing more money. To become a member in a co-op, you usually have to buy at least one share. Some co-ops will let you buy more than one share, many will *require* that you buy more, but these additional shares will **not** provide you with more votes.

3. Member Economic Participation

Members should contribute equitably and control democratically the capital of their co-operative. At least part of that capital is usually the common property of the co-operative. A number of approaches are used to ensure that capital is controlled democratically and equitably.

Limited return on share capital

Typically, co-ops are required to pay only a limited return on shares. In a conventional company, profits are distributed in proportion to the number of shares you own; not so in a co-op. In co-ops, you are paid no more than a fixed rate of interest on the money you have invested in shares. At most, co-ops pay a return on share capital that is similar to the interest rate you would get on your money in an ordinary savings account at a bank.

Co-ops distribute profits in proportion to members' use of the co-op.

Instead of distributing profit according to shares owned, which is what happens in the conventional business, co-ops typically distribute profits according to how much members have used the business. In a consumer co-op, for example, profits are distributed to customers in proportion to the amount they have bought from the co-op during the year. In a dairy co-op, profits are distributed in proportion to the amount of milk farmers supply to their co-op.

Issue bonus shares

Some co-ops, when distributing profits according to use, issue those payments in the form of bonus shares. Typically, these shares cannot be redeemed for cash immediately, but must be retained within the co-op for an agreed period. This enables the co-operative to reward members for their use of the co-op, while continuing to have the use of the allocated capital.

Reinvest profits in the co-op

Of course, co-operatives are not obliged to distribute any profits at all. It all depends on the wishes of the members and the financial state of the business. Members may choose to reinvest all of the profits in their co-operative to help build the business and expand its range of services.

4. Autonomy & Independence

Co-operatives are autonomous, self-help organisations controlled by their members. When they deal with other organisations, they should do so on terms that ensure democratic control by their members and maintain their co-operative autonomy. For example, to safeguard their autonomy, they should avoid becoming too dependent on government grants and subsidised services.

5. Education, Training & Information

Co-ops should invest in building the abilities and capacities of their members' and employees. Because co-ops exist to encourage the development of people, they should spend some of their profits on developing their members (to improve their ability to run their own affairs). They should also try to inform the general public (to show them how the techniques of co-operation can be applied to the solution of societal problems).

6. Co-operation among co-operatives

Co-ops should co-operate with other co-ops. Co-ops usually start out as tiny businesses set up by relatively poor people with very limited resources. They are much more likely to prosper if they work closely with other co-ops. This is why you find credit unions working together to set up a central body to provide affordable services to them all, and small retail co-ops co-operating to run a wholesaling organisation so they can enjoy the cost advantages of bulk buying. Co-operation between the different sectors of co-ops is less common, but could be one of the most effective ways of serving their users and building competitive advantage.

7. Concern for community

While focusing on members' needs and wishes, co-operatives also work for the sustainable development of their communities through policies approved by their members.

BIBLIOGRAPHY

Abell, P. (1983). "The Viability of Industrial Producer Co-operation", in Crouch, C. & Heller, F. (Eds). *International Yearbook of Organisational Democracy*, London: John Wiley & Sons Ltd.

Aebischer, S. (2000). "Prepaid Care, Third World Style: The Uganda Health Cooperative", *Managed Care Magazine*, June.

Béland, C. (1999). "Co-operative Banks in a Financial World of Mutation: Challenges and Outlooks", presentation to the *New Financial Services in a Global Environment Forum*, at the 1999 Congress of the International Co-operative Alliance, Québec City.

Bierce, A. (1971). *The Enlarged Devil's Dictionary*, London: Penguin Books.

Blackley, S. (1995). "The Future of Worker Co-operatives in the UK" in *The World of Co-operative Enterprise 1994*, Oxford: The Plunkett Foundation.

Bonner, A. (1961). *British Co-operation*, Manchester: Co-operative Union.

Böök, Sven Åke (1992). *Co-operative Values in a Changing World: Report to the ICA Congress, Tokyo, October 1992*, Geneva: International Co-operative Alliance.

Bornstein, D. (1995). "The Barefoot Bank with Cheek", *The Atlantic Online*, December. [Also www.theatlantic.com/issues/95dec/grameen/grameen.htm]

Bradley, K. & Gelb, A. (1983). *Co-operation at Work: The Mondragon Experience*, London: Heinemann.

Breen, R. et al. (1990). *Understanding Contemporary Ireland, State, Class and Development in the Republic of Ireland*, Dublin: Gill & Macmillan.

Briscoe, R. (1971). "Utopians in the Marketplace", *Harvard Business Review*, September/October.

Briscoe, R. et al. (1982). *The Co-operative Idea*, Cork: University College Cork, Centre for Co-operative Studies.

Browne, L. (1993). *History and Development of the Credit Union Movement*, Cork: University College Cork, Centre for Co-operative Studies.

Bruce, D. (2003). *Banking on Competition: Results of CFIB Banking Survey*, Willowdale, Ontario: Canadian Federation of Independent Business.

Calgary Co-op (2002). *Annual Report*, Calgary: Calgary Co-op.

Catell, C. (1996). "UK Worker Co-operatives: A Flexible and Innovative Option", in *The World of Co operative Enterprise 1996*, Oxford: The Plunkett Foundation.

Chambers (1999). *Chambers 21st Century Dictionary*, revised edition, Edinburgh: Chambers.

Coady, M.M. (1939). *Masters of Their Own Destiny: The Story of the Antigonish Movement of Adult Education through Economic Co-operation*, New York: Harper & Brothers.

Cole, G.D.H. (1944). *A Century of Co-operation*, Manchester: Co-operative Union.

Coll, M. (2002). *Ethical Policy and Co-operative Development: A Study Exploring the Impact of Ethical Commitment Statements on Two Canadian Credit Unions*, unpublished Master's dissertation, Cork: Department of Food Business and Development, University College Cork.

COOP (2003). *Annual Report*, Basel: COOP. [Also www.coop.ch/ueber/zahlen_fakten]

Co-op Group (1995). *Responsible Retailing*, Manchester: Co-op Group.

Co-op Group (2000). *Food Crimes: A Consumer Perspective on the Ethics of Modern Food Production*, Manchester: Co-op Group.

Co-op Group (2002). *Chocolate: A Campaign for Fair Trade Chocolate and an End to Exploitation,* Manchester: Co-op Group.

Craig, J. G. (1976). *Multinational Co-operatives: An Alternative for World Development,* Saskatoon: Western Producer.

Culloty, A.T. (1990). *Nora Herlihy: Irish Credit Union Pioneer,* Dublin: Irish League of Credit Unions.

Davis, P. & Worthington, S. (1993). "Co-operative Values: Change and Continuity in Capital Accumulation: The Case of the British Co-operative Bank", *Journal of Business Ethics,* 12, pp.61-71.

Department of Agriculture and Food (2003). *Agrifood 2010,* Dublin: Government Publications, Stationery Office.

Di Carlo, R. (Ed.) (1996). *Towards a New World View: Conversations on the Leading Edge,* Edinburgh: Floris Books.

Douthwaite, R. (1996). *Short Circuit: Strengthening Local Economics for Security in an Unstable World,* Dublin: The Lilliput Press.

Ellerman, D.P. (1990). *The Democratic Worker-Owned Firm: A New Model for the East and West,* Boston: Unwin Hyman.

Fitzgibbon, M. (1999). *Impacts of Financial Services on Small Holder Livelihoods: A Study in Moshi Rural District, Tanzania,* unpublished Master's dissertation, Cork: Department of Food Business and Development, University College Cork.

Fuglesang, A. & Chandler, D. (undated). *Participation as Process - What We Can Learn from Grameen Bank, Bangladesh,* Oslo: Norwegian Ministry for Development Co-operation.

Fukuyama, F. (1996). *Trust: The Social Virtues and the Creation of Prosperity,* New York: The Free Press.

Godoy, S.F. (1990). "More Mondragons", in *Worker Co-op,* Saskatoon: Centre for the Study of Co-operatives.

Gregory, L. (2002). "The Co-operative Experience", in *The Chronicle Online: The independent daily at Duke University,* October 30. [Also www.chronicle.duke.edu/vnews/display.v/ART/2002/10/30/3dbfafbd2abbd]

Group Desjardins (2003). *Annual Report 2002,* Montreal: Group Desjardins.

Hall, K.G. (2003). "Argentines Given Control of Factories: Judges have Turned 140 over to Workers", *Mercury News Buenos Aires Bureau,* 17 March.

Hampden-Turner, C. (1991). *Charting the Corporate Mind,* Oxford: Basil Blackwell.

Hansmann, H.B. (1980), "The Role of Non-Profit Enterprise", *The Yale Law Journal,* Vol. 89, 5: 835-901.

Hashemi, S. & Morshed, L. (1996). "Grameen Bank: A Case Study", in Wood, G. & Sharif, I. (Eds.). *Who Needs Credit? Poverty and Finance in Bangladesh,* Dakha: The University Press.

Holyoake, G.J. (1907). *Self-help by the People: The History of the Rochdale Pioneers,* London: Swan Sonnenshein & Co.

Hughes, C. (1998). "Passing on the Family Business", *Business & Finance,* 4 June.

Hughes, C. (2000). *The Evolution of the Worker Co-operative Concept in Ireland,* unpublished MSc thesis, Cork: University College Cork.

ICOM & Co-operative Research Unit (1993). *Directory,* Leeds: ICOM & Co-operative Research Unit, Open University.

ICOS (1989). *ICOS Annual Report 1988,* Dublin: Irish Co-operative Organisation Society.

ICOS (1990). *ICOS Annual Report 1989,* Dublin: Irish Co-operative Organisation Society.

ICOS (1999). *Share policy document,* Dublin: Irish Co-operative Organisation Society.

ICOS (2000). *A Strategic Review of the Irish Dairy Sector,* Dublin: Irish Co-operative Organisation Society.

ICOS (2003). *ICOS Annual Report 2002,* Dublin: Irish Co-operative Organisation Society.

Irish Government (2000). *Ireland National Development Plan 2000-2006*, Dublin: Government Publications, Stationery Office.

Jackall, R. & Levin, H.M. (1984). "Obstacles to the Survival of Democratic Workplaces", in Jackall, R. & Levin, H.M. (Eds.). *Worker Co-operatives in America,* Berkeley: University of California Press.

Jacobson, R.E. & O'Leary, C. (1990). *Dairy Co-op Issues in Ireland: With Special Reference to PLC Activities,* Cork: University College Cork, Centre for Co-operative Studies.

Jenkins, C. (2003). *Co-op Expands into Child-care: The Oxford Experience.* presentation to Annual Conference, UK Society for Co-operative Studies [Also www.co-opstudies.org/Conference/ Conf_03/Conference_Reports_03.htm]

Joy, P. (2003). "Co-op Planning Methane System at Landfill", *Times Argus,* 19 September.

Keating, C. (1983). "Plunkett, the Co-operative Movement and Irish Rural Development", in Keating, C. (Ed.). *Plunkett and Co-operatives: Past, Present and Future,* Cork: University College Cork, Centre for Co-operative Studies.

Kennelly, J.J. (2001). *The Kerry Way: The History of the Kerry Group, 1972-2002*, Dublin: Oak Tree Press.

Kinzer, S. (2002). "The Orchestra that Won't Give Up; the Players Own It, and Took a Paycut", *New York Times,* 20 March.

Knapp, J.G. (1964). *An Appraisement of Agricultural Co-operation in Ireland,* Dublin: Department of Agriculture.

Koch, R. & Godden, I. (1996). *Managing without Management: A Post-Management Manifesto for Business Simplicity,* London: Nicholas Brealey.

Korten, D.C. (1998). "Your Mortal Enemy", *The Guardian,* 21 October.

Krimerman, L. & Lindenfeld, F. (1992). *When Workers Decide: Workplace Democracy takes Foot in North America,* Philadelphia: New Society Publishers.

Kripalani, M. & Engardio, P. (2002). "Small is Beautiful", *Business Week,* 26 August.

Langer, E.J. & Rodin, J. (1976). "The Effects of Choice and Enhanced Personal Responsibility for the Aged: A Field Experiment in an Institutional Setting", *Journal of Personality and Social Psychology,* 34, pp.191-198.

Levin, H.M. (1984). "Employment and Productivity of Producer Co-operatives", in Jackall, R. & Levin, H.M. (Eds.). *Worker Co-operatives in America,* Berkeley: University of California Press.

Lietaer, B. (2001). *The Future of Money: Creating New Wealth, Work and a Wiser World,* London: Century.

Lincoln, M. (1960). *Vice-President in charge of Revolution,* New York: McGraw-Hill.

Lupton, M. (2003). "Shop and Save", *The Guardian,* 2 April.

Lutz, M.A. & Lux, K. (1988). *Humanistic Economics: The New Challenge,* New York: Intermediate Technology Development Group (Bootstrap).

MacLeod, G. (1997). *From Mondragon to America: Experiments in Community Economic Development,* Sydney, Nova Scotia: University of Cape Breton Press.

Manz, C.C. & Sims, H.P., Jr. (1993). *Business without Bosses: How Self-Managing Teams are Building High-Performing Companies,* New York: John Wiley & Sons.

Marshall, R.L. (undated). *Co-operative Education: A Handbook of Practical Guidance for Co-operative Educationalists,* Manchester: Co-op Union Education Dept.

Mathews, R. (1999). *Jobs of Our Own: Building a Stakeholder Society – Alternatives to the Market and the State,* West Wickham, Kent: Comerford & Miller.

McCarthy, O. (2002). *Micro-credit Strategies for Development,* Cork: University College Cork, Centre for Co-operative Studies.

McLagan, P. & Nel, C. (1997). *The Age of Participation: New Governance for the Workplace and the World,* San Francisco: Berrett-Koehler.

Mendez, L. & Salverda, M. (1999). "Mexico and Thailand: Community Currency Systems", Conference on *Economic Sovereignity in a Globalising World: Creating People-centred Alternatives for the 21st Century*, Bangkok.

Mitford, J. (1964). *The American Way of Death*, London: Hutchinson.

Mondragon Corporacion Cooperativa (2000). *Annual Report 1999*, Mondragon: Mondragon Corporacion Cooperativa.

Mondragon Corporacion Cooperativa (2004). *Annual Report 2003*, Mondragon: Mondragon Corporacion Cooperativa.

Morrison, R. (1991). *We Build the Road as We Travel*, Philadelphia: New Society Publishers.

O'Connell, P.J. & McGinnity, F. (1997). *Working Schemes? Active Labour Market Policy in Ireland*, Aldershot: Ashgate.

O'Hara, P. (1998). *Action on the Ground: Models of Practice in Rural Development*, Galway: Irish Rural Link.

O'Hara, P. (2001). "Ireland: Social Enterprises and Local Development" in Defourny, J. & Borzaga, C., (Eds.) (2001). *The Emergence of Social Enterprises*, London: Routledge.

O'Leary, C. (1983). "Agricultural Co-operatives since Knapp", in Keating, C. (Ed.) *Plunkett and Co-operatives: Past, Present and Future*, Cork: University College Cork, Centre for Co-operative Studies.

O'Rahilly, A. (1942). *Money*. Cork: Cork University Press.

Padmanabhan, K.P. (1996). *Rural Credit: Lessons for Rural Bankers and Policy Makers*, London; Intermediate Technology Publications.

Pam, A. (1992). *LETS: The Economic System of Giving*, www.glasswings.com.au/utopia/lets.html.

Parnell, E. (2003). *The Role of Co-operatives and Other Self-help Organisations in Crisis Resolution and Socio-economic Recovery*, Geneva: ILO Cooperative Branch and IFP/Crisis InFocus Programme on Crisis Response and Reconstruction.

Pateman, C. (1970). *Participation and Democratic Theory*, Cambridge: Cambridge University Press.

Pinchot, G. & Pinchot, E. (1996). *The Intelligent Organisation: Engaging the Talent and Initiative of Everyone in the Workplace*, San Francisco: Berrett-Koehler.

Porter, M. (1985). *Competitive Advantage: Creating and Sustaining Superior Performance*, New York: The Free Press.

Power, T.M. (1988). *The Economic Pursuit of Quality*, 1st edition, New York: M.E. Sharpe.

Prospectus (2003). *Strategic Development Plan for the Irish Dairy Industry*, Dublin: Prospectus.

Rabobank (2003). *Annual Report 2002*, Utrecht: Rabobank.

Reed, L. (2002). "Worker Control Breathes Life into Ailing Factories", *Sydney Morning Herald*, 9 November.

Rural Co-operation (2003). *Growing Rural Businesses through Collaborative Solutions*, Manchester: Co-operatives UK.

Russell, G.W. ("AE"). (1982). *The National Being: Some Thoughts on an Irish Polity*, Dublin: Irish Academic Press (first published, Dublin: Maunsel & Co. Limited, 1912).

Saul, J. R. (1995). *The Doubter's Companion: A Dictionary of Aggressive Common Sense*, London: Penguin Books.

Schumacher, E. F. (1973). *Small is Beautiful: A Study of Economics as if People Mattered*, London: Sphere Books.

Senge, P. (1990). *The Fifth Discipline: The Art and Practice of the Learning Organisation*, London: Century Business.

Seron. S. (1995). *LETS*, www.gmlets.u-net.com/resources/sidonie/home.html.

Smith, D. (2002). "Co-op will Replace Nuclear Energy with Methane", *Times Argus*, 13 May.

SolarNet (2001). "A Window to Kenya's SACCO's SHS Finance: The Michimikuru SHS Finance Project", Vol.3, No.3, September/December.

Temu, A.E. (undated). *Community Initiatives for Sustainable Financial Services: The Case of Kilimanjaro Co-operative Bank and SACCOs in Northern Tanzania*, Copenhagen: Scandinavian Seminar College, www.cdr.dk/sscafrica/temu-tz.htm.

Thirkell, D. (1998). Ignorance abounds on the worth of farmer co-ops", *Irish Farmers Journal*, 7 November.

Timmons, J.A. & Spinelli, S. (2003). *New Venture Creation: Entrepreneurship for the 21st Century*, 6th edition, Homewood, Illinois: McGrawHill/Irwin.

Torgerson, R. (1999). *Co-operative Year Book*, Oxford: Plunkett Foundation.

Tucker, V. (1983). "Ireland and the Origins of the Co-operative Movement", in Keating, C. (Ed.) *Plunkett and Co-operatives: Past, Present and Future*, Cork: University College Cork, Centre for Co-operative Studies.

Turnbull, S. (2001). "The Competitive Advantages of Stakeholder Mutuals", in Birchall, J. (Ed.) (2001). *The New Mutualism in Public Policy*, London: Routledge.

United Nations (1992). *Report of the Secretary-General*, Document a/47/216-E/1992/43, Geneva: United Nations.

Ward, M., Briscoe, R. & Linehan, M. (1982). *Co-operation between Co-operatives*, Cork: University College Cork, Centre for Co-operative Studies.

Waugh, E. (1948). *The Loved One: An Anglo-American Tragedy*, London: Chapman & Hall.

Webb, C. (1910). *Industrial Co-operation: The Story of a Peaceful Revolution*, 4th edition, Manchester: Co-operative Union, pp.68-69.

Woodin, T. (2003). *Working Co-operatively: Exploring Successful Co-operative Enterprises*, Lincoln: East Midlands Co-operative Council.

Young, M. & Rigge, M. (1983). *Mutual Aid in a Selfish Society: A Plea for Strengthening the Co-operative Movement*, Paper No. 2, London: Mutual Aid Press.

Zurdo, R.J.P. (1997). *The Main European Co-operative Banking Systems*, Madrid: Unión Nacional de Cooperativas de Crédito.

Websites

The website addresses given below, and in the footnotes, were all checked prior to printing. However, nothing is static on the Web and so, page references may change. If you cannot access a page reference cited, please contact the authors at b.briscoe@ucc.ie. All web references are preceded by http://.

attra.ncat.org/attra-pub/csa.html	CSAs
bcics.uvic.ca/youthzone/	BC Co-ops youth zone
www.acdivoca.org	ACDI/VOCA
www.action.org	CSAs
www.alternatives.org	Alternatives Credit Union
www.angelicorganics.com/farm.html	CSAs
www.appropriate-economics.org/materials/ Towards_An_Economy_in_the_hands_of_the_Peopl e.pdf.	LETS
www.bayarea.com/mld/mercury news/business/ (16.3.2003)	Argentinean co-ops

www.buildingcommunityassets.coop/en/model.html	Co-ops and community building
www.bwea.com/	Baywatch wind energy co-op
www.calgary-coop.com	Calgary Co-operative Society
www.cambrianorganics.com	Cambrian Organics
www.capricorn.com.au	Capricorn Garage Co-op
www.carsharing.net	Car-sharing
www.cartwheelholidays.co.uk/	Cartwheel Holidays
www.coop.co.uk	United Co-op
www.co-op.co.uk	Co-op Group UK
www.co-op.co.uk/ext_1/Development.nsf/	Co-operative Action Foundation
www.co-operativeaction.coop	Co-operative Action Foundation
www.co-operativebank.coop	Co-operative Bank, UK
www.co-opnet.coop	Co-opNet
www.coopscanada/newsletter/intersector/autumn2003/#item5	Saskatoon Youth Co-op
www.country-holidays.ie/english_index.html	Irish Country Holidays
www.cuco.org	Soil Association
www.dailybread.co.uk	Daily Bread Co-op
www.desjardins.com	Desjardins Group
www.dublinfoodcoop.com/	Dublin Food Co-op
www.dwrcyru.com/English/Results/Report_E.pdf	Glas Cymru
www.eighth-day.co.uk	On the Eighth Day Co-op
www.emes.org	Social enterprises
www.essential-trading.co.uk	Essential Trading
www.ghc.org	Group Health Co-operative, Seattle
www.gll.org	Greenwich Leisure
www.gmlets.u-net.com	Bantry Area Trading System
www.grameen-info.org	Grameen Bank
www.grameen-info.org/bank/index.html	Grameen Bank
www.healthpartners.com	HealthPartners
www.icos.ie	ICOS
www.iowarec.org/public/about/about.shtml	Rural electric co-ops
www.landolakesinc.com/corp_function/int_dev.asp	Land O' Lakes Co-op international development work
www.lincoln.coop	Lincoln Co-op
www.londontimebank.org.uk	Time banks
www.lso.co.uk	London Symphony Orchestra
www.macsac.org	CSAs
www.managedcaremag.com/archives/0006/0006.uganda.html	Uganda Health Co-operative
www.mcc.com.es	Mondragon

www.mcc.coop/ing/noticias/gdistribucion/n_0001.asp?id=479.	Eroski
www.mcc.coop/ing/noticias/gdistribucion/n_0001.asp?id=489.	Eroski
www.midsco-op.co.uk/	Midlands Co-op
www.migros.ch/migros_FR	MIGROS
www.mobility.ch/e/index.cfm?dom=2	Car-sharing
www.mobility.ch/e/index.htm	Car-sharing
www.moosejawcoop.com	Moosejaw Co-op
www.nabco.ie	NABCo
www.natfed.org	Credit Unions and Development
www.nearfm.ie/aboutus.html	Irish Radio Co-op
www.nochubank.or.jp.	Norinchuken Bank
www.nytimes.com/2002/03/20/arts/music/20LOUI.html	Louisiana Philharmonic Orchestra
www.osg.coop	Oxford, Swindon & Gloucester Co-op
www.plymco.co.uk/funeralsites/funerals	Funeral services
www.plymco.co.uk/index.htm	Plymouth & S.W. Co-op
www.rabobank.org	Rabobank
www.rdc.com.au/grameen	Grameen Agricultural Foundation
www.sclf-help.org	Development finance
www.suma.co.uk	Suma Co-operative
www.timebanks.co.uk	Time banks
www.timedollar.org	Time banks
www.umass.edu/umext/csa/.	CSAs
www.unicorn-grocery.co.uk	Unicorn Grocery Co-op
www.vancity.coop	VanCity Credit Union
www.washingtonelectric.coop	Washington Electric Co-op
www.weaverstreetmarket.com	Weaver Street Market
www.wisc.edu/uwcc/	Wautoma Co-operative Care case-study
www.wisc.edu/uwcc/icic/orgs	Credit Agriccole Mutuel
www.woccu.org	Credit Unions

INDEX